SONG OF THE REEL

GFC's grandson Stephen Homer fishing in Lane's Creek, Upper Woodstock, July 1964

SONG OF THE REEL

SECOND EDITION

GEORGE FREDERICK CLARKE

"You will find angling to be like the virtue of humility, which has a calmness of spirit and a world of other blessings attending."

— Izaak Walton

EDITED BY MARY BERNARD

CHAPEL STREET EDITIONS
WOODSTOCK, NEW BRUNSWICK

© Copyright George Frederick Clarke 1963

2nd edition by
Chapel Street Editions
Edited by Mary Bernard
© The Estate of George Frederick Clarke 2016

All rights reserved. No part of this publication may be reproduced, distributed, or transmitted in any form or by any means, including photocopying, recording, or other electronic or mechanical methods, without the prior written permission of the publisher and/or author, except in the case of brief quotations embodied in critical reviews and certain other noncommercial uses permitted by copyright law. For permission requests, write to the publisher at the address below.

Published by Chapel Street Editions
150 Chapel Street
Woodstock, NB Canada E7M 1H4
chapelstreeteditions@gmail.com

Library and Archives Canada Cataloguing in Publication

Clarke, George Frederick, 1883-1974, author
        Song of the reel / George Frederick Clarke ; edited by Mary Bernard.
— Second edition.

Includes index.
ISBN 978-1-988299-03-7 (paperback)

        1. Salmon fishing—New Brunswick. 2. Fishing—New Brunswick.
3. Outdoor life—New Brunswick. 4. Saint John River Valley (ME. and N.B.)
—Description and travel. I. Bernard, Mary, 1941-, editor II. Title.

SH685.C54 2016   799.1'755   C2016-904383-5

Cover illustration by H.E.M. Sellen.

Book design by Brendan Helmuth

To my wife, who for fifty summers has helped pack my dunnage, and not forgetting the smallest necessity sent me off to the rivers or the woods with the cheery words: *Have a good time. Take care of yourself. Good luck.*

Editor's Dedication

TO MY DEAR COUSIN
STEPHEN HOMER

THE SONG OF THE REEL

I am the song of the reel whose notes rejoice
   Be it rain or shine, on lake or brawling stream;
And I sing as I must, in soft or raucous voice,
   And waken the sleeping forest from its dream.

When the salmon strikes and both sharp hooks bite deep,
   And the line spins out as it starts its frantic race,
I shriek my song, then pause as it makes its leap
   To shatter like breaking glass the river's face.

Then on I sing, exultant and wild and free;
   And the kingfisher wonders what strange thing this,
And leaves his perch on the leaning cedar tree.
   But what reck I in my golden hour of bliss!

For he who holds me next his throbbing breast,
   And the guide behind who paddles the frail canoe,
Are both a-thrill with the carefree wilding zest
   The gods confer on only a chosen few.

With anxious, beating heart I sing as they fight;
   Now fast, now slow, now muted my notes reveal
My hope and fear and awe as the salmon's might
   The bamboo bends in an arc of amber steel.

I sing as I must, nor pause at the very end
   When the wide-mouthed net the silver form enfolds,
But deep in my heart I sing, and silently lend
   My voice to the good-luck-cheer that the hour holds.

                                              G.F.C.

CONTENTS

Editor's Preface. i
List of Illustrations. ix
Sources of Illustrations xiii
Foreword. xv
    Chapter I 1
    Chapter II 11
    Chapter III 17
    Chapter IV 23
    Chapter V 31
    Chapter VI 53
    Chapter VII 57
    Chapter VIII 69
Photographs: Part One. 77
    Chapter IX 91
    Chapter X 101
    Chapter XI 109
    Chapter XII 117
    Chapter XIII 133
    Chapter XIV 145
Photographs: Part Two. 153
    Chapter XV 167
    Chapter XVI 179
    Chapter XVII 187
    Chapter XVIII 199
    Chapter XIX 207
    Chapter XX 209
    Chapter XXI 223
    Chapter XXII 235
    Chapter XXIII 259
    Chapter XXIV 265
Afterword 271
Index 277

EDITOR'S PREFACE

George Frederick Clarke fished the streams and rivers of New Brunswick all his life. He was seven or eight when he first fished for trout in the Meduxnekeag Creek in Woodstock. He was over eighty when bursitis and an injured knee put an end to his angling.

His first angling memoir, *Six Salmon Rivers—and Another*, appeared in 1960. Writing it had been "almost as good as having six vacations." *Song of the Reel* was his second, and writing it was "a pleasure difficult to describe in mere words"—except for a few additions his publishers insisted on. They thought that anglers wanted a fishing book to be something of a how-to manual. GFC had learned from readers of *Six Salmon Rivers* that what they liked most was his stories—and stories were what he wanted to tell. (I call him GFC here and in the notes: his full name is a mouthful.) But the publishers were adamant, so he inserted some details about the flies, rods and reels he used, and his casting technique. He did not enjoy writing them.

But they are only a small part of *Song of the Reel*. His enjoyment, his love of both fishing and writing, breathes through the book. It is a rich, informal mix of anecdotes, vivid descriptions of his rivers, musings about the good life, and the robust tall tales and folk stories that he heard from guides. They sound like transcriptions of the men's own words, and often are, for he often took notes while his friends spun their tales. He tells vivid real-life stories—about the night he and Dr Grant caught poachers in a dugout named *The Drunkard's Doom*; or the time Levi Grant got stung by "tame bees;" or early fishing trips, up the Pokiok with a boyhood friend, or to Indian Lake with three pretty girls, with one of whom he fell half in love. He gives exciting accounts of playing and landing salmon or running treacherous rapids, and wonderful descriptions of the sights and sounds and smells of the wilderness, of gathering wild strawberries, of the river at night.

Sometimes he overloads his readers with allusions to classical mythology or barely apposite quotations from poetry or obscure seventeenth-century historians. But it is easy to skim past them and come to something like this:

> Twilight faded. Darkness settled over the hills; the moon climbed majestically into the blue, lighted up Grand Bar....My companion gave a deep sigh, then said, in a low voice: "How beautiful! 'It is not all of fishing to fish'."

"It is not all of fishing to fish." It is the motto of the Flyfishers' Club of England, and it was dear to GFC's heart. "Of course we all like to catch fish," he admitted; but fishing was more than just catching fish. It was "a day off with the companionship of dear friends; with the quiet and peace of a little river and its bird and animal life; with the flowers and trees along the shores, all of which impart to us a sense of tranquillity—a heart's-ease that drives away all distractions."

My brother, an ardent salmon fisherman, often meets anglers who feel that GFC, more than any other writer, captures "something they feel about salmon fishing: not just the sport, but everything they see, hear, smell, sense while they are on the rivers and in the woods." That "something" is GFC's overarching theme, his urgent imperative to us. Live fully, he says, in the senses and in the spirit. Do not ignore the beauty of the natural world. Look at it, listen to it, immerse yourself in it.

Readership

Six Salmon Rivers had sold well, and anglers loved it. They wrote to him ("I've had many letters from people I never knew," he told his daughter Jane: "more complimentary letters about that work than for all my others combined."), and they called on him. I was home every summer between 1960 and 1964, and I answered the door dozens of times to slightly bashful anglers, on their way to or from the great salmon rivers of the province, hoping to meet the author of their favourite fishing books. GFC was usually busy writing or correcting proofs, but he never turned them away. They probably expected no more than a hello and a handshake. What they got was an hour or more of animated conversation, and usually Mary Clarke's tea and cookies as well.

Editor's Preface

GFC had been writing in solitude all his life, with little recognition from reviewers and little feedback from readers. It was enormously gratifying to have written a book that brought readers to his door. *Song of the Reel* brought more. Twenty-nine anglers called on him in the summer of 1964 alone. By 1970, more than three hundred anglers had come knocking, and over four hundred and fifty had written to him.

Critical reception

It had bothered GFC that the reviewers of *Six Salmon Rivers* praised it but failed to sense what he half-apologetically called its "spiritual content." They must be, he thought, "mere sports writers whose main object in life is the catching of fish, and insensitive to the contemplative side which should be a part of fishing."

He had less reason to complain about reviews of *Song of the Reel*. Newspaper ads for the book might emphasise its straightforward sporting appeal (see Plate 11b), but reviewers were beginning to see him as an important regional writer. One started by declaring: "Dr. Clarke has done it again." Another said: "A new book by Dr. George Frederick Clarke is always a major event in the literary life of New Brunswick," and called him, "the dean of New Brunswick prose writers."

More to the point, several reviewers emphasised the book's "spiritual content." Here are three representative excerpts:

> Through all the laughter and the stories of salmon and trout fishing runs a serious—but appealing—vein of philosophy that pleads for conservation of the treasures of land and water.

> Not the less effective for its restraint in expression is Dr. Clarke's fear that the forested, well-watered New Brunswick, where people can not only fish but develop the book's philosophy that "It is not all of fishing to fish," will presently disappear, that it is indeed disappearing now. The danger is real.

> *The Song of the Reel* can be read for sheer enjoyment, [but] in a deeper vein, it is a plea for the preservation of New Brunswick's forest-fed rivers and the way of life that draws its strength from them.

They had recognised one of the principal messages implicit in the book. Don't just delight in the beauty of nature—work to conserve it. GFC had done so down the years, writing and speaking about ecologically responsible forest management; pollution of the province's rivers; over-fishing; and the disastrous effect of the hydro-electric dams at Beechwood and the Tobique Narrows on salmon stocks.

Mactaquac and after

Song of the Reel came out in November, 1963. Two months later the government unveiled a plan to dam the St John river at Mactaquac, creating a sixty-mile headpond that would stretch to Hartland. GFC was at the forefront of the battle against the dam. He and his fellow protesters lost the fight. In 1967 the sixty most beautiful miles of his beloved river became "a lifeless pond."

He lost; but he went on fighting for the future. In 1970 he prepared a second edition of *Six Salmon Rivers*; it came out in December 1971. Then he started revising *Song of the Reel* for a new edition. His reason for revision, he told me, was to point up the destruction the dam had wrought upon his once-majestic river and its once-rich valley, upon salmon fishing, upon agriculture, and upon human communities uprooted and scattered. He did not want to re-fight a lost battle, but to urge the people of New Brunswick not to let such destruction happen elsewhere. As he put it on the cover of the new edition of *Six Salmon Rivers*:

> Dr Clarke...is determined, if he can prevent it, that our remaining rivers, streams and lakes, with their enchanting environment that caused New Brunswick to be named "*The Picture Province*", shall not suffer the same tragic fate as the St John River.

Early in 1972 he had a mild stroke. He was eighty-eight and had written tirelessly since childhood. He struggled valiantly to finish revising *Song of the Reel*, but his eyes bothered him; he tired easily; and he was in and out of hospital, becoming slowly weaker.

When the journalist Jackie Webster interviewed him in late 1973, he seemed to be in fighting trim: "a dedicated environmentalist," who "sees Mactaquac as a triumph of politics over ecology. Now that it is a fait accompli, he is in no way reconciled." Speaking of the loss to anglers, he told her emphatically:

> They have ruined the St John River....Salmon fishing has been ruined on the river, at Hartland, and on the Tobique, and there is no way it can be restored. They bring the salmon up to the Tobique in trucks. They will survive there in those cold waters, but there is no sport to fishing. It is the same as catching gold fish.

He died in October, 1974, his changes to *Song of the Reel* unfinished. His manuscript revisions have not survived, but I know from our conversations in the summer of 1974 that he had already written passages about the effect of Mactaquac on the environment in general and on salmon fishing in particular. In this second edition I have tried to honour his intentions by pointing out in my footnotes passages that he would probably have amended.

The text

I have worked from the first edition, silently correcting a few typos.

I have kept GFC's footnotes; they are numbered A-N. I have corrected or amplified a few of them; the additional information is in brackets. My own footnotes are numbered 1-105. A few are about Mactaquac; the rest give dates, sources for quotations that GFC left unattributed, odd bits of information, and definitions of terms that may have become obscure in the fifty-three years since the first edition.

The word "Indians"

GFC lived before the term "First Nations" was in common use. He called First Nations peoples Indians, and it was what they then called themselves. I have not changed his usage. Nor have I changed his spellings of the names of First Nations peoples, such as Maliseet and Micmac.

The illustrations

The first edition of *Song of the Reel* had twelve illustrations. I have kept seven and added thirty-seven more. Most of them illustrate specific passages; I have given the number of the illustration in parentheses in the text.

H.E.M. Sellen was one of the best wildlife artists who ever worked in Canada. I have included his drawings of a moose and a bear. He also made the cover illustration of a fisherwoman and guide. All three were commissioned for stories by GFC about angling and animals published in magazines in the early 1930s; GFC bought the drawings from him.

The drawing of a beaver is by GFC's woodsman friend Fred Grant.

GFC had a keen eye for young talent. He spotted it in young Mike Saunders, who lived across the street and was just starting work as a photographer. GFC used three of Mike's photographs in *Song of the Reel*, and praised them in the text. Each was a full-page plate in the first edition. Mike would have given me high-quality scans of them, but he and his negatives are on opposite sides of Canada and won't be in the same place in time for this edition. I had to scan them from the book, and the moiré patterning was so obtrusive that I could not reproduce them full page. Sorry, Mike.

About myself

I am the daughter of GFC's elder daughter, Jane; GFC was my grandfather. In 2015 Chapel Street Editions published *The Last Romantic*, my story of his life.

About the George Frederick Clarke Project

Chapel Street Editions has undertaken a grand publishing project called the George Frederick Clarke Project. It will publish all of GFC's books over the next few years, at the rate of four a year. I am editing the series.

Three books launched the Project, in September 2015:

- my biography of GFC: *The Last Romantic: George Frederick Clarke, Master Storyteller of New Brunswick*
- GFC's first fishing memoir: *Six Salmon Rivers—and Another*
- the first collection of all his surviving short stories: *The Ghost of Nackawick Portage: the Collected Short Stories of George Frederick Clarke*

Editor's Preface

This fall of 2016 sees the publication of:

- GFC's second fishing memoir: *Song of the Reel*
- his two books for young children, complete in one volume: *Jimmy-Why and Noël Polchies: their Adventures in the Great Woods*
- *Someone Before Us*, 1967, his memoir of his archaeological finds and adventures

The next two book in the project will be *David Cameron's Adventures*, an exciting novel for youg adults, and its sequel, *Return to Acadia*.

Acknowledgments

I want to thank Ian Bernard for answering my questions about angling; Jean Haywood, Library Manager of the Dr Walter Chestnut Library in Hartland, for helping me identify the photograph of the Hartland Salmon Pool and the location of Patterson's Pool; Jackie Webster for permission to quote from her article, "Fred Clarke—Citizen", which appeared in the *Atlantic Advocate* of February 1974; and above all my publishers Keith, Brendan and Ellen Helmuth of Chapel Street Editions. They are beyond praise.

Mary Bernard
Cambridge, England,
June 2016

LIST OF ILLUSTRATIONS

Initials in parentheses are those of the photographer:
    GFC   *George Frederick Clarke*
    JME   *J.M. Elliot*
    SH   *Stephen Homer*
    MLB   *Mary Lord Bernard*
    MS   *Michael Saunders*
Photo credits follow the list of illustrations.

Stephen Homer fishing in Lane's Creek, July 1964 (MLB). . *Frontispiece*

1. a. GFC and Bill Kennedy, Gulquac Lodge, Restigouche, 1950s 78
   b. GFC with fishing friends at Gulquac lodge, Oct 7 1948

2. GFC with a twenty-nine-and-a-half-pound salmon, Restigouche, 1930s. 79

3. a. Charlie Clark, Dr Grant, Bill Kennedy, with guides, c. 1937 (*GFC*) . 80
   b. The Izaak Walton memorial window in Winchester Cathedral

4. a. Dr Grant 81
   b. Charlie Clark with salmon
   c. The Four Musketeers of Fish in 1937: Dr Grant, Bill Kennedy, Charlie Clark, GFC

5. GFC's sister, Ruby Clarke, at Ayers Lake, 1911(*GFC*). 82

6. GFC's fiancée, Mary Schubert, at Ayers Lake, 1911 (*GFC*) 83

7. a. GFC and guide with salmon, c. 1910. 84
   b. GFC and daughter Jane in a dugout canoe on the Miramichi, c. 1919

8. The Anglican church on the Lower Road below Woodstock, 2003 (*MLB*) 85

9. Russell Boyer, 1930s. 86

10. Russell Boyer, 1940s. 87

11. a. Anglers at the Hartland Salmon Pool, before Mactaquac 88
    b. Newspaper advertisement for *Song of the Reel*, 1963

12. a. The St John River near Woodstock, before Mactaquac (*MLB*) . . . 89
    b. Russell's camp, 1940s

13. a. The St John River north of Hartland, 1967 (*MLB*) 90
    b. The St John River above Woodstock, early 1960s, before Mactaquac

14. a. Earl Cole back view, with salmon (*MS*) 154
    b. Earl Cole silhouette (*MS*)
    c. Keith Wright, Patterson's Pool (*MS*)
    d. GFC as a bridegroom (*JME*)

15. Northampton Church steeple, summer 1967 (*MLB*) 155

16. The St John River at twilight, 1967, below Mactaquac (*MLB*) . . . 156

17. Noël Polchies 157

18. a. Child's snowshoes made by Noël Polchies in about 1921 (*MLB*) . . 158
    b. Salmon spear owned by GFC (*MLB*)
    c. Double-pointed blades excavated by GFC at Shiktehawk, 1932

19. GFC and friends at the Forks of the Miramichi, between 1915 and about 1925 159
    a. GFC, Murdoch Mackenzie, Dr Grant and unknown man beside the GFC-Grant-Clark camp, c. 1925
    b. George Greer and GFC with 2 trout, c. 1919
    c. Dr Grant in dugout canoe with trout
    d. Henry Wilson with trout, the Forks, 1916

20. a. Bear catching salmon, drawing by H. E. M. Sellen. 160
    b. Beaver gnawing birch stump, drawing by Fred Grant

21. a. The Forks pool, 1997 (*MLB*) 161
    b. The camp at the Forks in 2012 (*MLB*)

22. Bull moose, drawing by H. E. M. Sellen 162

23. Mist on the Miramichi, 1972 (*MLB*). 163

24. a. Ian Bernard poling at the Forks, 1971 (*SH*) 164
    b. Still water at the Forks, 2012 (*MLB*)

25. *Song of the Reel*: the sign above the restored camp at the Forks (*MLB*)165

SOURCES OF ILLUSTRATIONS

Plates 2, 7 a, 9, 10, 19 a, 24a: Stephen Homer collection.

Plate 3 b: digital image courtesy of 'The Hundred Books', www.thehundredbooks.com.

Plates 14 a-c: Michael Saunders.

Plate 17: Peter Paul Collection, MG H 151, Photograph 6-51(418), courtesy of Archives & Special Collections, Harriet Irving Library, University of New Brunswick. (I have cropped and edited the photograph.)

Plate 18 c: Archaeological Research Laboratory, Department of Anthropology, University of New Brunswick, Fredericton.

Plate 20 b: I am grateful to Ida Grant for permission to reproduce Fred Grant's drawing.

All other photographs and illustrations are from the editor's collection.

I have digitally edited and restored all photographs and illustrations.

FOREWORD

by K. C. Homer*

"It is not all of fishing to fish." Readers who made the acquaintance of Dr. George Frederick Clarke through the pages of *Six Salmon Rivers and Another* know how wholeheartedly he subscribes to this motto of a famous angling fraternity. They will be pleased to learn that in *Song of the Reel* Dr. Clarke again dons his fishing clothes and returns to his beloved New Brunswick rivers.

But confirmed anglers understand that he travels, too, in a country which knows no geographic boundaries...that world within a world inhabited occasionally by those whose passports are a rod and line, eyes that see, ears that are open, and hearts that respond to the quest for Nature's indefinable rewards.

As an ambassador of this boundless world, Dr. Clarke is without peer, and its special atmosphere informs and enhances everything he writes of it.

Here are tales of classic encounters between anglers and wily salmon told with masterful suspense and containing a wealth of disguised fishing lore.

Here are associations with fellow "Brothers of the Angle" and the professional guides who are at once mentors and companions, their campfire anecdotes and conversations ranging over a wide field, touched with humour and delight and filled with the peculiar philosophy of anglers everywhere.

---

* Ken Homer was the husband of GFC's younger daughter and the father of my cousin Stephen, to whom I have dedicated this edition of *Song of the Reel*.

Song of the Reel

Here are gleanings from a lifetime of familiarity with "the best that was thought and said in the world" presented deftly by a pen which puts the reader in a "taking mood" as surely as a salmon will respond to a neat cast from the same experienced hand.

Here are all the sights and sounds and scents of the out-of-doors…and as the exciting song of the reel thrills out over Dr. Clarke's New Brunswick pools and rapids, there is always present beneath it the gentle harmony of that "other river" which anglers seek, the river of heart's ease and content.

CHAPTER I

The days of late winter have begun to lengthen and warmen, and spring—like a long-absent housewife—is preparing to return and take up its age-old chores. It is at this time of year that we dedicated anglers feel a restless stirring in our veins and think of fishing. In fancy we see our favourite river (or rivers, as the case may be) or a brook pursuing its vagrant course through woods and pastureland, or a lake cupped in a vast wilderness which, we hope, the wheels of commerce will never invade. We remember that last half-hour of our stay on the river last year, and the big salmon (surely the biggest we had raised during fifty years of angling) that came from near the ledge on the right. It followed the fly, just beneath the surface, until it had completed its curve downriver. Then, disdaining the fly, it swung about in a half-circle, its huge body heaping up the water in a wide wake that extended back to its resting place.

What a mighty salmon! It had set our heart thumping. We gave it a short rest, then cast, but although we tried again and again—and even resorted to other flies—it refused all our offerings. Well, perhaps this year we may actually hook and land one just as big…

We think of old comrades (some of them, alas! gone from us for ever, but lovingly enshrined in the archives of memory) and of the many trips we took to our rivers, for we fished several. We recall the late evenings after the day's fishing, when Charlie, the Doctor, Bill and myself sang *The Big-Bellied Bottle, Banks of Devon, The Banks O' Doon, Coming Through The*

Rye, Annie Laurie, Old Black Joe, Mother Machree[1] and many others; and at intervals drank suitable libations. I can hear the voices as I write this. We sang for hours on the wide verandah of our little wigwam, at the Forks of the Miramichi, on the Tobique, on the Restigouche and the Kedgwick, while the moon and myriad stars bathed their reflections in the pool below. And finally, standing up with arms linked together, we sang *Auld Lang Syne*,[2] the poignant words and melody of which have echoed in camps of miners, lumberjacks and explorers in Newfoundland, the mainland of Canada to Hudson's Bay, the Arctic Sea and the Pacific Ocean; from the State of Maine to San Francisco; from Land's End to John o' Groats; in barracks and about campfires on the sands of Egypt and on the African veldt; and on shipboard, and wherever the lovely English and Scots tongue is spoken.

Aye—we each had some Scots blood, so that the skirl of the pipes and the swinging kilts and sporrans set the blood coursing in a wild tumult of unnameable excitement. Oh yes—ancestors of ours had come from that land of glens and crags and heather which, although we had never glimpsed it save in picture and story, is forever Scotland.

> *Whose songs are first to heart and tongue*
> *Wherever Scotsmen greet together...*[3]

* * *

What is it about fishing that induces in your true sportsman a happy, carefree state of mind? I believe it can best be summed up in the motto of *The Fly Fishers' Club*, England: *Piscator non solum Piscatur*. It is not all of fishing to fish. What a volume in that short sentence! It should be lettered in gold and hung in the den or library of every angler.

1　The first four songs are by Robert Burns. "Annie Laurie" is a traditional Scotch song. "Old Black Joe" is by Stephen Foster. "Mother Machree" dates from 1919: lyrics Rida Johnson Young, music Olcott and Ball.

2　By Burns.

3　From "The World-Mother (Scotland)" in *Beyond the Hills of Dream*, 1899, by William Wilfred Campbell, one of the Confederation Poets.

Chapter I

Of course we all like to catch fish; but there is something associated with the sport, as the Flyfishers' motto implies, that makes for the state of felicity about which philosophers and poets have written so much and attained only for brief hours. It is a day off with the companionship of dear friends; with the quiet and peace of a little river and its bird and animal life; with the flowers and trees along the shores, all of which impart to us a sense of tranquillity—a heart's-ease that drives away all distractions. Hazlitt tells us of the motto inscribed in an old sun-dial, near Venice: *Horas non numero nisi serenas*—"I count only the hours that are serene".[A] What a pleasing conception: to forget or to pass over the unpleasant things of life and charge our minds only with those that are pleasant; to take the day as it is (whether rain or shine) and find joy in it; to accept the loss of a good fish with philosophical calm; and lastly—remembering that "the vices we scoff at in others laugh at us within ourselves"[B]—to overlook the faults of our friends. Of course it is an ideal state of mind, difficult if not impossible to reach, but none the less a goal the striving for which should make us better sportsmen.

* * *

During the last six months I have received numerous letters from fishermen, all of whom spoke of the different rivers they had fished and referred in nostalgic terms to the happy hours they had enjoyed. One of my correspondents was Frederick Sturgess, Jr.,[4] of Wall Street, New York City. He had fished the Kedgwick—a northern tributary of the Restigouche—for many years and, although now nearing the four-score years and ten mark, is still young in spirit. His last letter contained a copy of a letter he had received, in 1904, from Henry James, in which that famous author said:

---

4 [*recte* Sturges], 1874-1977. His obituary in *The Princeton Alumni Weekly* (Volume 78, 1977) mentions the James letter.
   Sturges' letter to GFC has not survived.

A Hazlitt—*Sketches and Essays:* "On A Sun-dial" [1827].
B *Religio Medici*—Sir Thomas Browne. [It is in fact from his *Christian Morals*, 1716.]

"I am at last in a deep peace and a very beautiful spot, a rare New England Arcadia of mountain and forest and lake and crystal brook."

To recall from the corridors of the mind all the anglers and guides I have met and known would make this chapter too long. When many of the former arrived at the river they were fatigued both mentally and physically. But, like the weary woods traveller who eases his pack beside some bubbling spring, drinks of its life-giving nectar, resumes his pack and, lighter of foot and refreshed in spirits, goes on his way, so the fisherman sheds his load of cares, then returns home rejuvenated, more fit to grapple with his daily chore.

I well remember one man who came to the government reserved water on the Restigouche. That first night we stood for a few minutes on the terrace in front of the Lodge. Below us the river flowed past the shores as it had done from time immemorial. The moon, at its full, was reflected in and washed by the ripples. On the opposite hillside the trees stood in ranks from the base to the summit, where the lordly spruces and pines looked like etchings against the horizon. High in the realms of illimitable space the "slow-moving palaces of wandering light"[5] shone with indescribable splendour, not least that group of brilliant stars which form the constellation variously known as Charles's Wain, The Big Dipper and the Great Bear, alluded to by Matthew Arnold in *Balder Dead*:

> ...*the Northern Bear,*
> *Who from her frozen height with jealous eye*
> *Confronts the Dog and Hunter in the south.*[6]

And my new friend said in awed tones: "My God—how beautiful the night is, and how soothing the sounds of the waters, and how soundless and mysterious the forest! Do you realise, Doctor Clarke, what you possess in your wonderful country?"

I told him that I had long been conscious of it, that it was all a part of the heritage I enjoyed in New Brunswick.

---

5   Quoted in "Winter Stars," in *Where the Forest Murmurs*, essays by "Fiona Macleod" (William Sharp), 1906. I have not found the source from which Macleod quotes.

6   Matthew Arnold, "Balder Dead," ll. 155-157, in *Poems, Second Series*, 1855.

Chapter I

"I envy you," he said. Then, after a brief pause: "But for this week I shall share it with you."

*　*　*

One of the most memorable pleasures of my fishing trips is contained in the fragment of time when, with my companions, I first arrive at the Lodge: an oasis set in a wilderness of spruce, pine, the warty poplar known as the Balm of Gilead and, on the riverside, a row of white birches (*1a-b, 4c*) as though Mother Nature had placed them there expressly that they might view their lovely reflection in the fast-flowing waters. It is good to return to our river! Here is profound and abiding quiet—almost the same as that which prevailed before the white men saw the shores of North America. One needs only a little imagination to picture the Indian chipping his arrowheads, knives, scrapers and spearheads of flint, or standing in his birch-bark canoe at night—the water about him flooded with ghostly radiance from his flambeau—while he spears salmon around the mouth of Larry's Brook. We see the guides: perhaps a new face among them. We take their hands, hardened by lumbering during the long winter months, by driving the innumerable logs from the far headwaters to the booms a hundred miles distant in the spring, and by poling canoes through swift rapids. Their eyes look straight into ours, their faces lighten with a smile of recognition. "Glad to see you again," they say. "Yes, the fishing was good last week... Yes, plenty of fish in the river." Comrades in the most thrilling sport in the world! I have known as many gentlemen among the guides as among the doctors, the lawyers and businessmen. They judge us not by our clothes, not by the size of our pocket-books and the cars we drive, not by the gratuity (little or big) we give them at the end of the week, but by our gentleness and our ability to accept with good grace the loss of a fish: in other words by our good sportsmanship. Let us never undervalue them. Some of them fought in two world wars, others in one, performing deeds of gallantry unsung and unrecognised.

Yes, we do get something from the guides other than their service in helping us to catch fish. We get good cheer and that informing comradeship which is as abiding, in our minds, as faith.

A good guide is like a kindly dictator; he has fished from boyhood and knows his river and the lies of the fish. We deliver ourselves into his hands confident that he will work his head off to bring us good luck; he humbles us by his patience. The names of these men have gone far beyond the confines of the little villages where they were born, and the rivers where they spend so much of their lives. They live in our memories.(*3a, 7a*)

* * *

The salmon is the most unpredictable of fish: it is this, and the anticipation of a rise, that makes the sport so exciting; and if Lady Luck smiles on us and we finally hook and land one or more, we are wonderfully repaid for our patience. The game of chance has taken on a glamour that can never be erased from our minds.

Moreover, to the true lover of Nature the lilt of the rapids, the majesty of the hills, the melodious "Oh! Come! Come! Come-to-me! Come-to-me! Come-to-me!" of the white-throat hidden among the trees takes on new meaning, new sanctity. Our day off from office or business has brought its reward whose benefits are priceless and enduring. It is something not only of the mind but also of the spirit. Unfortunately some of us do not absorb the latter. Is it because we have not been born with the capacity to sense it? Or is it that, in our efforts to secure the material things of life, we have closed our minds and hearts to the spiritual? In any case we have to give something of ourselves in order to receive: otherwise we have lost that which is infinitely precious.

A few years ago a *blasé* man of the world was invited by friends to accompany them to the Miramichi for a week's fishing. He had accepted with little enthusiasm. As a young man he had gone to college. Subsequent years at an exacting profession and rounds of social activities had robbed him of his early zest for the out-of-doors. At this time he was middle-aged, tired, and fed up with life. But now the enchantment of the river and all the primitive beauty of the hills and the few fish he caught brought back nostalgic memories of his early boyhood when, with alder pole and worm-baited hook, he had fished a small trout stream in northern Maine. By week-end he had recovered some of the riches which the waters and the earth are so willing to share with us.

Chapter I

* * *

Thus our thoughts (several weeks before the ice in the rivers had broken up), resurrecting from the past the scenes and events that ever delight the fisherman. We get down certain well-thumbed books from their resting places; some of them dealing with the habits of salmon; with the authors' own particular choice of rods, flies and reels; with how to fish the wet and the dry fly. But we soon lay these aside: we want something quite different, so we once again browse through the pages of books that do not merely attempt to dictate what rods or flies or reels we must use in order to take more fish; books that ramble along like a delightful brook through woodlands; yarns replete with good fishing, interspersed with philosophical reflections, and all the scenes and sounds and sights of the various creatures who inhabit the shores of lake and stream. And choicest among these *The Compleat Angler* which, first published three centuries ago, has gone through many editions and is still read by an ever increasing body of anglers. For Walton is *Walton*.[7] Although he never caught a salmon and knew little about fly fishing, "whether we consider the elegant simplicity of his style, the ease and unaffected humour of the dialogue, the lovely scenes which it contains, or the fine morality it so sweetly inculcates, has hardly its fellow in any of the modern languages."[8] It always evokes new thoughts, new wonder—as when we gaze at the perfection of the various constellations, or the recurring miracle of dawn, and the sun pushing its crown over the far horizon.

Izaak Walton died in 1683 at the age of ninety, and was interred in the south aisle of Winchester Cathedral. On his tombstone are written these simple words: "Here lie ye bones of Mr. Izaak Walton."[9] There is also a beautiful stained-glass memorial window, which was presented to the cathedral[10] by fishermen of Britain and the United States.(*3b*) On it is this beautiful inscription: "The Lord God ruleth over the water flood." A fitting tribute to one who for more than three hundred years has given

---

7   Izaak Walton, 1594-1683. *The Compleat Angler* was first published in 1653.

8   Sir John Hawkins, in his life of Walton, 1760.

9   [*recte* "Here resteth the body of Mr Isaac Walton".]

10 In 1914.

pleasure to thousands. And if any of my readers have not read him, I would say with Charles Lamb: "Pray do so." Hazlitt, in one of his essays, has a very fine passage, in which he says: "I feel the same sort of pleasure in reading his book as I should have in the company of this happy, childlike old man, watching his ruddy cheek, his laughing eye, the kindness of his heart, and the dexterity of his hand in seizing his finny prey."[11]

* * *

Just as our remote ancestors of the stone and antler implement age overhauled their fishing gear, made new antler spears, and wove nets of fibre bark, so do we go over our boxes of flies and decide to tie or order from the tackle dealer a few extra. Yes, and we take down our rods from the wall where they have hung since we stopped fishing last season, and set them up and test them for possible loose ferrules. For there is nothing more annoying to the fisherman, who truly loves his tools, than to feel the wobble of a loose joint. Then the reels—we carefully dismount the working parts, remove the old, dry oil, and apply new. Finally, having reassembled them we spin the gears and listen, with a satisfied smile, to the mild music that will be accentuated a thousandfold when the fish takes the fly and, the line over its shoulder, rushes downstream to the guide's chortle of delight: "You've got him!"

Personally I use only a few flies of standard pattern: both large and medium (I do not like very small ones); some of both lightly dressed for low water. But in June I use a 1-0 or 2-0. Later, when the water slacks off, a No. 4 or 6. But let me add that I have often taken fish on large flies during low water conditions. And when late evening settles over the river, I always tie on a No. 2-0. Why? Ask the salmon! I seldom use a single-hook fly, nor do any of the guides I have fished with. As for the dry flies, I carry a few. I have seldom used leaders longer than nine feet—a preference I share with Hutton[12]—and like him, I have caught salmon on a three-footer. I use double-handed rods: one a steel-centre Wye, the other a twelve-foot Gold

---

11   From "Merry England," in *Lectures on the English Comic Writers*, 1819.
12   John E. Hutton, *Trout and Salmon Fishing*, 1949.

Chapter I

Medal rod that, although quite withy, has so much "life" that it casts a line with the least effort of any rod I have used during a period of fifty years. Often in making the back-cast I do not swing it up and towards my right or my left shoulder (I cast with equal facility with right and left hand), but lift it sidewise by a hand and wrist movement. Then, when the line straightens out, the butt and tip of the rod are on a line midway between my waist and shoulder. Then, with a quick upward movement of wrist and forearm I toss it forwards. The spring of the rod does the rest, and the line shoots out fifty, sixty or eighty feet. It is a cast that requires as little effort as tossing a bride's bouquet to a bevy of waiting girls. I enjoy making long casts, seeing the fly shoot out to the desired spot. But a long cast is not as sure of hooking a rising fish as a shorter one, say thirty feet.

I well know that many fishermen prefer lighter and shorter rods than those I use. All right, that is their privilege. Personally I do not like to play a fish an hour or more, and seldom take more than fifteen or twenty minutes to kill a twenty-five or thirty-pound fish. For to me the most thrilling moment is when the salmon makes the boil, when I feel the heavy tug and know it is on. Of course the leaps it makes and the wild music of the reel excite me; but I repeat, that *strike* is the thrilling moment. Nothing else in sport can compare with it.

Just as I concede the right of every man to choose his own particular form of religion, so too with flies, rods and leaders. I do not try to evangelise him. As an old Negro once said to me: "Doctor, I tell you 'bout dis religion business: it just like de spokes of a wheel—one spoke Methodist, one Baptist, nodder Anglican, nodder Roman Catholic, nodder Presbyterian… An' where does dey all lead to? Well, dey all leads to de hub, and de hub am Heaven."

To broaden the corollary, so it is with rods and reels and flies in respect to angling: they all lead to the river; and with almost each and every fly it is possible to take fish, if the fish are in the mood for taking.

* * *

We all have our theories, which may at times be upset by some wily old fish; and I have often worked an hour, trying all the art I possess, to lure a fish to take my confections, even adopting the suggestions of others. Once, on the Miramichi, I went to the head of the Forks Pool, tore chunks of sod and earth from the river bank, and threw a dozen or more into the water. Then, in a few minutes I renewed my casting and took two twelve-pounders. Perhaps they had been sleeping, for it was past mid-day. I believe it was Williamson, author of that famous *Salar The Salmon*,[13] who says that salmon often sleep. One day, about four o'clock in the afternoon, Jock Ogilvy and I fished the lower portion of Pool No. 3 on the Restigouche Reserved Water. We knew fish were there, but didn't get a rise until a motor-canoe rushed around the bend and passed us, the waves dashing against the side of our lighter craft and against both shores. After the turmoil had subsided I again began casting, took three salmon and lost two more. My theory—borrowed from Williamson—is that they had been sleeping. But J. A. Froude, in his essays on literature and history, says that "a theory is nothing more nor less than an imperfect generalization caught up by a predisposition."[14] But, the sods I threw into the pool at the Forks and the turmoil caused by the racing motor canoe, and the subsequent catching of fish, would seem to substantiate the theory that salmon *do have their sleeping hours!*

* * *

On one of my early trips to the Miramichi, I hooked more salmon in six days than during any other period of time on that or any other river. Most of them were taken on a double-hook No. 6 Parmachenee[15] Belle, sent me by a tackle dealer in Scotland. One fish refused to rise for the No. 6. So I tied on a single 2-0 (with enough feathers on it to adorn a picture hat of the gay nineties) and cast over the fish. It rose with a boil that set my every nerve atingle, was hooked and landed after a hot fight. The only other flies I had were Jock Scotts, and I took fish with them, but not as many as with the Belle. Why? Because I used the latter more than the former. How many salmon are taken today on a Parmachenee Belle? I doubt if it is ever used, at least in this country.

---

13   Henry Williamson, *Salar The Salmon*, 1935.
14   *The Lives of the Saints*, 1852.
15   Named for a lake in Maine. The word is also spelt "Parmacheene" and "Parmachene."

CHAPTER II

I remember a late evening's fishing I had during the second week of August four years ago, with Harvey Wyers as guide, in the Run or No. 1 Pool on the reserved water of the Restigouche. Harvey was in his mid-sixties, had spent most of his life on the river, and was one of the best guides I have ever fished with. He was dark-skinned and for the most part as taciturn as an Indian. He has since passed on to where, I hope, there is good fishing.

We had taken one fish, weighing 22½ pounds, midway down the pool, and night was fast settling over forest and river. A drop below I hooked and lost a good fish that came from near the left-hand shore, and in a few minutes I could hardly see where my fly was falling. I said to Harvey: "There's a submerged boulder (he knew it as well as I did) far to the right, exactly opposite those two leaning white birches. I think I can reach the place." So I began casting straight downriver, slowly lengthening line until I was quite sure I had out sufficient to reach the desired spot. Then, half turning, I made a far cast to the right a few feet above the unseen boulder and allowed the fly (a No. 2-0 Black Dose) to swing with the gentle current. I barely had time to think: "If I hook a fish now we'll have a difficult chore to land it in this darkness," when there was a big swirl as though the boulder had reversed the law of gravity and propelled itself upwards.

It is so difficult to wait for the strike, the impulse so strong to lift the rod-tip. My wait seemed minutes, rather than a couple of seconds, until I felt the heavy tug that told me the fish was on. Only then did I lift the rod. The reel screamed, and above its glad notes I heard Harvey's low voice: "You've got him!"

I could feel the immense strength of the fish and knew it was a big one. It ran downstream and towards the left shore, then swerved into the middle of the river, made a long run, leaped four or five feet into the air and fell back with a smack that sounded like that made by a beaver when it dives and strikes the water with its flat tail. I had dimly seen the fish leap; for although the shore-trees were shrouded in black night, the water, for some distance, reflected a little of the lighter sky.

Harvey had already lifted the lead kitty and was poling after the speeding fish in the effort to get even with or below it. For neither he nor I wanted to leave the pool, run into Cheyne, and possibly go over the bar below into the rough waters at the head of Pool No. 3. I lifted my rod high and put as much pressure on the fish as I thought wise; but it was impossible to stop its wild rush. I glanced down at my reel and saw, to my dismay, that the hundred yards of backing was at least two-thirds out. So I tried a trick I learned from a Scot I had met years before on the St John River and lowered the tip of the rod, thus releasing most of the pressure on the fish. Magically it worked. Perhaps the salmon imagined it was free, for it ceased its downward course, paused. Harvey continued poling along the right-hand shore while I slowly reeled in, keeping only slight pressure on the fish. In the intense blackness of the river I could only guess where the fish was, but presently saw faintly a swirl in the water not fifty feet away. Then, with a rush that bent my rod almost double, it dashed first to the right, then to the left, paused again, shook its head as a terrier does a rat, and once more started downriver and into the deep water at the head of Cheyne where it rose to the surface and darted leftwards, leaving a wrack of troubled waters in its wake. Then it slowly worked its way between the boulder-strewn swift shallows and into the lower end of the pool. Again my backing was more than half out, but fortunately, while Harvey unerringly manoeuvred the canoe abreast of the shore, I was able to retrieve a good bit of it, at the same time giving the fish the butt as hard as I dared. But I could no more see where it was than I can at the moment I write this—four years after that hard-fought battle.

I could now feel the casting-line between forefinger and thumb and, breathing a sigh of relief, tilted the tip of the rod hard to the left, which caused the fish to change its course upriver where I wanted it; although if

Chapter II

we were ever to land it, it must be below, where there is a small rocky beach exactly opposite the turbulent water at the head of Pool 3. So alternately snubbing the canoe with his setting pole, and allowing it to slip downwards, Harvey edged it foot by foot along the shorewater with its ghostly line of trees, as black as the pit of Cerberus; and at the same time I let the salmon have its way upstream taking out line slowly, for I felt that I could now turn it whenever I chose—if the hook held. That was my worry: would it hold, or work loose?

It seemed hours before we reached the little beach and heard the sound of the tumbling waters over the hidden boulders, one of which, in midstream, would weigh half a ton. Harvey beached the canoe, threw his anchor, sprang out into the shallow water, seized his long-handled landing net, and I got out on the beach. "Have you got your flashlight?" he asked: perhaps the only words he had spoken since the fish was on.

"No," I answered. "I...I forgot it."

He said nothing. So I began reeling in line, not too fast, and putting little pressure on the fish. "He's coming," I said.

The salmon was: but whether it was dropping backwards tail-first or head, I didn't know, although I think the former. At any rate it only made short rushes towards the centre of the river while the reel whined its protesting notes. Nearer it came, and I walked still farther up the beach a little above where Harvey stood, the bag of his net in the water. And as I reeled in, and gave the fish the butt, I dimly saw a great boil just above Harvey's black form silhouetted against the blacker water.

He saw the boil, made a scoop with his net and drew it up—empty! He wasn't to blame for his miss, and the startled fish rushed out into the head of the boiling rapids, then stopped, and I again began reeling in. It came slowly, nearer, yet nearer, then, to my dismay, I heard a faint click that told me that I had reeled in the line past the knot in the leader. The rod bent almost double. I sprang forward, at the same time lowering the tip until it almost touched the water. Then, wonder of wonders, the knot disengaged itself from the ring; the tip sprang upwards, the reel whined like a buzz-saw as once again the salmon sped out into the swift water. But I stopped its rush and again reeled it in, keeping my left forefinger and thumb on the line while my heart thumped like a trip-hammer.

Song of the Reel

The fish came slowly but surely, foot by foot, inch by inch, and my right forefinger and thumb on the reel-handle felt numb and lifeless. But this time I was determined not to reel in past the knotted leader, and slowly backed yet farther up the beach. Dimly I could see a slight momentary turmoil a few feet out and above where Harvey stood, his net again submerged, waiting for the right moment when the fish should be over it.

I backed up another foot or two, not putting too much pressure on the fish, but I couldn't see it, nor any motion of it. and neither could Harvey, though as a matter of fact it was not in more than a foot of water. Then, to my great joy, I dimly saw the net quickly lifted with my fish in it and breathed a deep sigh of contentment.

Harvey waded to shore, and well up on the beach, drew his priest from his hip pocket and with a few quick blows on the head despatched the still-struggling fish, then he lifted it from the net and, while I lighted a match, held it up for me to see. "Thirty pounds?" I said. *(2)*[16]

It was twenty-eight, and what a fighter! Then came Harvey's nonchalant voice: "The hook came out of its mouth when I netted it."

Sure enough: it was caught in one of the meshes of the net. Harvey deposited the salmon in the bottom of the canoe, pushed off a little, and I took my seat; he followed. At my request he didn't start the motor, but swung the paddle with clock-like regularity.

The moon soared over the tops of the spruces and pines that lined the crest of the ridge on the left-hand shore. It threw a path of gold on the water over which we floated like a dream. A few stars, heralds of those restless caravans of radiant light that would later appear in countless millions, were reflected in the river and looked as though one had only to reach down with a landing-net and dip them into the canoe. The shores were silent save that once we caught the sharp bark of a fox, and a little later the raucous voice of an owl stuttered his enquiry to know who we were.

The sweet, resinous odour of the Balm of Gileads on the right met our nostrils. Times past the Indians gathered the sticky buds and used them for

---

16 Photograph *(2)*, of GFC with a big salmon, was taken beside the government reserved water on the Restigouche, but on a different trip, in the 1930s, when his guide was Adelard Gallant, not Harvey Wyers.

Chapter II

healing cuts and bruises. So did the natives of Arabia and Abyssinia make an ointment of them. And Jeremiah laments, saying: "Is there no balm in Gilead? Is there no physician there? Why then is not the health of the daughter of my people recovered?"[17]

How many times, seated in a canoe while the guide poled or paddled it, I have wished that I could roll back the years for a few hours to that time before the white men dreamed that America existed, that I might sit beside the Indian at his camp-fire and listen to him recounting the legends of his forefathers: learn what impulse caused them to cross Behring's Strait to Alaska: and the record of their travels across the vast continent to this land of Acadia. Alas! they left no written records, and the past is now hidden in the mists of unnumbered centuries.

We rounded the bend between Lower Three and the Home Pool and saw on the verandah of the Lodge the bright electric light, which Allie Murray had turned on to guide homing anglers to the wooden float. It threw into silhouette the tall flag-pole, the Lodge itself and the cabins grouped about it, and in front the slim white birches and the spruces and firs and poplars, silent and inexpressibly mysterious.

As we came nearer Harvey shipped his paddle, seized his long setting-pole, swung the bow of the canoe upstream, brought it in until the side of it touched the logs of the float, got out and held it while I disembarked. And I thought of the countless other men and some women—who after a morning's and evening's fishing, had landed at this same place during the past thirty years; then, carrying the precious rod, and the guide lugging the fish and tackle box, slowly climbed the hill to the Lodge where they were met by their waiting companions eager to learn what luck they'd had.

* * *

That night I did not have to woo Morpheus, son of Sleep and god of dreams, he came unbidden soon after my head was on the pillow, and for hours, it seemed, I relived the evening's battle with the big fish; although it was not the salmon that Harvey finally landed more than five hundred

---

17 Jeremiah 8:22.

yards below where I had hooked it, but a great star; and I cried out in my sleep: "Orion—we've got him!" and awakened on the instant. Then I heard Bill Kennedy's voice: "That last drink was too much for him… Wake up, Doctor!"

"I'm wide awake, Bill," I said.

He gave a low chuckle and said: "Who was Orion?"

"Well," I answered, "according to Greek mythology Orion was a giant, very handsome and a mighty hunter. He was blinded by Enopion for his sins, but Vulcan sent Celadion to be his guide, and his sight was restored by exposing his eye-balls to the rising sun. Later he was killed by Diana. He was transferred to the heavens as a constellation. Three other stars, in a row, are his belt, and three others his sword. And the gods, knowing Orion would be lonely without his favourite hound, named Sirius, placed it near by as the dog-star. Very fittingly, perhaps, the brightest star in the heavens… You understand, Bill?"

"Yes…yes, Doctor," was the soothing reply. Then in a barely audible voice: "I put too much in that last drink, but a cup of black coffee will set him right in the morning."

CHAPTER III

Doctor Grant, Charlie Clark, Bill Kennedy[18] and myself were seated one evening in our little camp at the Forks of the Main Southwest Miramichi. The lamps had been lighted and we were suitably celebrating a good day's fishing. For each of us had taken a nice salmon, and the Doctor a three-pound sea trout.

We talked of many things but principally about fishing, and then sang several songs. Finally Charlie suggested I sing a solo. Now I was the poorest singer of the lot, and tried to beg off. But they declared that I must sing or have cold water poured down my sleeve—a punishment to which Sir Thomas Dale, one-time Governor of Virginia, subjected any of the colony who were heard swearing. So I said: "Well, boys, you'll have to forgive some doggerel of my own composition; but since it's about fishing, I hope it will go down."

Of course they applauded, but insisted that we first have a drink. Lusty brimmers had been coming rather frequently, and I said so, but consented to take a very small one. Then, when we were settled, I began in my faulty baritone the following:

> *O there was a wee boy*
> *Who fished in a brook*
> *And caught a wee trout*

---

18   Nelson Parker Grant (1876-1942) was a doctor in Woodstock. Charles Wilmot Clark (1887-1951) was a Woodstock grain dealer. William Leslie Kennedy (1883-1965) kept a general store in Debec, and was Dr Grant's brother-in-law. GFC, Dr Grant and Charlie Clark co-owned the lease of the camp at the Forks.

Song of the Reel

> *With a worm and a hook:*
> *O high-diddle-diddle*
> *And diddle-de-dum*
> *It wasn't much bigger*
> *Than the wee boy's thumb;*
> *"But a mighty fine fish!"*
> *Said the proud little man:*
> *"A mighty fine fish!"*
> *Said the proud little man.*
>
> *O hurrah for the Garden,*
> *And three cheers for Eve;*
> *Hurrah for the Apple*
> *She poached from the Tree,*
> *And gave it to Adam*
> *(While she smiled in her sleeve),*
>
> *O high-diddle-diddle,*
> *And diddle-de-dan,*
> *If it hadn't been for Adam*
> *And his wily wife Eve,*
> *Who gave him the Apple*
> *(While she smiled in her sleeve),*
> *There'd ne'er have been boy*
> *With his worm and his hook*
> *To catch a wee trout*
> *From a small singing brook:*
> *To catch a wee trout*
> *From a small singing brook.*

"Now—all together!" I said. And they filled the time-browned room with the words:

> *O high diddle-diddle,*
> *And diddle-de-dan,*
> *If it hadn't been for Adam*

Chapter III

And his wily wife Eve,
Who gave him the Apple
(While she smiled in her sleeve),
There'd ne'er have been boy
With his worm and his hook
To catch a wee trout
From a small singing brook:
To catch a wee trout
From a small singing brook.

There was a noisy clapping of hands and thumping of feet. When it had ended the Doctor said: "That's splendid, Fred. Congratulations. But", he added, "haven't you made an historical error? At the time of the Apple episode Eve was quite naked, so how could she smile in her sleeve?"

"Oh," I said, "you *would* light on *that*. But cannot a writer indulge in a metaphor?"

"Of course," he said, with one of his winning smiles. "So I most humbly apologise, and with my apology suggest that it's just about time for a little touch of something, and we can use the occasion for a suitable toast." He picked up the bottle of whisky, poured a portion into each glass, added a little water, and having passed them around, said: "You know, boys, I've never forgiven Adam for attempting to lay the blame on Eve after he had eaten the apple. If you remember, he said: 'The woman tempted me and I did eat.' However, perhaps having been persuaded longer than he had the capacity to endure, he finally came to the conclusion—arrived at umpteen centuries later by Lady Christian Bruce—that 'the best way to get the better of temptation is just to yield to it.'"[19] The Doctor paused, rose to his feet, lifted high his glass, waited until we had followed his example, then, in a ringing voice said: "I propose a toast to the little boy who first caught a fish."

"To the little boy who first caught a fish," we repeated, and all drank… I have no doubt that it was a toast unique since first the custom was started.

* * *

---

19 In Clementina Stirling Graham, *Mystifications*, 1865.

Someone once referred to us as the Athos, Porthos, Aramis and D'Artagnan of fishermen; for we were always together. *(4c)* Alas! the Doctor was the first to leave. His had been a life of unselfish devotion to his patients. Summer or winter he never refused to respond to their appeal, and so he wore himself out on the altar of what he considered his duty. Men and women who had no physical ills came to him with their troubles, confessed their sins of omission and commission, and from the inexhaustible dispensary of his understanding mind and soul there issued the balm of kindly counsel and good cheer. *(4a)*

His shibboleth was play the game; and he himself played if to the very end. His opinions were of the strongest kind; right was right, wrong was wrong, and he never compromised. He had one recreation—fishing. His favourite poem was Gray's Elegy. I well remember one evening, after we had fished a lake, we came out of the woods as twilight was settling over the valley of the St John, and began walking the two miles to a farm house where he had left his car. Suddenly he began quoting the poem nor ceased until he had given it all. And, perhaps because he had spent his boyhood and young manhood on a farm, he was especially captivated with the two opening stanzas:

> *The curfew tolls the knell of parting day,*
> *The lowing herd wind slowly o'er the lea,*
> *The ploughman homeward plods his weary way,*
> *And leaves the world to darkness and to me.*
>
> *Now fades the glimmering landscape on the sight,*
> *And all the air a solemn stillness holds,*
> *Save where the beetle wheels his droning flight,*
> *And drowsy tinklings lull the distant folds.*

For several years following the beginning of our friendship, I didn't know that he was familiar with Shakespeare. Then, early one morning at two-thirty, while we were at the Forks of the Miramichi and enjoying good salmon fishing, a message was brought him by Murdoch MacKenzie, saying that one of his patients was in labour. His only remark was to say that he was sorry to take me from the river, and prepared to leave. It was a fifty-mile drive to Woodstock, and another twelve miles to a sparsely inhabited settlement.

Morning light was dispelling the dark as we passed through the town of Hartland. A couple of miles farther on he stopped the car, and, pointing to the opposite horizon, said:

> "But, look, the morn, in russet mantle clad,
> Walks o'er the dew of yon high eastern hill."[C]

And then:

> "Night's candles are burnt out, and jocund day
> Stands tiptoe on the misty mountain tops."[D]

Two years before he died he told me that his secretary had lately gone over his books, and found that some eighty thousand dollars were owing him. "But," he said, "although some of my patients can afford to pay, for others it would be a hardship... So let it go."

* * *

Charlie Clark followed him five years ago, and was laid to rest where he chose to be—in the little hillside cemetery in the Parish of Wakefield, whence can be seen, in the deep valley below, his beloved St John River pursuing its journey to Fundy Bay. Like the Doctor, Charlie had hosts of friends. Whenever he walked down the main street of our little town he was sure to be stopped half a dozen times and held in conversation. He had a fund of quaint humour, and in fancy I can now hear his Rabelaisian laughter that was like a tonic to all who heard it. *(4b)* The late Fred C. Squires[20] wrote some verses to his memory. If I remember correctly two stanzas go thus:

---

20   1881-1960. He was a lawyer and, from 1925 to 1935, an MLA.

C   Horatio to Marcellus, *Hamlet*, Act I, Sc. I [where the hill is "eastward" not "eastern"].
D   Romeo to Juliet, *Romeo and Juliet*, Act III, Sc. V.

E'en now I hear his gladsome laugh,
His gleeful shout, his winsome jest;
With glowing hand he touched the need
Of the lone soul with grief oppressed.

And so the heralds of the heart
Can draw his lineage complete;
He was a prince of high renown
Who held his Court upon the street."

Thus, of that gay and devoted little band of brothers—who for more than three decades foregathered each year to fish the most famous salmon streams in New Brunswick—Bill Kennedy and I remain. *(1a)* But, whenever we drive along the Stewart Highway (winding through forty miles of wilderness) to get to the Restigouche River, we pause beside a spring of bubbling water which of old the four of us never passed without stopping to quaff of its cold purity; and here, after drinking, we take off our hats, and with bowed heads observe one minute of silence in memory of two of the most faithful comrades fishermen ever had.

CHAPTER IV

It is not at all strange that the majority of the people I remember best have been those who accompanied me, or whom I met during my fishing excursions. For these delightful days off have been so many in my life.

I had a cousin, Ada Bonner, who taught school a few terms in a farming district named Maplewood some twenty-five miles from Woodstock. She was a pretty thing not more than twenty-two years of age. One of her eyes was brown, the other grey: the brownest of things brown, the greyest of things grey, to paraphrase one of Swinburne's alliterative lines.[21] During the first week in August, almost sixty years ago, she came to Woodstock to spend a few days with my mother, and knowing that fishing was one of my main interests, she said I should come to Maplewood, thence go to Indian Lake and catch some of the big trout for which it was famous. The school term would begin the fifteenth of the month; should I come any week-end after that, she would guide me over the old portage road to the lake, and show me one of their favourite resting places where a tiny, ice-cold brook cooled the waters of a small cove. She told me that there was a punt at the lake. We could anchor it to an enormous pine log that had fallen halfway across the middle of the cove and, save for the loss of its branches, had endured the ravages of ice and waves beyond the memory of the oldest inhabitant of Maplewood. She would, she said, make arrangements for me to stay at the home where she boarded.

I needed no coaxing. So on Friday afternoon, two weeks later, I boarded the train, got off at Woodstock Road siding, shouldered my pack, and

---

21   In "Félise," *Poems and Ballads*, 1866.

carrying my rod in one hand, walked along the gravelled highway towards Maplewood. Five miles, but I didn't mind that. I had often walked fifteen miles to reach trout water.

* * *

At six o'clock I reached my destination where I was graciously received by Mr. Newel and his wife, and with expressions of joy by my cousin Ada. "I wasn't sure you'd come," she said.

After supper, she told me that she and Pearl Palmer and a visiting fifteen-year-old cousin, Bessie Palmer—who lived somewhere near Boston, Massachusetts—had arranged to go to Indian Lake on the morrow, and she hoped I wouldn't mind the extras. Then, with a roguish smile, she said: "They are beautiful girls, cousin Fred. I'm sure you'll adore them. We'll take sandwiches, and a kettle to make tea in, and spend the day." *(5, 6)* [22]

"I'm quite sure not more beautiful than you," I said.

"Oh," she said with a shy smile, "you say that because I'm your cousin."

"Not at all," I protested. Then: "It will be exciting to have three beauties for my companions."

"At least there's safety in numbers," she said, and smiled again. I was then nineteen.

* * *

The following morning Ada and I walked up the highway to meet the girls with whose beauty she had sought to impress me. I must admit that she had not exaggerated their charms. Pearl was my own age, her face peaches and cream with large, melting brown eyes, a lithe figure and dark-brown hair braided in two long plaits. Bessie—how shall I describe her? She was shorter than her cousin, her figure inclined to plumpness which remained throughout her life. She was as light on her feet as a fawn. Her dark-brown

---

22 About photographs *(5)* and *(6)*: In 1911 GFC photographed his sister, Ruby, and his fiancée, Mary Schubert, at Ayers Lake. In 1963 he used the photographs in the first edition of *Song of the Reel*, though without referring to them in the text. I think he meant Ruby and Mary to stand for all the happy young fisherwomen of his youth, including Ada, Pearl, Bessie, and the barefooted girl in chapter XXII.

Chapter IV

hair curled about her brow and hung in lustrous waves to her shoulders. Her eyes were bluish-grey, with little darker flecks that gave them a dancing expression when she spoke or laughed. Her face was rounded and tanned a delicate brown. But it was her exquisite good humour—the laugh that came from the very springs of her being—that enchanted me and all who knew her. Indeed, like Falstaff, she laughed her way through life even when cares and illness laid their heavy hand upon her and would have crushed a less valiant spirit.

North and northeast the fields, separated by snake fences of grey-weathered cedar rails, sloped gently downward to Fiddle Brook. Beyond its winding course the terrain rose to high, forested ridges and imposing hills—a vast wilderness which stretches unbroken (save by brooks and lakes and deadwaters) to the Nashwaak, the Miramichi and the Tobique country. These hills seen from Maplewood bear the names Petong Mountain, Big and Little Spruce Peaks, Bear Trap, Lawrence Peak, Fish Lake Mountain, and Oak Hill. Between Oak Hill and a high ridge is cupped that enchanting body of water Indian Lake.

We crossed the little corduroy bridge which spans Fiddle Brook, and began our journey along the old portage road, two of us abreast, or in Indian file when huge boulders made that impossible. We walked between palisades of spruce and hemlock, birch and maple, and in the swampy areas between the sombre files of ancient cedars. Several times we flushed partridges; and once a doe with two fawns bounded up the ridge with a flash of white flags. Near the ground the bunchberries spread a carpet of red, close-clustered fruit. The earth, the trees, the moss, the ferns filled the air with their combined fragrance.

The girls chatted or sang or laughed all the way through that peaceful wilderness. Cities and towns had ceased to exist for all of us. Our world was in its youth.

Suddenly, descending a ridge, we glimpsed through the boles of the trees the sheen of blue water that could have been the sky. With shouts of joy we hastened our pace, presently came to the margin of the lake and saw its whole lovely expanse—like an immense opal—shimmering in the sunlight. And as we put down the picnic baskets beside the spring that bubbled from the cool earth at the base of an ancient birch tree, a loon from near the lake's outlet sent up its strange, almost human call which echoed and re-echoed against the sleeping hills.

The Micmac and Maliseet Indians have a legend that Gluskap, their ancient deity, friend and adviser, made the loon his friend. And then, in the long ago, he left the eastland and went no one knew whither. And the loon is forever lonely, and so, they say that whenever it sends up its weird, far-reaching notes, it is calling for its old friend Gluskap.

I remember that Bessie cupped her hands on either side of her lips, and repeated the call with such perfection that the distant bird heard it, and rose to its feet on the surface of the water, and flapped its wings, while once again the lonely and expectant call shivered into the silent air, and against the hills, and was repeated by others more distant, then died away into nothingness.

* * *

I cut alder poles for the girls, strung the lines and tied on the hooks (for they had brought worm-bait), then set up my little fly rod. We bailed the rain water from the boat, got in and paddled to the little cove where I tied the painter to a long spike some former angler had driven in the pine log. Then, safely anchored, began fishing.

The trout seemed to prefer the worm-bait to my flies, for I caught none during the hour we fished. The girls got five between them: none less than a pound each. And what fighters! They bent the withy alder poles almost double and strove by every trick they knew to break away. Even when pulled into the boat they displayed amazing energy, and twisted their bodies in the girls' hands quite as though they knew their ultimate fate and were determined to struggle to the last to elude it. Beautiful creatures with small heads and tapering bodies spotted with gold and carmine moons.

Then cousin Ada's line straightened: the tip of the alder pole vanished beneath the water. She cried out: "Oh, I've got a monster!" and pulled an eel into the bottom of the boat. A chorus of shrieks from Ada and Pearl. Bessie laughed until the tears ran down her cheeks. Then I lifted up the writhing creature, took the hook from its lip and flung it into the lake.

Shortly after the noon-hour we went to shore, made a little fire, boiled spring water for tea, then, seated in a circle, started on the egg and tomato

Chapter IV

and ham sandwiches. After we had eaten these Pearl brought out a blueberry pie her mother had put in her basket, and we spoiled that; and after a second mug of tea called it a meal. And there was laughter and jest, and I got a ragging for not having caught a trout. And turning to Ada, Pearl said: "I thought you told me he was a good fisherman!"

I told them to wait; that perhaps I'd do better later in the afternoon. And while we laughed and talked, a squirrel leaped from another tree to that by which we sat, and scolded us and scolded us with such vehemence that its whole body shook.

And Bessie and Pearl sang one of the current sentimental things about a young man who was entreating the girl he loved to return his affection. I remember the title, "Maybe", but of the words only the following lines:

> *Maybe in the dreary winter,*
> *When the storms sweep land and sea;*
> *Maybe in the gentle springtime,*
> *Maybe you will say "Maybe".*[23]

But that was almost sixty years ago. However, I better remember the verse Bessie quoted and the song she sang the following Monday morning. For both were familiar to me.

When we renewed our fishing later in the afternoon I regained my laurels, for I hooked and landed a pound-and-a-half trout, then a smaller one. But Bessie and Ada and Pearl bettered me with worm bait, each catching three more. Then, after another lunch, we began the return journey over the old portage road.

As we descended the hill to Fiddle Brook the sun was withdrawing his radiant brow below the opposite horizon.

That evening Ada and I went up to Pearl's home, and she played the piano and we sang songs until almost midnight.

* * *

---

23   Lyrics by Frank Tannehill, Jr., music by George Rosey, published 1901.

About eight o'clock Monday morning I was ready to take the highway to Woodstock Road siding to catch the train home, when Bessie and Pearl appeared at the door. Pearl told me that back of her father's house an old woods-road led to the railroad and a small siding at Nackawick. It was much shorter than the way I had come, and she and Bessie would like to guide me.

Of course I was delighted, so I said goodbye to my hostess, and to Ada, who had to take up her weekly duties in the little schoolhouse.

So Pearl and Bessie and I walked back to the home of Charles Palmer, and soon entered the woods.

The narrow road, which had not been used for many years, was in places partly grown up with alders, but the deep-rutted tracks made by waggons and horses that had hauled logs to the railroad made it easy to follow. I remember patches of blueberries (gentian-coloured globes of imprisoned nectar). Now and then we snatched a hasty handful, munching them with that enjoyment which only youth knows. And Bessie and Pearl sang. Once Bessie stooped, picked up a crow's feather from the middle of the road, and stuck it in her thick, wavy hair.

* * *

We reached the railroad and the little siding. I looked at my watch. The train would not arrive for an hour. So the three of us sang and talked and sang again. Then Bessie jumped up on a big granite boulder, and facing us, her cheeks flushed, and the black feather still jauntily fixed in her hair, recited Tennyson's *Ulysses*. Almost sixty years ago, but I can still remember the vibrant tones of her voice as she spoke the lines:

> *'Tis not too late to seek a newer world.*
> *Push off, and sitting well in order smite*
> *The sounding furrows, for my purpose holds*
> *To sail beyond the sunset, and the baths*
> *Of all the western stars, until I die.*
> *It may be that the gulfs will wash us down:*
> *It may be we shall touch the Happy Isles,*
> *And see the great Achilles, whom we knew.*
> *Tho' much is taken, much abides; and tho'*

Chapter IV

> *We are not now that strength which in old days*
> *Moved earth and heaven; that which we are, we are;*
> *One equal temper of heroic hearts,*
> *Made weak by time and fate, but strong in will*
> *To strive, to seek, to find, and not to yield.*

Then that mere child—but old beyond her years—recited portions of that beautiful and soul-stirring poem Tennyson wrote in memory of his friend, Arthur H. Hallam.[24] Finally she raised her rich contralto voice in perhaps the most tender and perfect love song ever written in any language ancient or modern:

> *Oh, wert thou in the cauld blast*
> *On yonder lea, on yonder lea,*
> *My plaidie to the angry airt,*
> *I'd shelter thee, I'd shelter thee;*
> *Or did Misfortune's bitter storms*
> *Around thee blaw, around thee blaw,*
> *Thy bield*[E] *should be my bosom,*
> *To share it a', to share it a'.*
>
> *Or were I in the wildest waste,*
> *Sae black and bare, sae black and bare,*
> *The desert were a paradise,*
> *If thou wert there, if thou were there:*
> *Or were I monarch o' the globe,*
> *Wi' thee to reign, wi' thee to reign,*
> *The brightest jewel in my crown*
> *Wad be my queen, wad be my queen.*[25]

---

24 *In Memoriam A.H.H.* 1850.

25 By Burns.

E Bield—shelter, a sheltered place, the sunny side of a wood.

Then, far down the track, came the hoarse whistle of the train, and soon the thudding of the wheels over the tie-joints, and the giant puffing of the engine. It came into view devouring space with every thrust of its mighty pistons. I stepped to the side of the track, waved my battered old hat. With a creaking of brakes and a hissing of steam, the train came to a stop.

I thanked the girls for their kindness in guiding me through the woods and Bessie for her poems and song, then, although loath to leave them, climbed the steps of the last coach, and the train started off.

Hastily I ran to the rear, opened the door and stepped onto the platform. (I wonder if they knew I would do that?) They were standing as I had left them, their eyes following the moving train. I waved my hand. They waved back. And that was the last I ever saw of Bessie Palmer.

CHAPTER V

It was late afternoon of a day in the last week in July. A purple haze spread its broad banner along the eastern horizon as far as the eye could reach. It was a lovely day, warm, but not too warm. The St John was at its low level. I was standing, rod in hand, a few feet below the mouth of Clark's Brook, which is ice-cold and as clear as crystal.[26]

At this place Grand Bar stretches its three-quarter-mile length in midstream. On its eastern side the river is deep, rock-strewn, turbulent, but on its western border the water is more shallow and the current flows swift and waveless until it swings around the lower end of the Bar. In former times Grand Bar was a famous rendezvous for the Maliseet Indians, who in their bark canoes speared the salmon that rested in the low, swift water.

My stand was at the upper angle of a small cove (not more than a long cast across it) whose northern border swings westward about forty feet, then curves southward and finally completes a three-quarter circle past a granite ledge where it meets the river-current. At the western border a cold spring bubbles out of the gravelly beach, and there are numerous tiny rivulets which trickle into the cove. In very hot weather salmon often enter this little place to refresh themselves in the low, spring-fed water.

I had a No. 6 Brown Fairy tied to my gut leader, and three times a nice salmon had slowly risen without taking.

I thought I was quite alone when a voice, unmistakably Scottish, said: "That was a good fish. He came short."

---

26   On the west side of the St John, just above Wakefield.

I half turned and saw the speaker standing on the small terrace at the foot of a declivity that ascends at an angle of eighty degrees to the intervale above. The terrace was only a couple of rods long, surrounded by large trees. It was an ideal camping ground. "Yes," I said. "He came short. They often do at this season of the year."

"Will you pardon me if I make a suggestion?" he asked.

"Of course."

He clambered down the eight-foot-high embankment and came towards me. He was probably a trifle under six feet and spare of frame; his sandy hair needed cutting. His face, tanned by long exposure to sun and wind, was slightly tapered, with a strong chin; the eyes blue, set beneath sandy brows. He had on a khaki shirt open at the neck, khaki slacks, and heavy-soled brown army boots. He was a perfect stranger to me.

He came close and, for I had reeled in my line to rest the fish, looked at the fly and said: "As I thought. It has too many feathers; it might do to cut some of them off...I have scissors in my kit."

Evidently he was a fisherman, so I told him I was willing to try anything.

"I'll be back in half a mo," he said, strode to the bank, climbed up, and presently returned with a small pair of scissors. "Will you allow me to perform the operation?" His smile was charming.

"Yes. Of course."

I handed him the fly. He took it, gazed at it a few moments in silence then said: "If you'll pardon me for saying so, I'd prefer a fly with a much longer shank. Do you happen to have one?"

I took my fly-box from my pocket and opened it. He carefully looked over the lot, finally picked out a long-shanked (so-called low-water) Jock Scott—one of several an English dealer had sent me two years earlier.

"What a mess of feathers!" said my new friend. "Dinna tell me this fly was made in the old country! It might do on a river in spate, but never in low water. You're quite sure you have no objection to me transforming it?" He opened the scissor-blades, gave me a quick look, and I knew he was anxious to begin the operation.

"No, no, go ahead!" I said. "I'm always willing to learn."

"Many aren't," he murmured. "That is, they think they know all there is to learn. None of us do. The little I know about salmon fishing I got from my father, who was gillie two seasons for A.H.E. Wood."[27]

As he spoke he was snipping off some of the feathers that had decorated the fly, pausing every moment or so to hold it to the light to inspect it.

"Wood?" I said. "Oh, yes, the greased-line man." And wondered what freak of fortune had transferred my chance acquaintance to this part of the world.

"He was one of the best," he said, snipping off another feather and some of the hackles. "Perhaps the *very* best… You live in New Brunswick?"

"On this river, six miles below here, at Woodstock; a small town, and very beautifully situated."

"Woodstock," he repeated, "the same name as the English Oxfordshire town, and reminiscent of the fair Rosamond and the silken cord by which her royal lover found his way to her bower." He paused a moment, then: "Of course you've read Sir Walter's novel of the same name?"

"Yes."

"How did your Woodstock get its name?" he asked.

I told him that none of the present generation knew, but that probably Governor Sir Thomas Carleton had suggested it following the end of the American Revolutionary War when members of various loyalist regiments settled along the valley.

"Oh," he murmured, "that was a sorry mess! An unnecessary affair." He again inspected the fly and said: "A few more and I fancy it will do."

I told him that most of the villages and settlements had English place-names: such as Northampton, Grafton, and Southampton.

"And Perth," he said, "Scots."

"As are Kilmarnock, Kincardine, and Kintore."

---

27 A legendary Scotch fisherman, died 1934, who developed and popularised the "greased line" technique of fly-fishing. At that time fishing lines were made of silk or linen, which absorbed water, got heavy and sank. Coating the line with a grease, such as lanolin, let it stay afloat.
Wood also developed a technique of casting that makes the fly seem to drift with the stream. It was, and still is, known as greased-line technique, though modern fishing lines, light and waterproof, need no grease.

"Ah!" he said. "What bonny names!" and his blue eyes shone. He snipped off the ends of a few more feathers and hackles and said: "That's enough. I fancy his or her salmonship will like that," and held it up to me. Only a few short feathers and hackles now remained near the eye of the hook; the rest of it was quite bare.

"You see," he said, "the fish often makes a short rise at the feathers, and if the hook—as now—has a long shank, he'll be more liable to hook the barb in his jaw. At least that's the theory; take it or leave it. I notice that your line floats well."

"I'd like *you* to fish," I said, holding out the rod to him.

"Oh, no, no," he said. "I canna…I saw you casting; it was a good line."

But for all that he had demurred, I knew—by that sixth sense, which no words can explain—that he would like to feel the thrill of a fish taking. So I pressed the rod into his hands and backed away from him.

His eyes brightened as he flashed me a winning smile. "It's a bonny tool," he said. "Not too heavy, nor too light, and the action…perfect." He pronounced it "pairfect".

So he stepped to the edge of the pool just above the mouth of the brook and, as he began casting, I knew that he was an expert. Slowly, carefully, he covered the water. His back-casts performed a beautiful curve, and not until the line had straightened out behind him did he make the forward cast. It was mostly all wrist work, a poem of movement. A delight to watch. He was as unhurried as though taking part in a casting tournament.

Gradually he worked downstream until he had reached the place where I had raised the fish. He did not cast from the reel but with forefinger and thumb on the line which he held a little below the reel-seat, with a dozen coils lying on the beach at his feet. He made another cast and I watched with almost-held breath as the fly again made its curve to the desired area. Then I saw a huge "boil" that set my heart hammering.

The fisherman stood like a statue, made no effort to lift the rod tip, but I saw the forefinger and thumb tighten on the line and hold for a brief second or two then, as the fish swung out into the current, he raised the rod, paid out the coils of line at his feet, and allowed the reel to sing its glad notes.

He turned his tanned face to me and said: "Will you no take the rod and play him?"

"No; thanks," I said. "This is your chore. I'm having a wonderful time."

The salmon leaped, and he quickly lowered the rod-tip. Then, as it plunged back into its native element, sending up diamonds of spray, he raised it again; not too high—just enough to keep a light but steady pressure on the fish. It took out fully one hundred feet of line, ran upstream, swung back and towards us, then, as the fisherman quickly reeled in the slack, "felt" the fish, and canted the rod sideways, it again swung out into the strong current. That, I was sure, was where he wanted it. Like his casting, every movement was unhurried, nor did he betray the least excitement.

I have seen anglers, with a fish on, running up and down the beach, and backwards and forwards like demented creatures.

* * *

In fifteen minutes he had the salmon on its back, slightly above us, then let it drop down to where, gaff in hand, I stood knee-deep in the water. With one quick stroke I had it, lifted it high, waded to shore and deposited it well back on the beach. It had only a few kicks left. I killed it with a tap on the head with a beach rock, then removed the fly; both hooks had been well-set in the back of the jaw.

My new friend, standing beside me, said: "A bonny fish. Fifteen pounds?"

"All of that," I said, and held out my hand to him. "Congratulations. I have never seen a fish played more handily."

He took my hand in his, gave me the sign which all members of the *craft* know, and, his blue eyes on mine, waited expectantly for my answer. Then assured, he said: "I had a wee inspiration that you had travelled the road."

So we were brothers![28]

* * *

Going over to my knapsack I took out a pint bottle of Grant's Special, two small paper cups and came back to him. "Will you have a drink to celebrate your victory?" I asked.

Again his face lighted with a smile. "Grant's Special!" he said. "Och! but

---

28 Masons.

it's a bonny whisky. Smooth as cream. You are very good to me—a complete stranger. Yes, yes, a wee drop."

I half filled the cup I had given him, and said: "I've left room for some spring water—if you want it."

I think it had been his intention to take it straight but, since I was watering mine, he courteously did likewise. Then, raising his cup, he said: "Here's to your continued good health, and may we always have fishing in this worrld and the next."

"And the next," I repeated. And we slowly drank to each other.

When we had finished I said: "I have some sandwiches. I only wish we had a boiling kettle and tea."

He gave a low chuckle, then: "I have a wee billycan and tea at my camp-place."

"And a frying pan?" I asked.

He nodded, and I said: "Then we'll fry some of the salmon."

He laughed with boyish pleasure. "Splendid!" he said. Then: "If you'll gut the fish I'll run up and make the fire. Someone has been there before and lunched, if the heap of ashes is any sign."

"That would be my friend Russell Boyer," I said. "The fish warden. He often camps here on his way down river. Grand Bar is an old drifting ground for the poachers, as it was for the Indians to spear salmon." And, picking up our fish, I went down to the river, gutted it, scraped off the scales, then turning, saw the friendly smoke of the camp-fire floating above the trees that environed the little terrace.

The Scot had already filled the billycan with water from the spring and placed it on two boulders on either side of the blaze. So I cut four slices from the salmon, put them with butter he gave me into his frying pan, then began cooking it.

* * *

What a feast we had! We sat opposite each other on a wide plank set on a couple of short logs Russell Boyer had retrieved from the river. And when the Scot and I had quite finished he offered me a cigarette. I thanked him but said I only smoked a pipe, and took my tobacco pouch from my

Chapter V

pocket. As I did so I saw a pipe-stem protruding from his jacket that was hanging from a tree branch behind him.

"*You also* smoke a pipe," I said.

"Yes; but I happen to be quite out of baccy," he confessed.

"Will you accept some of mine?" I asked, and passed him my pouch. He thanked me and said (with that rolling of his r's I loved): "You are generous... Salmon steak...whisky, and now your baccy." Slowly, meditatively, he filled the bowl of his pipe, then picked up a half-burned stick from the fire, held the glowing end over the tobacco in my pipe, lighted his own, and with a sigh of contentment said: "If I may make a guess, it's an English mixture."

"Garrick," I said. "I've smoked it for years."

"So did our ain Jamie Barrie," he said; and added: "He wasna big, but he had a hairt of gold, and I wad rather have written *Peter Pan* and *A Window in Thrums* and *The Little Minister* than be made king of England."

* * *

We smoked in silence for a few minutes then he said: "I hae no doubt you've been wondering who I am, and what I'm doing in this country so far frae hame... Weel, my name is MacGregor." He paused a moment then, "Robin...Rab, for short. When the war broke out I joined the Black Watch, was in North Africa, Italy, then France. I met some of your Canadian Black Watch men, and they talked so much of this country that I decided to come and see it for myself. I flew to Montreal, then footed it to Winnipeg, took the train to Vancouver and back to Winnipeg. Then I did Ontario—the southern part on foot—and back to Quebec City, crossed to Levis; finally down this valley, and am now on my way to Halifax, where I hope to work my way home on some freighter. I didn't specially care for Ontario, nor the prairies, but British Columbia—well, the mountains, though bigger, reminded me of home; the same with pairts of Quebec, but, of all the places I've seen, this valley of the St John suits me best. The rivers are so clear and free of silt." He paused. I told him my name, that I was of Scottish descent on two sides of my family, and that one was a Sutherland who had served in the Royal 42nd or Black Watch before and during the American Revolutionary War.

MacGregor beamed me a happy smile and said: "That's another link between us."

"So few people in this country now walk," I said. "So I'm curious to know how you happened to find this spot. It's almost a mile from the highway."

"I didna travel the highway, at least from that small town I last passed through: Hartland? Yes. I crossed the bridge—the longest covered bridge in the world I believe—then walked along the upland flanking the river. In some respects the gradual rise of the hills reminds me of parts of England. I crossed several little burns and finally, coming to this place, thought it a good camping-ground and decided to spend the rest of the day and the night. I have a wee silk tent in my pack I'll set up later."

"You'd hardly find a better spot," I said. "You have seclusion, the music of the brook and the river and, when the moon comes up, one of the most beautiful sights imaginable."

"You have affection for the river," he said.

"Yes, Robin (if so I may call you). I was born within a few hundred yards of it. But I also love other New Brunswick rivers," and told him about the Tobique, Miramichi, Restigouche, Kedgwick and Upsalquitch, and that I had fished them all.

"The names are strong names—like prose poetry," he said.

"Yes; they are Indian names. For the most part Indian place-names are euphonious. As a matter of fact the Indian name for the St John is *Wul-ahs-tuk*, and means beautiful or pleasing.*(12a, 13a-b)* It flows into the Bay of Fundy at Saint John, and has numerous tributaries of which, in the old days, some were good salmon waters, but today, due to dams and pollution, only two or three contain salmon."

"That is a pity," he said. "Salmon must spawn, and if they canna get over the dams you speak of they'll gang to some other river in another part of the country and you'll be robbed of the best sport known to man…although I'll put trout fishing next in order. But", he added, "fishing is only part of the game to your true fisherman. The other part is the song of the water in a little burn or salmon stream, the beauty of the trees and the songs of the birds…all make for contentment, for that peace of mind and soul that is more worth seeking than anything else in the world."

Here was a man after my own heart. "I take it, then, you have long been a fisherman?"

Chapter V

"Aye," he answered, "ever since I was a wee laddie: first with my father then, when I was a little older, by myself or with my brothers and sisters,—who loved the sport. But in those early days I was, like John Buchan when a lad, far from being a contemplative angler (few are except born poets). My object, like his, was to catch fish and as many as I could by fair means or foul: with worm-bait or by tickling. An old poacher showed me how to do the last. But I must unconsciously have absorbed all that which goes to make fishing not merely a day off... Do you know the motto of *The Flyfishers' Club*: It is not all of fishing to fish?"

"Since reading John Buchan's autobiography," I answered.

"Ah," he said, "he was an outstanding type of your true fisherman. So were Marston and Wood and Sir Edward Grey and Lang. Of course old Izaak is the patron saint of all anglers. Not so much because of what he said about fish—for he often erred—but for his sweet, gentle and cheerful philosophy. Every time I read him (and it has been scores of times) I draw in something new. And as he refreshes me so does he humble me, and I would fain be as he was... Pardon me for going on at this length. Now *you* talk."

He had expressed my own thoughts.

"Will you have a drink of Mr. Grant's Special?" I asked.

"With you, gladly... I'll get water from the wee spring." So saying, he rose to his feet, picked up his billycan and swung himself down the bank to the beach.

He was back in less than a minute, and we drank to each other. He was a charming companion... I have made many chance acquaintances both on the highways and beside my rivers and brooks, but among them all none who so appealed to me as did this sun-tanned Scot. (I once met a graphologist, but of him later.)

Seated again he relighted his pipe and, for I had been smoking while he talked, I recharged my own with Mr. Garrick's mixture. But I didn't light it immediately. Instead: "I know the kind of rod you like, but what is your choice in flies—salmon flies?"

He blew out a cloud of smoke and said: "A very few do me—six or eight at most. And the standard patterns; among them the Jock, Highlander, Black Dose, Silver Doctor, Brown Fairy, Mar Lodge... It doesn't much matter which one of them I use, but in low water I often cut off half or more of the dressing—as today."

"A bright fly for a dark day? And a dark-coloured one for a bright day?"

"Not at all," he answered. "On the brightest days I've taken salmon on a Silver Doctor or Wilkinson—It doesn't matter which… I'm afraid the makers of flies wouldna approve of me. But their business is to tie and sell flies."

"Double-hook or single?" I asked.

"Personally I prefer the single hook," he answered. I laughed and said: "We differ in that. I like the double."

"It's a small matter," he said.

"And rods—?" I asked. "I know you approve of mine, but what do you think of the two, and the three-ounce rods that some of our piscatorial friends use?"

He smiled, then: "Every one to his fancy, as the old woman said when she kissed the coo… When I was with the forces we always liked to have just as big or better artillery than the enemy. What I mean is that I dinna care to send a wee laddie on a man's errand. If it's trout, a light rod. If salmon—the king of freshwater fighting fish—a rod with length and backbone."

"Reels?" I questioned.

"Yours is good," he said. "I prefer the single action, but a few times I've used the multiplying reel. But I do like a reel with a good drag you can regulate as occasion requires. As you doubtless observed, I prefer to fish with thumb and forefinger on the line."

"Except for my preference of fishing from the reel and using the double fly-hook, we agree on all the rest," I said, and rose to my feet. "It's time I was starting for home," I added.

"Oh," he cried, "dinna say that! I was hoping you'd stay the nicht. I havena had such a pleasant time for mony a day."

I thought a few moments then said: "My wife is on a holiday… Yes, Robin, I'll stay, thank you. And just before dark we'll try for another fish. But in the meantime I'll take a walk back to my car and get a rug."

"May I go with you?" he asked.

"Certainly. I'll be glad to have company; but first I'll put the salmon where it will keep fresh." So we descended to the beach, and in the bed of the brook scooped out a trench big enough to contain it, laid it in and covered

Chapter V

it with gravel. Then we went back and clambered up the steep path to the field above, that for more than a century had yielded crops of either hay or oats, but was now grown up with clumps of poplar and birch saplings four or five feet high. That tireless matron, Mother Nature, is never idle, and when man's efforts at cultivation relax, she again takes up her task of providing a new forest.

As we threaded our way between the saplings I told my companion that in prehistoric days the field had been the site of an Indian encampment, doubtless while they were engaged in spearing salmon along Grand Bar; and that I had dug up many stone implements such as arrowheads, spearheads, knives, scrapers, stone axes, and some rounded pebbles that might have had some religious significance. Then I showed him the place where earlier in the afternoon I had left the field and travelled along the brook to the river.

He asked me many questions about the first inhabitants of North America which I gladly answered as best I could. He had seen Indians hanging around railway stations in the far west garbed in decorated tunics, fringed trousers, and feathered bonnets that came below their hips. Of course their garb was similar to pictures he had seen in English magazines. As a lad he had read Cooper's Leatherstocking tales, and confessed that he had quite fallen in love with Uncas, son of the Delaware sagum, Chingachgook, and had actually wept when he had been killed by Le Reynard Subtil, the Huron chieftain.

"And so," he said, "I and my brothers and sister used to play Indian and whites over the same craggy hills and glens where, at an earlier date, my Highland ancestor, Rob Roy, and his clansmen, made their way to plunder the cattle belonging to the Duke of Montrose. Of course Rob always claimed that he was only recompensing himself for the illegal confiscation of his ancestral estates."

* * *

On our return to the river we broke off enough boughs from some fir trees to make a mattress, and gathered drift-wood to keep our campfire going. Then we set up his little tent, big enough for only one. The Scot insisted that, when it came time to sleep, I must occupy it; but I refused his offer and said I preferred to sleep under the stars.

I now got my rod, went down to the river and soon hooked and landed a five-pound grilse. So, having gutted it, we dug another trench in the bed of the brook, laid it in and covered it with gravel.

The sun sank below the cliff behind us, and in a short time the eastern sky was saffron-coloured from the reflected afterglow. My companion gazed at it with awe and admiration. "Beautiful!—Beautiful!" he repeated. "It makes me homesick for the hills and the heather. Please do not misunderstand me," he hastened to add, "I love this place, and your gracious company. But you must come to Scotland some time and see the mountains and glens that your ancestor knew—a Sutherland, you told me, and a Black Watch man."

"That's right," I said, "and the Clarkes were also Scots."

"It makes us all the more kin," he said. "And if you should make the journey, bring your rod, and I'll arrange for you to have some fishing or my name isna Robin MacGregor."

I thanked him. Some time, I assured him, I would make the journey. Alas! That was fourteen years ago, and I have not yet made it. Perhaps next year…or the next…

Twilight faded. Darkness settled over the hills; the moon climbed majestically into the blue, lighted up Grand Bar. Its washed reflection in the fast-flowing river looked like an enormous cauldron of molten gold. The stars swung into orbit—distant jewels in the immensity of space. My companion gave a deep sigh, then said, in a low voice: "How beautiful! 'It is not all of fishing to fish'." Then after a slight pause: "Oh man…man.. 'Canst thou bind the sweet influences of Pleiades, or loose the bands of Orion? Canst thou bring forth Mazzaroth in his season? Or canst thou guide Arcturus with his sons?'"[29]

* * *

A little later he said: "You were telling me, as we walked across the field this afternoon, that you had found several curious stones. I dinna mean the arrowheads and such-like, but the others—the ones you thought might have some religious significance. I would ask why you think so."

---

29 Job 38:31.

Chapter V

"Well," I answered, "the early Jesuits, who ministered to the Indians, seeing that they set great store by them, and being under the impression that they represented some pagan cult, tried to induce them to throw them away. But they stoutly refused to part with them even though they had accepted Christianity."

"Ah," he said, "so did our Scottish ancestors treasure certain stones. Some thought they contained the souls of people. You've heard of the bannock stone—a flat, round stone which, even today, some Scots put in front of the fire, and when heated cook their cakes of oatmeal and barley on? Well, it was thought one in particular contained the soul of a giant."

"Yes," I answered, "I've read of bannock stones, and know of one having been used in recent years for such a purpose in this province. Our Indians used stones on which to bake their corn-bread, although sometimes they placed the raw cakes in hot ashes. Of course they had clay pots as did the prehistoric peoples of Britain, but they were not suitable in which to cook their corn-bread. Our Indians say that their ancient deity Gluskap, or Gluskabe, shot arrows into trees, and out of the trees came Indians. Thus he peopled north-eastern America."

"That's a nice conceit," said my companion. "It has its near parallel in the homeland. We also believed that the souls of people abode in trees—especially in thorn trees. Not only in trees, but in butterflies, birds, and bees, and even in salmon. Strange—wad you believe it?—I always feel like apologising to the bonny fish when I land it and hit it over the head with the 'priest'. I try to be as gentle as possible. It micht be an atavistic inheritance from the remote past."

I didn't smile. "Our Indians used to believe that certain animals were their brothers. So they actually said to the bear and the beaver: 'I am sorry, brother, to kill you.'" I paused a moment, then went on: "When I was a child we had in our family a maid-of-all-work named Margaret McIntyre. She used to tell me ghost and fairy stories, and tales of warlocks who turned people into other forms. Although I loved them I was afraid to go to sleep, and if I awakened and found my toes out of the bed coverings I was terrified."

The Scot chuckled. "Aye," he said, "so was I, when I was told that there were certain old green women called *water wives* who seized people as they were crossing a burn or river, and drowned them. But it was not long before

I found that there were trout in the burns, then not even my fear of the *water wives* was enough to keep me away from them with hook and worm. Then there were the banshees—little people three or four feet high—who warned you of approaching calamities. Many people had these familiars, as they often called them. And mind you, many people in Scotland even now believe in these little people."

"Same here," I said. "I know of a family that has a banshee. This family is of Irish descent, and claim that when their ancestor came from the old country—more than a century and a quarter ago—the banshee followed him. He or it was a little man with a face like a wrinkled apple that has hung on the tree all winter. He was always dressed in snuff-coloured jacket and knee breeches, and his coming always presaged a death in the family. The man or the woman of the house would suddenly awaken during the night and see the 'familiar' standing by the bedside. The next moment he had vanished. And shortly afterwards some one of the family or a near relative died.[30] This particular family was quite proud of their banshee; possibly felt that it conferred on them a certain aura of nobility. But, joking apart, there are people who, when a dog howls at night, say it means death. And others who have the same superstition if a bird flies into the house. And I know of people who will never begin a journey on a Friday."

"In Scotland," said MacGregor, "the banshees live in caves on high cliffs or mountains. Sometimes they come to the houses and give their warning of death by most doleful wailings."

"Do you believe in them?" I asked.

"I dinna rightly ken," he began, paused a moment, then went on: "There are certain superstitions that have their origin in the very matrix of time, and some of us—most of us—are heir to some of them. But,"—he pointed his pipe stem at me—"wad you believe that I saw you coming down the little burn this afternoon even before I heard your splashing footsteps? You were carrying your rod in your left hand and your knapsack over your right shoulder. Once you paused to examine a small hole in the high bank. And the face—it was yours. You winna believe that?"

---

30   GFC used this banshee in his unpublished novel *The Last of the Middletons*, c. 1933-1935.

Chapter V

I gave an involuntary shiver. It was quite true; I had paused to look at a muskrat hole in the clayey bank!

Taking out my tobacco pouch I opened it, then realising that his own pipe was empty, handed him the pouch and said, with a low laugh: "Shall I have many more fishing years?"

"A good many," he answered. "You are still young."

"Sixty-four," I said.

"That is nothing," he said, smiling. "Your spirit is young. I canna imagine you getting old."

That was thirteen years ago. I am still fishing.

He filled his pipe, restored the pouch to me and said: "Mony thanks." He picked up a glowing brand by its unburned end, leaned forward, held it over the bowl of my pipe until it was going nicely, then lighted his own.

The souls of men abiding in salmon! Possibly that accounts for its dual nature; for like man the noble fish is both very wise and very foolish. A man runs after a pretty face, and a salmon after a fly, and both often get hooked.

* * *

Before turning in for the night I poured a couple of nightcaps—the remainder of Mr. Grant's Special. Before drinking, the Scot rose to his feet, and standing tall and straight at one side of the glowing embers of our campfire, said in vibrant tones: "I wad drink—" he paused until I rose to my feet and stood opposite him, my paper cup raised to his—"I wad drink a toast to the memory of twa men: one a Scot, the other English: both of whose names posterity will continue to honour as long as this auld worrld spins on its axis—to Isaak Walton and Robbie Burns!"

"To Izaak Walton and Robbie Burns!" I repeated.

A little later I rolled myself in my rug upon my bed of resinous-smelling fir boughs, and he crawled into his little tent. The moon and the light from the still-flickering campfire made the place almost as light as day. I lay for a long time, my face to the stars, and thought of my companion. On the morrow we would part, like ships that, having spoken each other at sea, go on their separate ways. He was a delightful chap and I didn't want to lose him. We meet such lovable people occasionally.

* * *

Daylight had dawned when I awoke to the odour of frying bacon, and found Robin on his knees beside the little fire over which, between the two stones, he had set his billycan filled with spring water. "Good morning," I said. "How long have you been up?"

He half turned me his face, smiled, then: "Good morning," he said in his cheery voice; "a half hour. Will you have one, or two eggs—? One—righto. Did you sleep well?"

"Like a dormouse," I said. "And you?"

"Like a hibernating badger," he said. Then, as I rose to my feet, he said: "I laid out a fresh towel for you—there—on the beach. As a matter of fact I had a swim. The current was verra strong but I enjoyed it."

Going down to the beach I washed face and hands then returned to our little camping ground. The Scot was on his feet. He smiled and held out to me a wallet I recognised as mine. "It was lying near the edge of the bank," he said, "and I took the liberty of picking it up."

It had my name stamped on the flap, and contained something over one hundred dollars. "My wife", I said, "has always chided me for being careless with money, and keys—I'm forever losing them. Thank you," I added, took the wallet from his outstretched hand and restored it to my pocket.

He said: "When I went down to the beach I saw the wakes of two fish leaving the shallow water close to the little cold spring near the cove. Evidently they heard the vibration of my feet on the ground."

"Yes," I said, and told him that once my friend Doctor Grant and I had disturbed at least three fish from the same spot. "At present," I said, "the ones you saw are very probably in the swift water just below the brook. We'll try for them after breakfast."

"It's a grand hour," he said.

* * *

And so, after we had eaten our bacon and eggs and drunk two cups of tea, we went down to the beach. I held out my rod to him. "You try," I said.

"Nay—nay," he protested, backing away from me. "It's your rod, and your river."

Chapter V

"And yours…now," I said. "You've fallen in love with it. So please give me the pleasure of watching you fish. I can come here any time I choose."

He gave me a long look, smiled, then said: "It would give me as much pleasure to watch *you* fish."

"Let's toss a coin," I said.

"I…I'd rather not." He looked troubled. "Why?" I asked.

"Because," he answered, "*I'll* win."

I laughed. And taking a penny from my pocket, said: "Will you choose head or tail?"

"It doesna matter. It winna make any difference," he said. "Well, I choose tail.

"A fish has both head and tail," I said; and tossed the penny a few feet into the air, caught it in the palm of my hand then held it out for his inspection.

"Of *course* it's *tail*," he said. "I'm sorry," and reluctantly took the rod from my hand.

"The same fly as yesterday?" I asked.

"Yes. Why change?" He inspected the knot, tested it, and nodded. "It's all right," he said.

"One week on the Restigouche I fished with the same fly for three days in succession. It was taking salmon," I said.

"And why did you change it the fourth day? Or was it the last three days of your trip that you used it?"

"The first three. Just as dusk was settling over the river my guide, who was then fishing, hooked an enormous salmon. He hadn't noticed, nor had I, that the line was caught around the reel-handle, and before he could release it the fish broke the leader and went off with the fly in its mouth. It was the last one of the type that I had. My guide, an expert angler, was almost inconsolable. The fly was a Cow-Dung. But we took fish the following day on a Mar Lodge."

The Scot said nothing for a few moments, then: "I once had the same experience. I wished his salmonship guid luck and prayed that the hook was not in his gills. It was a bonny fish." So saying, he walked up the beach beyond the mouth of the brook and began casting, while I sat on a flat boulder and watched him.

* * *

Slowly, covering the water with meticulous care, Robin MacGregor worked down past the mouth of the brook to the upper angle of the little cove. But there was no answering swirl. He lengthened his cast and gradually reached the ledge of rock which formed the extreme lower arc of the cove. There was swift water. Thrice he cast to his left, and I watched the line make its curve and straighten out several feet below where the fish had taken the day before. Then there was a "boil" that set my heart thumping. But the fish didn't take.

The Scot half turned me his face and said: "The fly wasna moving just richt for his honour," reeled in his line, came and sat down beside me, took out his pipe, then replaced it in his pocket. I knew the reason, so handed him my tobacco pouch.

He took it, thanked me, filled the bowl, struck a match, smoked a few moments in silence, then said: "Sometimes I rest a fish, sometimes no. I had out too short a line. We'll give him a bit rest, then make another try. That fish came from a distance, made the turn deep in the water. That's why the boil wasna big. I'll try a different trick in a few minutes."

We sat and smoked. Across the river, half-way up the hillside, we could see a farmer seated on a mowing machine while he guided his horses through a field of golden-coloured grain. In the nearer distance, along the rail tracks that ran along the river bank, a long freight train thundered towards Woodstock, then silence reigned, save for the clacking of the mowing machine and the lilt of the river over the bar.

The Scot tapped the tobacco ash out on a beach pebble and restored the pipe to his pocket, picked up the rod, walked to the edge of the river and began casting, slowly lengthening his line until he had out about seventy feet. Then he cast, not out into the current opposite him, but at only a slight angle from the ledge of the rock. As the current caught the line and it swung towards the ledge, he began drawing it in towards him. Almost immediately a salmon rose with a swirl that heaped up the water. For a moment I saw the broad tail. As on the day before, he held the line between forefinger and thumb until he felt the tug that told him the fish was on, then wound

Chapter V

up the two or three yards of slack line dangling from his fingers. The whole operation had consumed a few seconds.

The salmon ran into the strong current; the reel hummed. Seventy-five yards out the fish leaped into the air, fell back in a shower of spray and tore off another twenty or thirty yards of line, rose again, turned a somersault then, as the reel-gears screeched, it ran upstream with the speed of a thunderbolt, taking off more than half the backing.

It was, I thought, a twenty-five-pounder or better. Suddenly the Scot lowered the rod tip—taking off most of the strain on the salmon's mouth—and it stopped its wild rush as suddenly as it had begun it and came slowly upstream while the Scot reeled it in.

Nearer and nearer it came. I could distinctly see the huge torpedo-like shape only a few inches beneath the surface of the water. Now it was in the calmer water just where that of the cove and river current met, and I reached for the gaff lying at my side. Then it sculled farther into the quiet cove as though it were on a tour of inspection. But suddenly it made an abrupt turn to the left, breasted the ledge of rock, again rushed out into the strong current, and upriver while the reel sang its protesting notes. Then it stopped its rush, sank to the bottom, gave its head a few shakes, and the tip of the rod sprang upwards.

Robin quickly reeled in the slack line, turned to me and said: "It was a bonny fish." Then quoted a few lines from the book of Job:

> *Canst thou draw out leviathan with an hook?*
> *Or his tongue with a cord which thou lettest down?*
> *Canst thou put an hook into his nose?*
> *Or bore his jaw through with a thorn?...*
> *Shall the companions make a banquet of him?*
> *Shall they part him among the merchants?*
> *Canst thou fill his skin with barbed iron?*
> *Or his head with fish spears?...*
> *Remember the battle, do no more.*[31]

---

[31] Job 41:1-9.

*   *   *

A little later, the grilse and the remainder of our catch of yesterday enshrouded with shore grass and ferns, and Robin's little tent, the billycan, his blanket and other things in his pack, we climbed the high path to the field above and made our way to Noddin's and my car. For I was taking him as far as my home, whence he would resume his solitary journey to Saint John.

Solitary, did I say? In one sense yes, in another no: for no man is solitary whose mind—like a good book—contains many delightful passages.

At my home (after we had washed up) he looked at my English water-colours, done by Hannaford.[32] That of Tavy Cleave, Dartmoor, with its rolling hill and high peak, and the moss-covered boulders and purple heather and the little burn between, he stood in front of for two or three minutes. Then he said: "The *heather!* The *heather!*" The words were more eloquent of his homesickness than a whole volume.

I showed him some of my choice stone blades, arrowheads and spearheads, and he said: "Not sae long ago our ain ancestors used similar objects."

I gave him a can of Garrick's mixture to take with him, and while he wandered about the room looking at this and that, I was in the kitchen preparing a salad with lettuce and tomatoes from the frigidaire. Then I took a bowl from the cupboard, and was just about to go into the garden where we had a stand of raspberry bushes, when he joined me. I told him I was going to pick a few raspberries for lunch. "Oh," he said. "Splendid. May I help?"

We filled the bowl with the luscious fruit, and he was as delighted as a child. Then we returned to the kitchen. The water had boiled in the tea kettle and I made a pot of tea, but I swear it was not so palatable as that we brewed in his billycan beside the little brook.

*   *   *

Afterwards I urged him to take the grilse with him, but he protested that it would spoil before he could eat it all. So I cut off several slices from

---

32   English water-colourist, 1863-1955.

Chapter V

the big salmon, wrapped them in waxed paper and he accepted them with thanks. Then I said: "I'll drive you a few miles below town, then let you off." He accepted the offer.

I drove slowly down Main Street, reached the outskirts of the town, went along the river-road flanked by farmsteads, many of whose owners were the descendants of those early pioneers who had left their homes following the American Revolutionary war and, coming to this peaceful valley, had carved out new abodes in the virgin wilderness.

Below the little Anglican church,[8] known as Christ Church, with its ancient cemetery, where the ashes of so many of the old loyalists have long since mingled with the dust, I stopped the car and the Scot got out, shouldered his heavy pack, then turned and held out his hand. I took it in mine. He said: "It's all been wonderful. Guid luck. Thank you again." He gave my hand another grip, his kindly blue eyes on mine, then turned and, stick in hand, started off.

"You'll have the river in sight for fifty-five miles at least," I called after him.

He turned. "And memories longer than that," he said.

CHAPTER VI

A man never forgets the experience of hooking and landing his first salmon, although he may, on some rare occasion, forget the day (much to his wife's justifiable but secret chagrin and annoyance) when their wedding anniversary once again rolls around. Women, God bless them, never forget it; and, if they have become disciples of Father Izaak, will always treasure memories of the first salmon they tangle with. Thus it is with Helen Gilbert.

Two weeks ago my wife and I were guests of Doctor Oscar Gilbert and his wife, Helen, at Pemaquid on the coast of Maine. Both are ardent anglers and have been coming to different New Brunswick and Gaspé rivers during a period of twenty-five years. One of their first trips took them to the Main Southwest Miramichi River, where Helen caught her first Atlantic salmon. She is a splendid *raconteur*, and one day, during the lunch hour, told us of her unique experience.

"At that time," she said, "I didn't know any more about the habits of salmon than I do about the moon. The first morning my guide took me in his canoe three miles upriver to a good pool, and I hadn't fished long before I was into a good fish. It raced this way and that, and took out a lot of line. I was as excited as a girl waiting for her boy friend to come and escort her to her first visit to the opera. I felt that I could bring it in as easily as I had trout on our Gaspé river. But I didn't know salmon. I raised the rod as high as I could and started to reel in line. I could hear the guide repeating some words I was too excited to understand. Finally he cried in a louder voice: 'Let him go, Mrs. Gilbert! Let him go!'"

"'But I don't want to let him or she or it go!' I almost screamed. 'Why do you say that? I want it—my first salmon. I want it,' and held the rod higher, if that were possible, and continued trying to reel in while the fish was near the top of the water beating it into foam. Of course it was well hooked and the leader a good strong one or I'd have lost it.

"'Let it go! For Gawd's sake let it go!' repeated the guide, and again I cried out: '*I won't let it go.* I'm paying twenty-five dollars a day to catch a salmon, and now I've got one on you say let it go.'

"'Oh, my Gawd!' he said; 'don't you understand? I mean take your hand off the reel, lower your rod a bit, and let the fish run. You can't pull in them babies like you do a chub!'

"'Oh!' I said. 'Why didn't you say that in the first place, instead of let it go?' So I gave the fish its head.

"'Well, Ma'am,' he said, 'I thought you understood the English language!'

"What could I say to that? Then, seeing that almost all the line was off the reel, I cried out: '*He'll get away! He'll get away!* What'll I do now?'

"'Don't worry,' said the guide, who was now paddling after the monster. 'We'll get below him. There's a nice beach below the bend where we'll land an' play'm. Now, reel in…slow…not too fast. But don't let'm git slack line. There…let'm go—I mean let'm run. There…he's going to jump again. When he does, drop the rod tip so if he falls on the leader he won't break away.'

"Of course I didn't know exactly what he meant, so I said: 'How can I do that when it's fastened to the rest of the rod?' And just then the fish made a beautiful leap and fell back throwing up a shower of spray.

"He gave a deep groan, then said something half to himself that sounded like 'By the three blind orphans, and the golden peavey-stock!' which seemed utter nonsense to me; but I imagined it was yet another example of Miramichi guides' type of profanity. Then he said: 'I meant lower the tip of your rod.'

"'Oh!' I said, and just then the salmon took another long run, leaped about four feet out of the water and fell back on its side with a terrific smack. Then it swung to the left and continued its course downriver while the guide paddled the canoe after it as fast as he could go.

"Finally, at the head of the beach he'd spoken of, he got below the fish, and it worked its way upstream. He let me out on the sandy beach, from which I played it. I should say it played me, for my arms and wrists ached,

Chapter VI

the perspiration flowed from my forehead into my eyes and almost blinded me, and I could hear my breath whistling between my clamped teeth. I guess my guide saw I was near exhaustion, for he asked me if I wanted him to take the rod. But I gasped: 'No! no! no! I'll land him myself...thank you.'

"He said 'OK', filled, lighted his pipe, and, hands on his hips, stood just back of me, puffing away and only pausing occasionally to offer some advice in a voice that was as emotionless as the monument on Bunker Hill... You know, the place where the Americans beat the British—or the British the Americans, whichever was which; and all the while my heart was thumping like an electric egg-beater. Calm, did I say he was? Yes, as much so as the big spruce trees behind him.

"Well, after I'd reeled in the creature a dozen times within twenty feet of the beach, and as many times it had gone back to the middle of the river, it suddenly came in as quiet as a kitten. The guide stepped into the shallow water, lowered his landing net, dipped up the fish and had just reached the beach when the mesh of the net broke, my salmon slithered through the opening and fell flop to the beach within a foot of the water.

"Quick as the guide was, I was quicker. I dropped my rod to the beach, gave a wild shriek of dismay, and dove head-foremost, like a baseball player sliding to base, and fell flat on top of the fish, my face over the shallow water. Luckily it was no more than three or four inches deep. But when my head bobbed forward, I gulped up half a pint which almost strangled me. In the meantime my guide was on his knees beside me trying to get hold of the salmon's tail, the while he was roaring with laughter. Then some of the hot ashes from his pipe dropped on the back of my neck, and I gave another shriek, released one hand to brush it off, toppled sideways, face down, and gulped down some more river water. But it gave my guide a chance to grasp the fish back of its tail, draw it from beneath my body and fling it a good distance up the beach. Then, again muttering something about three blind orphans and a golden peavey stock, he lifted me to my feet. 'Gosh, Mrs. Gilbert,' he said, 'you sure took a header!'

"'But I...I saved the fish after it had gone through your rotted net,' I gasped.

"'That's right,' he said. 'I deserved to lose it. But, Mrs. Gilbert, I didn't know it was rotten.' Then he went to where the fish lay and tapped it over the head with a leaded stick he carried slung to his belt. Both hooks were set in the thick gristle of the salmon's mouth, and the guide said we could have played it to Blackville."

Helen paused in her tale. My wife and I and Oscar were convulsed with laughter, in which she joined more soberly. Then she said: "Wasn't I a mess! Half of me wet to the hide, and the rest of me covered with salmon scales. I must have looked like a…a"… She paused, and Oscar filled in: "Like a mermaid."

She smiled. "That's what I was trying to think of," she said. "But your mermaid was the only one of our party that took a salmon that day."

"And the next," he said.

She nodded happily, then: "But I handled it better than the *first*. My guide—really an awfully good sort—talked all the way upriver to our pool and told me a lot I needed to know about fishing salmon… Will you have another cup of coffee, Mary? and you, Fred? and you, Oscar? Good."

CHAPTER VII

Some pages back I made mention of the graphologist and promised that I'd tell about him in due course. Now a promise made is like an unpaid debt and is as disturbing to one of my temperament as was the sword suspended by a hair over the head of Damocles by the tyrant Dionysius of Syracuse. And so I shall now discharge the debt and attain that peace of mind which is the ideal of all anglers.

A story that is now common currency in the Maritime Provinces tells how a traveller inquired of a young man where he was born, and he answered: "*The Island.*"

"What Island?" the other asked.

"Prince Edward Island," was the somewhat haughty reply. "What other island is there?"

"Any fishing there?"

"Of course; the best in the world. And potatoes—oh, man! They always bring a higher price in Montreal and Toronto than do Nova Scotia and New Brunswick potatoes."

"How about apples?"

"Best in the world. Once a dealer imported a carload of British Columbia apples. Couldn't sell them except for hog feed, and they gave the hogs some sort of colic."

"I take it, then, that the people are remarkably intelligent?"

"Smartest in Canada," the other averred soberly. "Doctors, lawyers, politicians, farmers, you can't beat 'em."

The young man's answers were characteristic of all the Islanders. I have been amazed at the large number of pedestrians I have picked up on my journeys to some fishing stream or prehistoric Indian camp-site—dozens of them, and seven out of ten were from *The Island*. So I wondered what the population would be if they had remained there. They must be a very prolific race. The remainder of those who have made the exodus to get work were, of course, from New Brunswick and Nova Scotia.

No wonder, then, that the people of Ontario—and especially of that hub of culture, Toronto—hold their chins up, look down their noses at all other Canadians not blessed of Providence by being native Torontonians, and declare that *they are the people!* God bless them! But what would "Tawranta" be without The Islanders, New Brunswickers and Nova Scotians?

* * *

Which is all by way of prelude to saying that when I saw James Strange walking with light, springy step along the highway two miles north of Woodstock, stopped my car and offered him a lift, I would have bet seven dollars to one that he was from *The Island*.

He was about five-feet-eight, slight of frame, his face tanned, and had nice brown eyes. He was well-dressed, bareheaded, and carried a small knapsack by a strap over one shoulder.

He seated himself beside me, slammed the door, and as I started the car, said: "Are you going far—Quebec, Montreal, Ontario way?"

"No," I answered, "only ten miles—the village of Victoria—where I expect to meet Russell Boyer and ask him about the prospects of fishing a week hence."

My companion gave a low laugh, then said: "After leaving Saint John, I was picked up by three different motorists, and all of them were bound to some stream or lake to catch fish. Is that all New Brunswickers do in the summer?"

"A good many of us do just that," I answered. "We have the best salmon rivers and trout streams and lakes in North America."

"I'm from *the Island*," he said. "I doubt if you can beat Island fishing."

I let it go at that, and said: "Do you expect to get work in Toronto?"

"Oh, no—that is, not what you may think. I'm a graphologist."

"So you read handwriting? That's interesting."

Chapter VII

"Yes. As you say, an interesting profession. I can tell a man's character and what work he does by his handwriting. You can always spot a doctor by his writing—it's rotten. I mean the worst in the world. Yes; I've travelled all over England and Europe, analysed the handwriting of all types of professional men, not to mention the crowned heads of several different nations. Most of them—I mean the kings and princes—always gave me a private audience. Evidently they didn't want any of their attendants to hear what I said. Of course I always told the truth, because above all I am an artist in my profession. One king, whose handwriting I read, didn't like it a bit, and threatened me with imprisonment; but after I had told him that his secret sins were as safe with me as if he had confessed them to his father confessor, he cooled down, but warned me to get the hell out of his kingdom and stay out."

The graphologist paused a few moments to flash me a twinkling smile. As much as to say he knew I knew he was pulling my leg a bit about the king. Then he went on, his whole manner as friendly as an English sparrow: "This is my fifth trip across the mainland of Canada. I've read the handwriting of most of the Canadian politicians (I can show you their cards); but Mackenzie King's script was the most puzzling of any. At first I didn't know what he was; felt like I was in a fog or a trance, but finally I made him out and told him. He was a bit huffed but had to admit that he *was* a politician.

"You know, it's odd how many people like to have their handwriting analysed; just like people (women in particular) will travel miles to have their fortune told either by the teacup or cards. If you'll allow me, when we get to our journey's end, I'll analyse your handwriting, without charge. I appreciate the lift."

I thanked him, but told him that save for a few things that were wholly between me and the Deity, he could only deduce from my handwriting that I was one of the most ardent fishermen in New Brunswick or, for that matter, in North America. No doubt my handwriting would reveal fish-hooks; mostly flies; because although for the most part I was a fly fisherman, I occasionally, when on some small brook, reverted to the worm bait of my younger days.

He gave a merry laugh, then said: "I'm sorry you're not going on to Quebec."

"And Montreal and Toronto?"

"Oh, no. To be quite frank, you'd have to do quite a bit of waiting. I have an appointment with the Roman Catholic Bishop of Quebec and the Anglican Bishop. Then, in Montreal, with the president of the Canadian Pacific Railway, as well as some other dignitaries. It's a very old and honourable profession. The Chaldean were especially expert, but they were outdone by Daniel. You remember that *Mene, Mene—Tekel Upharsin* business. That was real smart. It rubbed the noses of all the Egyptian, Chaldean and other astrologers and wizards. Aye, it's a very ancient craft."

"So is fishing," I said. "You'll find it mentioned in Holy Writ. Four or five of the disciples, among them St. Peter, were fishermen. The Pope wears a ring on his finger with a fish engraved on it in commemoration of St. Peter. Then there was Mark Anthony, a most ardent fisherman—if we credit Plutarch's report."

"Oh, yes. The chap who was fishing with Cleopatra, and she had one of her attendants dive over the opposite side of the galley, tie a salt herring or whatnot on his hook, then give the line a tug and suddenly let go; and Mark tumbled backwards to the deck. I fancy that wasn't the only occasion that she put one over on Mark."

"You must admit that he took the herring episode like a good sport," I said. "If you remember, when he had hauled it on board, he remarked that it was a good fish, but much smaller and older than he had thought. But the sport goes back much farther—to the most remote times—thousands of years before the Cro-Magnons did their picture writing on the walls of the grottos in France and northern Spain."

"It was good work," said my companion, "and far superior to much of what passes for art in these so-called enlightened days. At least you know that the bison is a bison; the mammoth a mammoth. Nor did those old chaps draw out of scale as did some of the Florentine artists who represented the infant Christ with the physical proportions of a ten-year-old boy. But let's get back to fishing and handwriting. I admit that fishing is an older craft, but writing is a close second. Witness the hieroglyphics on the temple of Horus, and the temples of the Aztecs in Mexico. Then there is the Runic alphabet of the Scandinavians, probably adapted from the Greek or Roman letters; and—"

Chapter VII

Just then we had reached the village of Victoria and a man on the roadside hailed me with: "Hullo, Doc! Where you going?"

It was Russell Boyer. I brought the car to a stop. He came forward, took my hand, wrung it heartily, and said: "If you think of the angels you hear the rustle of their wings. I was thinking of you."

I have described Russell's personal appearance before[F], but it will bear repeating: he was of medium height, broad-chested, brown of face and eyes, short moustache, and was as strong as a moose.*(9)* A man who had lived all his life in the out of doors as woodsman, guide and on occasion a fishery warden. No man could pole or paddle a canoe better than he. Every spring, since his wife died, he had taken his tent and cooking utensils to the long island opposite his home, and on a narrow terrace on the east side remained until mid-October.

Now he said: "The first run of salmon is on. I hope you brought your rod."

I told him I had only come to Victoria to enquire if the fish were up, and to see if he were alive and kicking; but I'd come up Wednesday afternoon next at six o'clock.

"Me alive!" he chortled. "Why, Doc, I could trim the northern lights. Yes, there's a good run of fish."

Then I introduced him to Mr. James Strange. As they shook hands I noticed that the graphologist winced. Said Russell: "Any friend of Doc's is mine."

Mr. Strange got to earth, slung his knapsack over his shoulder, thanked me for the lift, and both he and Russell stepped to the side of the road while I turned the car. Then, with a wave of the hand, I began the journey home.

* * *

A week later, at sharp six p.m. I was on the beach opposite Russell's island summer home. He was waiting for me. He gave me a broad smile, shook my hand, then lifted the canoe into the water and, when I was seated, picked up his long-handled setting-pole *(10)* and poled upstream along the shore for a few hundred yards, then shipped his setting-pole, and seizing his paddle struck a diagonal course against the strong current towards the

---

F *Six Salmon Rivers and Another.*

island shore. At its lower extremity he swung around it to the water on the eastern side then, discarding paddle for setting-pole, poled along the shore until we were opposite his camp-site, where I could see smoke from his campfire filtering above the tree tops.

We climbed the high bank, came to the little terrace I knew so well. *(12b)* And there, a long apron suspended from his middle, was Mr. James Strange.

He flashed me a happy smile, his eyes twinkling. "Welcome," he said. "The griddle is heated, the pancake-batter ready for the griddle. The water boiled for a brew of tea."

"What about your appointment with the bishops of Quebec—Roman Catholic and Anglican?" I asked.

"Ah," he replied, with a wave of the big spoon in his hand, "their Graces can wait. I couldn't resist Russell's invitation to spend a week with him. Haven't had such a good time in years. Shall I begin frying the flapjacks, Russell?"

"Just a moment, Jim," said Russell. He stepped over to the little cupboard standing left of the table, opened the door, brought out a bottle of rum, one of lime juice, then a small decanter of vermouth.

He was about to mix one of his famous Vesper cocktails.

Presently he poured a small drink for me (for from past experiences he knew I didn't care for big ones), then almost filled two other glasses, one of which, with a bow that would have done credit to the caterer of *L'Ordre du Bon Temps*—established at Port Royal by Champlain three and a half centuries ago—handed it to the graphologist. Then, lifting his own glass, he said in a reverent voice: "Here's to us. May the river always flow and the salmon always run up from the Bay. And may there always be good sports to fish for them." Then, when we had emptied our glasses, he said: "Carry on, James."

And so, seated on a wide plank set on two boulders in front of the fire, with the cast-iron griddle resting on an iron oven-frame over the coals, Mr. James Strange poured the mixture of buckwheat batter in four large rounded portions. Then, as the small bubbles rose to the surface, broke and left numerous indentations, he slipped a large wide-bladed knife beneath each one in turn, deftly turned them over, and in less than two minutes the under-sides were cooked a beautiful seal brown. "Now, boys," he said, "fall to. They're better hot from the pan."

Both Russell and I offered to cook the next lot, but the graphologist said no. He was an *Islander*, and knew better than we how to cook griddle cakes.

So Russell and I shared the first cooking, buttered and spread over with maple syrup, while James cooked more on his hot griddle.

They were delicious, and although we didn't eat twenty-four, as the story book tells us Little Black Sambo did, we each had four helpings before James consented to allow me to cook for him; and when I put them on his plate and he began eating them he admitted that, for a New Brunswicker, I had done very well indeed.

There are griddle cakes and griddle cakes, but I maintain that the best are those made from buckwheat meal mixed with sour milk or buttermilk; and Russell had got the latter from a farmer on the Brighton side of the river. Of course griddle cakes should always have maple-syrup spread over them, or good Barbados molasses.

After the graphologist had said he had had quite enough, I opened a carton I had brought and lifted out a rhubarb pie my wife had baked and given to me.

"What have you got there, Doc?" asked Russell.

I told him, and he chortled: "Rhubarb pie! Nothing better."

So I cut three large wedges while Russell poured a second dipper of tea for each of us.

When he had eaten his first mouthful the graphologist smiled happily and said: "Your wife must be an *Islander*. No one but an Island woman could make such delicious pie."

"No," I answered, "she was born in Philadelphia."

"And," said Russell, turning to Mr. Strange, "if you don't say she's the best cook in the Maritimes or in all Canada, I'll take you down to the river and drown you."

"Oh," said Mr. Strange, "it's a big country. But yes...yes, she's the best cook in Canada."

"That's better, Jim," said Russell. "You've saved yourself from a watery grave. May I have another piece, Doc?"

"Of course."

"And me also?" said the graphologist.
"Certainly. There's enough for a second helping for all of us."

* * *

It was seven-thirty when we had quite finished, then, while James Strange washed the few dishes, I set up my rod and Russell took me in his canoe downstream a short distance, where a brook vents into the river on the left-hand shore, dropped his anchor and I began casting.

Now no good canoeman attempts to pole his canoe upriver against the heavy current but along the less turbulent shallow shore-water. So does the salmon on his migrations to the spawning beds, swim close to the shores, stopping at times to rest near some suitable boulder, which may or may not be nearer midstream. But when he continues his course he invariably seeks the less heavy water. Stake-net fishermen and guides are well acquainted with his habits. Both fish close to the shores in very high water.

It was not long before I had a strike that made the reel sing, and after a short fight landed a two-pound sea trout—a beautiful fish, small mouth, with carmine and gold spots along its sides. A few minutes later I hooked a salmon that leaped half a dozen times, much to Russell's delight, and took out half the backing of my casting line. It was a small fish—about a ten-pounder, the average size of the first run of salmon known as the "Serpentine run". Although, let me hasten to add, I have taken twenty-pounders at that season of the year.

Finally Russell landed me on the beach from which I played the fish; but as with all early salmon, small or big, this one was a fighter and it took fifteen minutes to bring in close to shore where Russell netted it. Then we went back to the camp-fire.

* * *

Night settled over the valley. The sky was thick with stars; the moon swung over Brighton hills and was reflected in the fast-flowing river. The air, as always in early June, was cool. Russell piled more drift-wood on the fire. Occasionally a shower of sparks shot upwards and winked out.

Flanking the western side of the twenty-foot-wide terrace was an enormous yellow birch tree; opposite it a maple of almost equal girth.

Chapter VII

Their branches interlocked, forming an arbour high above us. Northward and southward was a thick growth of alders and hazel bushes, and the odour from the foliage commingled with the newly fallen dew and the wood smoke combined to make a magic perfume.

Here was the peace and freedom and contentment such as man longs for and so seldom achieves. The only sounds those of our voices in conversation and the music of the river where the two currents met at the lower end of the island.

Before we entered the tent for the night, Russell asked us if we would like him to recite a poem. We said yes. I suggested Kipling's *The Mary Gloster*[33]—one of perhaps a hundred poems that comprised my friend's repertoire.

And so, standing on the opposite side of the fire, the light playing over his bronzed face, he began.

I have heard others recite *The Mary Gloster*—once Lionel Barrymore, over the radio—but never did any of them render it with the same compelling fervour as my friend, Russell Boyer. He made you see old Sir Anthony lying in his bed while he told his ne'er-do-well son of his struggles to make a fortune; the first freighter he owned; the yards and the foundry he erected; the influence exerted on his life by his wife Mary. Then his appeal to the son to take his body in that first ship in which—while they were both young, they had sailed the seven seas—and at a certain latitude and longitude in the Macassar Straits to drop him overboard to rest in the deep beside the wife of his bosom.

* * *

There were two cots in Russell's tent. He insisted that the graphologist take one, and I the other. He laid a buffalo robe on the ground between us for himself to lie on.

I awakened only once. It may have been that the owl (perched on a high tree on the Brighton side) had glimpsed the yet-glowing embers of our camp-fire and insisted with raucous voice that we tell him who we were.

---

33   From *The Seven Seas*, 1896.

The following morning, after Russell had mixed his Matutinal cocktail—the ingredients of which were the same as his Vesper cocktail—and drank to "good fishing and contented minds," we had a breakfast of fried salmon steak. Then I said farewell to James Strange. Russell took me in his canoe to the Victoria shore and accompanied me up the hill to my parked car.

Before I got in he said: "What do you think of him—Strange, I mean?"

"As strange a creature as his name," I replied. "He's all right…a good head. But I wonder if he actually has an appointment with the Bishops?"

* * *

A month later I had a letter from Mr. William Dawson, then managing editor of *The Canadian Home Journal*, Toronto. Mr. Dawson, with his wife and two young sons, Bill and Mickey, had visited me two years before[34] and while Mrs. Dawson remained with my wife—I took her husband and the boys for a fishing trip to the Miramichi, picking up Russell and his canoe on the way. They had a wonderful time, and quite fell in love with Russell.

The letter read thus:

> *Dear Doctor Clarke: Yesterday a man entered my office and introduced himself as James Strange, a graphologist. He said that you had picked him up and taken him to Victoria where you introduced him to our mutual friend, Russell Boyer, and that, after you had left, Russell invited him to spend a week on his island. During his stay Russell told him about me, Mickey and Bill, and that while in Toronto, Mr. Strange might care to call on me. We had a long conversation during which he told me about the many important individuals whose handwriting he had read, and showed me some of the cards they had given him. It was quite an impressive list. To make a long story short I invited him to come around at five o'clock and accompany me home to meet the boys and my wife and stay for dinner.*

---

34 About 1931. The letter GFC quotes has not survived, but in a letter of 3 February 1932 Dawson says that his sons are "ever talking about their trip with you to the Miramichi." GFC probably met Strange in the summer of 1933.

Chapter VII

"You already know the profound impression Russell made on Mickey and Bill, and they showered Mr. Strange with questions about him. I must say Strange filled their ears with his experience while with Russell, and he spoke kindly about you. I envied him the griddle-cakes, maple-syrup, rhubarb pie and fried salmon."

* * *

Russell Boyer died five years ago.[35]

The little terrace on what was known as Russell's Island is now grown up with hazel and alder bushes, but the yellow birch and the maple still spread their enormous limbs over the trench where he had built so many campfires, boiled the kettle, fried flapjacks, bacon, eggs and an occasional salmon; mixed with meticulous care what he had christened his Vesper and Matutinal cocktails; and so often, as on that night the graphologist and I were with him, rendered in impassioned voice the lines of *The Mary Gloster* and numerous other poems.

---

35   In 1950.

CHAPTER VIII

It has been my good fortune to fish the most famous salmon rivers in the Canadian province of New Brunswick: some of them over a period of fifty years; others less. Rivers with "strange, strong, fascinating names," as Lord Tweedsmuir recently referred to the Restigouche, Kedgwick, Upsalquitch, Tobique and Miramichi.[36] Strange, strong, fascinating—what a happy combination of adjectives! They should be spoken slowly, rolling them (as it were) to convey the full significance of each enchanting name. Just as one allows a rare wine to linger on the papillae of the tongue in order to sense its whole delicious flavour.

But there is no R in the dialect of the northeastern Indians; hence they call the Restigouche *Lust-a-gooch*. The original of Kedgwick is that singing word *Quat-a-wam-kedge-i-wick* which, through a series of corruptions, has finally reached the more recent shorter form. *Upsalquitch* is also an Indian corruption of *Ap-set-kwetch* meaning "narrow going" because of the high hills which environ the delightful little river. *Tobique* was called such by the early English settlers after an old Indian named Tobit who, in the late eighteenth century, had his wigwam on the point of land where the river vents into the St John. The Indian name is *Na-goot-tuk*. *Miramichi* is a beautiful and euphonious name, its origin lost in the mists of time; but it is not Indian. Both Micmac and Maliseets know it as the *Lust-a-gooch-cheech* or Little Lust-a-gooch (Restigouche).

---

36 Tweedsmuir wrote an enthusiastic review of *Six Salmon Rivers* in the *Journal of the Flyfishers' Club*, reprinted in *The Daily Gleaner*, probably in the spring of 1961. GFC wrote to thank him for the review, and the two became pen friends.

"Strange, strong, fascinating," tongue-twisting names, but, when spoken slowly, they enchant the ear and evoke images of times and scenes when, in his bark canoe, the Indian first explored his New Brunswick rivers and gave them names which in his own tongue were descriptive of their beauty or of physiography, or of some battle between him and his foes. However, I wouldn't advise anyone to try to repeat them if he has imbibed anything approximating in strength the rare whisky-punch brewed by auld Thomas O'Tuzzilehope, which was (according to Sir Walter Scott) "more fatal to sobriety than any bowl in the parish".[37]

* * *

I have yet another favourite river—the St John, on whose banks I have lived practically all of my seventy-seven years; and at the early age of nine fished it for salmon and caught a lowly sucker. It, too, has its Indian name: *Wul-ahs-tuk*. Happily we know its meaning: beautiful or pleasing; probably it also refers to the lovely intervals and gently-sloping hills that environ it. *(12a)* Indeed, Doctor Boteler's famous eulogy of the wild strawberry might with justice be paraphrased thus: Doubtless God could have made a more beautiful river than the St John, but doubtless God never did![38]

It has always been a splendid salmon river, for its great tributary, the Tobique—with its cool, widely-divergent lesser tributaries, which have their sources in the very heart of north central New Brunswick—was their favourite spawning resort. But the huge Beechwood dam, recently constructed[39] fifteen miles below the mouth of Tobique, has no fishway, thus blocking the passage of the fish to the river above it. True, some of them are lifted out of the basin below, put into tanks, and then transported by truck to Red Rapids, on the Tobique, where they are released. Some of these are caught by fly-fishermen, the others seek the age-old spawning grounds farther up. But it looks as though a period has been put to the once famous Tobique as a salmon resort.

---

37 John Gibson Lockhart, *Memoirs of the Life of Sir Walter Scott*, 1837.
38 In *The Compleat Angler*.
39 Completed in 1955.

Chapter VIII

However, what has been Tobique's loss is gain for the St John, since the myriad fish that escape the "netting system" in the tidal waters mill around in the pond above Beechwood dam for a time, then back downriver. Some seek lesser tributaries than the Tobique, others spawn in the many gravelly shallows of the St John itself.

This, then, has made for even better fishing than formerly in the St John River; especially the fifteen miles of water below the dam at Beechwood. Indeed, one day last summer (while motoring between Hartland and Beechwood), I saw at least forty fishermen, some wading, others in canoes, patiently casting their feathered lures over likely pools and runs. But, during the June migration of fish, almost any stretch of water is fishing water. This is particularly true of Patterson's Run (incorrectly called a pool), and many local as well as visiting anglers fish it with extraordinary success until the river drops to low summer level, when the fish do not stop there.[40]

The accompanying photograph of Earl Cole, with a salmon on at Patterson's, is most interesting. The photographer—nineteen-year old Michael Thomas Saunders, did a masterly job that is more than just another fishing picture. *(14b)* The two other snapshots of anglers and river are even more enchanting: things of compelling beauty perhaps unique in the history of photography. *(14a/c)*

When Michael presented me with the photographs, he said that his ambition was to make good and artistic pictures rather than to make much money: a remark that at once endeared him to me. When he snapped the angler playing the fish, the hour was eight-thirty in the evening, and the setting sun cast its vivid reflection over the water and against the bank of clouds above. He used a Minolta camera, the shutter stopped down to F-32 and exposed it at 1/500th of a second. Some one, he said, had criticised the picture—on page 154—because he couldn't see the man's face. But Michael told him (as he told me) that the man's back and the fish were what he wanted. *(14a)* Then with a droll smile he said to me: "You know, Doctor, the face of a man, when he holds up his prize fish, has the same self-conscious,

---

40 These paragraphs were written before Mactaquac put an end to salmon fishing on the St John. Patterson's Run was on the Grafton side of the river at Woodstock, just north of the old Woodstock-Grafton bridge and Island Park.

smug expression as that of a bridegroom when he poses for his portrait beside his elegantly dressed bride!"[41]

Remembering my own portraits both as bridegroom and fisherman I quite agreed with him.*(14d)*

* * *

A few years ago the shopkeepers, barbers and craftsmen of Woodstock decided that fifty-two Sundays, and the usual holidays were not enough days-off, so they held a public meeting and agreed to cease all business every Wednesday afternoon in the year. For the most part this is strictly abided by; for the *majority* of them realise that an extra half-day pays dividends both mentally and physically. And so, many go fishing or indulge in some other form of recreation. Thus, whatever the rest of the world does or thinks, the citizens of Woodstock would not subscribe to the recent criticism of labour and management by an eminent Canadian banker, who is reported to have said: "One may wonder whether there is a tendency not only by labour but also by management to like leisure too much, to prefer a less arduous life to one of unremitting attention to business, to be unwilling to sacrifice our relaxed hours on our golf courses, in our homes or in our vacation environments."

Of course my golfing and fishermen friends wouldn't want *too much leisure*; but occasionally they do want certain hours of leisure in contradistinction to an existence of unremitting toil. The latter would be a dull life and not worth living. Moreover, they would doubtless argue that bankers and government employees cease work every Friday afternoon until the following Monday, and retire at the age of sixty-five with a comfortable living pension; while they, because of the very nature of their employment and its smaller remuneration, must continue working until advanced old age puts a period to their efficiency!

* * *

---

[41] This wording sounds more like GFC than Mike; but the droll smile is Mike's own.

Chapter VIII

Until twenty-five years ago, those farmers owning riparian rights along the St John non-tidal waters were allowed to set stake-nets.[42] Only a few at wide intervals availed themselves of the privilege. One of these was Harry Dale, and usually he had good luck. But the total number of salmon taken by all of the netters made up only a very small fraction of the multitudes that then reached the Tobique and its tributaries to delight the fly-fishermen.

One morning, thirty years past, as I was about to enter my office I saw Harry Dale in his car parked by the curb, and stopped to bid him good morning. He returned my greeting, then drew my attention to five salmon (two of the smallest twelve-pounders) lying on the floor between the rear and front seats. They were beautiful fresh-run fish. He asked me if I had any idea how old they might be. I replied that, if he would allow me to remove scales from two of them I'd soon tell him.

Of course he thought I was pulling his leg; but when I assured him I was not, he told me to help myself. So I took out my penknife and carefully removed a scale from the two small fish, and telling Harry that I'd soon be back, entered the near-by jewellery store.

Aubrey Hood allowed me to use his microscope.[43] I put one scale under the glass and read the series of rings that indicated the year-growth of the fish. Then I tried the second scale, and it gave the same identical reading. The dark concentric close-spaced rings in the centre of each scale indicated that, from the time the fish had been hatched from the egg, and during their parr and smolt life, they had remained three years in the river of their nativity. Then they had gone down to the sea where, feeding on innumerable smaller fish, their growth was more rapid. They had returned the following early summer as grilse (in the St John waters, five pounds is the usual weight of grilse). They had remained in the fresh water that summer and winter, and the next spring had again sought the sea where, as the more widely-spaced rings plainly showed, their growth had been much accelerated. Then, the present year, they had returned on their first spawning migration.

I got Aubrey (who was a keen angler) to read the markings on the scales, and we both arrived to the conclusion that the fish were five years old when

---

42 A fishing net hung on stakes set upright in the river.

43 Aubrey Hood died in December 1932.

caught in Harry Dale's stake-net. So I returned to him and told him of my findings.

"Are you joking, or is it just another of your fish stories?" he asked.

Then briefly I told him the story as unfolded by the scales.

"Well, I'll be damned!" he said. "You say they have rings on the scales just like the rings you see on the butt of a felled tree? I've seen hundreds of them."

He had: he had lumbered since boyhood. "Yes," I answered. "But whereas the rings seen on the cross-section of a tree indicate a year's growth, those on the scales of a salmon register its monthly growth (or perhaps a little better) until it reaches the smolt stage and goes down to the sea when, since it grows more rapidly, the rings are spaced farther apart."

He bedamned himself again, then said: "Why are grilse bigger in the St John River than they are in the Restigouche?"

I told him that possibly it was due to the greater abundance of food in the River St John and its tributaries. As evidence of this the parr and smolt reach a greater size than in the Restigouche. Then, when they reach the Bay of Fundy on their first sea journey, they are physically better able to catch their food in the form of small sardines and tiny smelts that inhabit that great body in untold numbers. "Mind you," I said, "that is my theory. I have not heard nor read the opinions of fish biologists."

"Well," he said, "it sounds all right to me." He paused a few moments then: "There's always things to learn, aren't there?" (He had learned, as Sir William Hamilton put it that "the grand result of human wisdom...is only a consciousness that what we know is as nothing to what we know not.")[44]

"Along with other things, about fly-fishing for salmon...." I said. I could have told him much more about the noble fish whose life history is so filled with romance and tragedy; but just then I saw a patient entering my office door, so I bade him good-bye, and was about to leave him when he said: "Come down some night while I'm tending my net. I'll have a little fire and we can sit in front of it and talk."

---

44 Hamilton was a mid-nineteenth-century Scottish philosopher.

Chapter VIII

"Thanks a lot," I said. "I'd much like that. Do you happen to know any old-time yarns you can tell me about happenings in the woods or along the river?"

He smiled and said: "Yes, Doctor. I can tell you a rare one about the ghost said to have haunted the horse-hovel in the Kilmarnock woods, and about Smokey-Joe and his card trick, and his strange disappearance. And I can tell you how Peter Loler, the Indian, raced the stage coach from Fredericton to Woodstock—sixty-three miles."

"Splendid," I said. "I'll come down tomorrow evening, do some fly-fishing a few miles below you, then, about dark, call on you—if that's convenient."

"OK," he said. "You know where I have my stake-net; but anyway, I'll have a fire going so you can't miss the place. Park your car off the side of the road, give a whoop, and I'll run up and show you down the path."

PHOTOGRAPHS

Part One

1 a. Fred and Bill Kennedy, Gulquac Lodge, Restigouche, 1950s

1 b. GFC with fishing friends at Gulquac lodge, Oct 7 1948
L to R: Charlie Clark, 2 unknowns, Bill Kennedy, unknown, GFC, unknown

2. GFC with a twenty-nine-and-a-half-pound salmon, Restigouche, 1930s

3 a. Charlie Clark, Dr Grant, Bill Kennedy, with 4 guides, Restigouche, c. 1937
The guide on the left is one of the Ogilvy brothers. Photograph by GFC (his is the empty canoe seat).

3 b. The Izaak Walton memorial window in Winchester Cathedral

4 a. Dr Grant

4 b. Charlie Clark with salmon

4 c. The Four Musketeers of Fish in 1937: Dr Grant, Bill Kennedy, Charlie Clark, GFC

5. GFC's sister, Ruby Clarke, at Ayers Lake, 1911

6. GFC's fiancée, Mary Schubert, at Ayers Lake, 1911

7 a. GFC and guide with salmon, c. 1910

7 b. GFC and daughter Jane in a dugout canoe on the Main Southwest Miramichi, c. 1919

8. The Anglican church on the Lower Road below Woodstock, 2003

9. Russell Boyer, 1930s

10. Russell Boyer, 1940s

11 a. Anglers at the Hartland Salmon Pool on the St John River *before Mactaquac*

Miramichi salmon are renowned fighters. This illustration, from The Song of the Reel, depicts a scene above Juniper on the North Branch of the Main Southwest Miramichi.

GIFTS RICH
in
ATLANTIC PROVINCES
TRADITION

THE SONG
OF
THE REEL

by George Frederick Clarke

Dr. Clarke is becoming generally known as the modern day successor to Izaak Walton. A book for those who love fishing, for those who love the out-of-doors.

$5.00

11 b. Newspaper advertisement for *The Song of the Reel*, 1963

12 a. The St John River near Woodstock, 1964
before Mactaquac

12 b. Russell's camp, 1940s

13 a. The St John River north of Hartland, 1967
above the Mactaquac headpond

13 b. The St John River above Woodstock, early 1960s
before Mactaquac

CHAPTER IX

The following evening, after an early dinner, I took my rod, reel, gaff and a few flies, and drove down the east side of the St John River until I arrived opposite a nice run a short distance above the Northampton parish Presbyterian Church.*(15)*

I parked the car well off the highway, set up the rod, tied on a twelve-pound-test leader, then a double No. 4 Silver Doctor, and descended a path to the river where I began casting just as the sun sank below the opposite hills.

Far above the river a pair of ospreys, with a patience as old as time, soared on tireless wings in wide and lesser circles while their keen eyes searched the depths below for their evening meal. Thrice one of them paused in flight, sustained itself almost stationary on wide-beating pinions for a few moments, then dropped like a plummet towards the surface of the water. But, when only a few yards from it, it suddenly banked, and again soared into the heavens and once more took up its tireless patrol.

In a few minutes the western horizon was filled with the rose-pink of afterglow which gradually mounted higher and higher into the sky, until the whole firmament was carpeted with the magical and breath-taking splendour, and was reflected in the windows of the few houses strung along the opposite highway, and in the hurrying river, and danced along the crests of its myriad ripples.

The ospreys, now unable to see any object beneath the crimson flood, took off downriver, hoping perhaps to find some lagoon where they could find a more favourable fishing ground.

Song of the Reel

As for myself, I didn't care to cast while sky and water were crowned with that radiant colour. So I waded to shore, sat down on a boulder and absorbed the beauty and the wonder of it. And, as though Mother Nature must give something more of her bounty to the enchanting hour, a hermit thrush in the thicket behind me loosed his tender, tranquillising litany, the notes rising and falling in melodious cadences: "O spheral, spheral! O holy, holy!—sweet!" I listened, hoping for a repetition of the song; and presently, from a distance, it came once more, a mere thread of melody, but wholly distinct; and with its passing there was no sound save the gentle rippling of the waters.

* * *

The colour in sky and river faded,*(16)* so I renewed my casting, and presently hooked a nice fish that sped with the rapidity of a jet-plane far out into the river. Then back it came, and ran downriver, leaped, and again sought the stronger water opposite me, where it stopped and began those dangerous jigging tactics so nerve-racking to fly-fishermen. So I gave it line and it ran upriver, jumped again, ran a little farther and repeated its performance. Then, to my dismay, the line went slack.

"Good-by, Sal,"[45] I said, quickly reeled in the line, took down the rod, restored the reel to my pack and the rod to its case, and climbed the path to the highway and my car. It had been a wonderful evening—an evening I have never forgotten. For the beauty and the peace were beyond price. As for the salmon—well, it was not the first I had lost, nor was it to be the last. It's a part of the game of chance in the most exciting sport in the world.

* * *

And so, a little later, I sat beside Harry Dale on the beach near his stake net, and while we talked the flames of his little friendship fire licked the dry driftwood he had gathered for the occasion, and gave off tiny golden stars which, I liked to think, winked brief friendly signals to those greater stars that studded the bowl above, seemingly so near and yet millions of

---

45 Probably from the Latin name of the Atlantic salmon, salmo salar.

Chapter IX

miles distant. The moon, at its full, cast a long silver pathway across the hurrying river and lighted up the opposite shore-line with ghostly radiance. And there were no sounds save the occasional howl of a dog from the Indian reservation a mile upstream, and near by the incessant gurgling of the waters against the wooden stakes which held Harry's net in position. Once, much later, we descried the shadowy outline of a canoe, with two men in it, stealing along the opposite shore, and decided they were probably my old Indian friends—Peter and Noël[46] Polchies—out to spear salmon to augment their meagre diet, just as their forefathers had done.

Although it is against the law for anyone (Indian or white) to spear salmon, I didn't blame my Indian friends for taking a fish, or two or three. For it had always seemed to me an injustice that their white brothers could lawfully net them while they were denied their ancient right to take them with the spear.

I told Harry that I had once watched a female salmon in her spawning bed. "It was on the north branch of the Main Southwest Miramichi," I said, "the middle of October. I was hunting partridges and finally came to a high, level terrace above the stream. Above me, where it made a sharp bend, the water was deep, then shallowed off to a depth of not more than two feet, and from shore to shore was about sixty or seventy feet in width. The water was as clear as crystal, and in the centre of the gently gliding current a female salmon was in her bed—a space a little longer than her body which she had hollowed out of the gravelly bottom. She looked to be about a twelve-pounder. A male fish the same size was beside her. I could see plainly the long projection that rose from the front of his lower jaw. Even as I gazed on them a three-pound grilse swam leisurely down from the deep part of the pool and approached the pair. Then, Harry, something happened that I wouldn't have missed for a good deal. When the intruding male was within four or five feet of the female and her mate, the latter—its mouth wide open—rushed at him with the speed of a torpedo. With the quickness of light the grilse swung in a half circle, dashed across the stream where the water was only a few inches deep, then sped up the shore leaving a wide wake until it had reached the deeps of the big pool, where the female's

---

46 His name is pronounced "Newell", not "Nowell".

mate didn't follow it. Instead he swung back and again took up his former position beside his motionless mate.

"I waited to see if the grilse would make any further attempt to disturb them, but evidently he had got a sufficient fright to cool his ardour for some time. The female fish was very red on her sides and heavy with spawn. Her consort had not been so long in the river. But I was quite convinced that as soon as she had deposited her eggs and he had covered them with milt, and all were covered with rocks and gravel, both would drop back to the sea.

"No, Harry, not all salmon remain in the rivers during the winter months!"

"Now that," said Harry, "was an interesting experience. I'd like to have been there with you. I'm learning something about fish all the time—things I never imagined possible!"

* * *

Four times during the following hour I went with Harry in his boat to "tend" the net from which he gathered six beautiful silver salmon; one a twenty-pounder, another sixteen, the others twelve-pounders. Then, again beside the fire, we resumed our talk.

He said: "Do you believe that salmon know enough to return to the same river where they were spawned?"

"The salmon is the wisest of all fish," I said; "and I firmly believe that, if it survives the numerous dangers to which it is exposed in its sea-life, it almost invariably returns to the same river in which it is born."

"That's marvellous," he said. "Instinct or reasoning, Doctor?"

"If birds reason, and I believe they do," I answered, "as well as beavers and other animals, why not fish—in a limited way? Most men believe that they alone have reasoning power. But study the ants. At any rate there is no doubt that in the spring and summer the salmon cruises along the coasts, and when it smells the river of its nativity it ascends it to deposit its spawn just as its predecessors did for years past."

"Well, I'll be damned," said Harry.

"And do you know," I said, "that a salmon is the only fish that was ever responsible for a man and his wife becoming reconciled following a serious domestic upheaval?"

Chapter IX

"No," said Harry with a laugh. "How was that?"

"Well", I began, "it happened a long, long time ago. On the site of the present city of Glasgow, Scotland, there lived a king named Rederith and his wife Langaureth. She fell in love with one of the king's soldiers, and gave him a ring the king had presented to her on some happy occasion (perhaps on one of her birthdays). The King, knowing of the whole illicit affair, went to the room in which the soldier slept, took the ring from his finger and threw it into the river Clyde. Then, like a cunning old fox, he returned to the castle and asked his wife for the ring. Evidently she put him off for the time by some pretty subterfuge. But she was aware that it must sooner or later come to a showdown. So in her despair she went to St Kentigern (who well knew of her unfaithfulness) and asked him what she should do. So the kindly old Saint, who among other virtues possessed that of being a fisherman, got his rod, went to the river and caught a salmon; and behold, it had the ring in its mouth. Then he returned and gave it to the queen. The result was that she was able to produce it when next the king asked her for it. No doubt he was dumbfounded and thought he had only dreamt that he had thrown the ring into the river. At any rate—after the repentant wife had promised to reform—it was the means of restoring peace to the royal household. And it is to be hoped that they lived happily ever afterward. But, Harry, after its good turn, I hate to think that the salmon became food for even the good St. Kentigern."

When I had ended, Harry's fat sides shook with laughter. Then he said: "That's a good one, Doctor—almost as good as the yarn I promised to tell you about the haunted horse-hovel and Smoky-Joe. But there's a flaw in yours. How in blazes could the gal's husband get the ring off her boy-friend's finger without waking him?"

"I thought of that," I said. "Really, I don't know, unless he'd first given him an overdose of Scotch whisky."

Harry's long-drawn: "We-l-l" seemed to imply doubt in the efficacy of whisky to drown a Scottish soldier into insensibility. For several moments he gazed into the fire as though seeking inspiration from that quarter. Then, with a bright smile, he turned to me and asked: "Of course in those days it was more potent than what we get now."

"You've got it," I said.

"But," he went on, "there's something else that puzzles me: why didn't the salmon swallow the ring like they do any fly or bait?" Then, before I could make reply he added: "Unless it was using it as a teething ring."

"That's a brilliant suggestion," I said. "And perhaps the origin of the present custom of giving children rubber rings to chew on. That's another star in the crown of the salmon. But, Harry, joking aside, there must be some truth in the story, because eventfully the finding of the ring leaked out, with the result that, among other emblems in the Arms of Glasgow there is that of a salmon with a ring in its mouth."

"I'll be damned!" muttered Harry. "That seems to tie up with the rest." He paused again, then said: "This talking of teething rings reminds me about the Moriarity family that once lived at Upham Creek. There were about twenty-two children and all boys. When the first one was about six months old it became fretful, and Mrs. Moriarity said the poor dear must be teething and needed something to chew on to help them through the gums. So she let it have her bare knuckle. It soon found her wedding ring and chewed on that until its teeth were all in. It was the same with the other twenty-one kids. By that time Mrs. Moriarity's wedding ring was worn so thin she told her husband that the least he could do, after all she'd gone through because of him, was to buy her a new ring. So he did.

"Well, Doctor, about all those boys did was fish and hunt. Worst poachers in the country. They fished the trout brook and its deadwater and sold the fish they couldn't eat to the neighbours; the same with the deer meat, and the salmon they got from the river by spear and drift-net.[47] With part of the money they bought chewing tobacco, because each one of them, when five years old, had learned the cussed habit. Mrs. Moriarity said it was inherited from their father, and that it would stunt their growth. But after the first two or three had sprung up to six feet in their moccasins, she changed her tune. Her husband said the habit was formed because she'd allowed them to cut their teeth on her wedding ring.

---

47 Drift nets hang vertically in the water without being anchored to the bottom; they are kept vertical by floats attached to a rope along the top of the net and weights attached to another rope along the bottom. [Wikipedia]

Chapter IX

"Well, Doctor, when the world war broke out in 1914, they were all six-footers, and all enlisted in the Carleton Light Infantry, but it was soon nicknamed Moriarity's Brigade. Not long after the regiment reached England, word came that Big Ben was missing. Of course it wasn't true. But Mrs. Moriarity got the news and said to her husband: 'There! I knowed them boys of ours would be up to their old poachin' tricks. Just you wait till they git to France, an' they'll steal the Kaiser.'"

Harry let up until my laughter had ceased, then went on: "But, Doctor, those Moriaritys *could* use a rifle, and if the whole British forces had been made up of Moriaritys the war wouldn't have lasted more than a year. They not only shot Germans, they'd go out at night and come back each one lugging a German on his shoulders, just like they used to lug deer from the Upham woods. And chew tobacco—they bought, begged or stole it, which all came from Mrs. Moriarity allowing them to cut their baby teeth on her wedding ring. Strange to say, Doctor, all but three came back after the armistice. They had their packs filled with regimental badges from every regiment in both the allied and German armies. But they didn't stay long at Upham Creek. They just drifted away up north where there was better hunting (or so they thought). I've heard since that there's a settlement up there called Moriarity-ville where the people are all six-footers. I've no doubt that they are the former members and descendants of Moriarity's Brigade."

* * *

Although I have not fished Marven's Brook for sixty years or more, I believe that I could make a fairly accurate chart of its pools and ledges and various windings, small bridges that spanned it, and the remains of the old dam where, years before I ever waded it, there had been a mill-site. It is the same with stories my mother told me and the books I read during my early boyhood. I am quite sure that I could write a complete synopsis of a serial story, *The Smuggler's Beacon,* by Henry Frith, published in the *Boys' Own Paper* in 1890. The same with Stevenson's *Treasure Island* with its respectable characters Jim Hawkins, Doctor Livesay and Squire Trelawney, and those less worthy but none the less interesting characters, Captain Billy Bones, Blind Pew, Israel Hands; and, the greatest villain of them all, Long John

Silver and his parrot he named after that other wicked old sinner, Captain Flint. "Fifteen men on the dead man's chest, Yo! ho! ho! and a bottle of rum!" How the old jingle rings in the memory!

I remember scores of poems. Two evenings in succession (fifty years ago) I took my volume of Kipling's *The Seven Seas* with me, and walking back and forth over the half-mile-long bridge which links Woodstock with the village of Grafton (there were no motor cars in those days to bother me) I memorised the seventeen pages of *The Mary Gloster*. I can repeat the whole of it today.

It is the same with rivers. I remember them all, and the guides I met and the yarns they told and the songs they sang. I remember an odd character I picked up thirty-five years ago and gave a lift in my car: a middle-aged sailor hiking his way from Sydney, Nova Scotia, to Ontario in the hope of signing up on one of the lake freighters. I took him as far as Levis, opposite the city of Quebec. Were I an artist I could paint a portrait of him with his one drooping eyelid and a scar that stretched from his left cheek-bone to his chin: a knife wound, he told me, he had got in an affray with a lascar[48] while on a voyage from Melbourne, Australia, to Liverpool. I met many other characters, among them Indians, on my drives and while tramping beside the rivers, and from all of them I obtained interesting and, in some cases, tragic stories of adversity which I remember as if it were yesterday.

It is said that people of advanced age dwell more in the past and remember its events more clearly than those of more recent years. If this be a criterion of old age then I have always been old. At any rate, I have always had the same insatiable curiosity and love of the folklore and history of my native province as had Sir Walter Scott for the old ballads, odd characters, castles, ruins and other antiquities of his beloved Scotland. What is of interest we retain; the rest we conveniently forget.

---

48 A sailor or militiaman from the Indian subcontinent or other countries east of the Cape of Good Hope, employed on European ships from the 16th century until the middle of the 20th century. [Wikipedia]

Chapter IX

The reader will doubtless be aware that the foregoing is a digression from Harry Dale's yarn, and charge me with rambling. But, as Lord Bolingbroke wrote in his *Reticence in Criticism* to Alexander Pope: "To digress and to ramble are different things, and he who knows the country through which he travels may venture out of the highroad, because he is sure of finding his way back to it again."[49]

---

49 "A Letter to Alexander Pope," in *The Works of Lord Bolingbroke*, 1754.

CHAPTER X

Harry now told me about the haunted horse-hovel in the Kilmarnock woods near the deadwater of the same name, and about Smoky-Joe. The yarn had been handed down by an old Ulsterman who had migrated to Canada almost one hundred years ago, and after some vicissitudes had done well in lumbering operations. But there, I'll allow Harry to continue the yarn in his own way, which he did with a fidelity to detail that won my admiration.

"If I remember correctly," he said, "his name was Montgomery. But names don't matter: it's the story. Well, he had a crew of twenty men besides the cook and cookee, and three horses he kept stabled nights and Sundays in the hovel about three or four rods from the camp. Then, one night, the middle of November, while the men were all seated at table and the cook and cookee serving them supper, the camp door suddenly opened and a man with pack and snowshoes strapped to his shoulder came in. He shut the door, then stood with his back to it and looked at the men. He was a big tall man with red hair and beard. He had lost an eye, and wore steel-rimmed spectacles with a smoke-coloured glass that covered it. He never said a word until the boss got up from the table, then he spoke: 'I want to hire,' he says.

"'Well,' says Montgomery, 'if you're good with axe and crosscut saw I'll take you on. What's your name?'

"'Joe,' said the stranger.

"'What else?' says the boss.

"'Just Joe,' he said. 'Adam didn't have no other name, did he?'

"The boss and the crew gave a short laugh. Then the boss said: 'Now that you mention it, I never heard that he had. Nor, for that matter, did Mother Eve. Well, Joe, off with your gear and come and have supper with us. Tomorrow we'll see if you know the work.'

"Just Joe," repeated Harry. "But until he disappeared in a most mysterious manner, the crew called him Smoky-Joe. He proved a good worker, was a very silent man, seldom spoke except when he was playing cards, then only a few words. And he knew card games, especially poker. They played for matches and he won hundreds of them but always gave them back to the men at the end of the game.

"But, Doctor, the very first morning after he came a most curious thing happened—only the beginning of stranger things. The teamsters had harnessed the horses and were just about to go to the place where the crew had been cutting logs, when Smoky-Joe walked over to a big roan horse, put his lips to its ear and whispered something not even the teamster could hear. And the beast turned its head, laid its muzzle over Smoky-Joe's arm and gave a little whinny. And the boss said: 'It seems the creature knows you, Smoky-Joe.'

"'Aye,' he says. 'Aye: he ought to. I rode him when I fought at Naseby under the great Cromwell.'"

Harry paused a few moments, then said: "Naseby and Cromwell was a long time ago, wasn't they, Doctor?"

"More than three hundred years," I said. "To be exact, the battle of Naseby was fought June 14, 1645."

"Oh!" said Harry, "that long? Of course Smoky-Joe was crazy or else an awful liar or…well…I don't know…But at any rate that horse was mighty fond of him: so much so that whenever he was near the beast, it would whinny and try to get to him. And the boss, old Montgomery or whatever his name was, had to send Smoky-Joe to another part of the cuttings.

"Smoky-Joe came on a Monday, and Thursday morning, when the teamsters went to the hovel to feed the horses, the halter ropes that fastened them to the manger were untied and knotted about their necks. Of course suspicion fell on Smoky-Joe, but the fellow who slept next to him in the long bunk was a light sleeper, and said he was sure that Smoky-Joe hadn't got up during the night. Then it was thought that the cookee, a mischievous lad of sixteen, was the culprit. So the boss decided to sit up that night and watch. He admitted that he might have dozed off two or three times, at least long enough to allow the boy, or anyone else, to steal out to the hovel and untie the halter ropes. At any rate, before any of the crew were up the next morning he lighted the lantern, and going to the hovel found the beasts untied as before. So after breakfast he told the crew what had happened, and said that if he found out—and he would—which one had done the trick, he would have to pack his bag and leave. Of course they all swore by all that was holy that they were innocent: the hovel was haunted or the devil was in the horses, and they were of a mind to leave anyway and get work elsewhere.

"Well, Doctor, that would have spoiled old Montgomery's winter operations, because it would take considerable time to collect a new crew, and so he soft-pedalled a bit and said how foolish they'd feel when they learned that some one was trying to throw a scare into them. Then he asked if any one of them had ever seen a ghost. All but one of them said no, and he declared that one night he'd seen one riding a white horse on the island opposite the Indian Reservation, where there were remains of a house so old that not even the oldest settler knew who built it; and that old coins and other things had been ploughed up near it at different times. Then a Scot who'd only been in New Brunswick a couple of years spoke up and said that in his country there was little fairy-men who cut up all sorts of mischief. And perhaps some of them were in Canada.

"At that Smoky-Joe gave a low laugh; some of the others joined in, and so the affair passed off for the moment, and they got their axes and saws and went down to the cutting.

* * *

"About three in the afternoon it started snowing; the wind sprang up, rocked the trees and made them moan and creak one against the other, so the boss ordered the crew to stop work and go back to camp. You know, Doctor," said Harry, "it's dangerous felling timber with the wind blowing a gale, because it's liable to fall any direction but the right one and wound or kill a man.

"As they trekked back to camp the boss thought to himself that there'd not be any horses untied the next morning, because footsteps in the snow would be a dead give-away.

"At any rate, after supper, when the dishes had been washed and put away, the men had a game of cards. Then the boss got Billy Jones to play his fiddle, hoping it might cheer them up a bit, because he knew that they were still jittery over the queer doings in the hovel.

"That night, before they all turned in, the boss lit the lantern, went out to the hovel and inspected the horses. Everything OK: halters on, ropes through the holes in the manager, and each tied in a clove-hitch. So he tramped back to the camp through snow almost a foot deep.

"Well, Doctor, he was up next morning even before the teamsters and the cook, opened the camp door, went outdoors and found the tracks made the night before were all filled in with snow. So he floundered through it, opened the hovel door, entered, and—what do you think he saw, Doctor?"

"Of course, Harry," I said, "the ropes were tied as he'd left them the night before."

"Yes," he replied. "The ends of the ropes were tied to the manger all right, but the halters had come unbuckled and lying on the floor."

"Good heavens!" I exclaimed. "Are you joking, Harry?"

"No, no," he said earnestly. "Not a bit. I'm telling it as I heard it. I admit the yarn made me feel queer in my innards. At any rate, old Montgomery put back the halters and buckled them safe, then he goes to camp. The men were already seated at the table and the cook and cookee serving breakfast. Says the boss, in a cheerful voice: 'Well, boys, the ropes were not untied this morning, so you can rest easy.' At that Smoky-Joe looked up and gave a low laugh.

* * *

"So the days passed and every morning Montgomery got up before any of the others, went to the hovel, and each time he found the halter ropes untied and loosely knotted about the horses' necks; or the halters unbuckled and lying on the floor.

"Then he got a dose of flu: chills, headache and all, and had to stay in his bunk, drinking hot ginger tea a dozen times that first day. And the next morning one of the teamsters, who'd been to the hovel, came in, his face as white as snow, and cries out: 'It's come again, boys!—halters on the floor this time! So I'm gettin' outa this place after breakfast.'

Chapter X

"All the other men, except Smoky-Joe, said they'd follow him. One said all the goings-on was a forerunner of some calamity if they stayed. But Smoky-Joe spoke up and said they couldn't leave a sick man alone. Well, Doctor, at that they calmed down a bit and said they'd hang on till the boss was better, but not a day more, so they ate their breakfast and then went down to the cuttings.

"That evening it started snowing again but had stopped, the wind down and stars out, when the cook went to the door at nine o'clock to throw out potato peelings.

"In the meantime the men began talking about ghosts, and little fairy men and forerunners. And if there was any sudden noise, like the creak of a tree outside, or some one of them dropped something on the floor, or the boss coughed, they all jumped to their feet and each looked at the other as though they expected the devil to walk into the camp. All of them except Smoky-Joe, I mean.

"At length he sprang to his feet, told them they were a lot of miserable cowards. 'As for me,' he says, 'I've had too much to do with spirits to be afraid of them. They ain't yet hurt anyone, so far as I know.' Then he whipped out a deck of cards from his pocket, and dealt them face-up on the table until he came to the Jack of Clubs. 'Now,' he said to the cook, 'put one of the crew's name on the back of that Jack, add two or three numbers and put it in the pack while I have my back turned.'

"So the cook got his lead pencil, wrote his own name on the back of the Jack, and three numerals, 2-1-6. Then he gathered up the cards and says: 'OK, Smoky. What now?'

"Smoky-Joe turned, took the cards from the cook's hand, and said: 'If you fellows think untied horses is the work of ghosts or little fairy men, I'll show you something that'll start the eyes from your head!' Then he walked over to the big cylinder stove, opened the door, threw the pack of cards into the flame, muttered some gibberish no one understood a word of, then crooned in a louder voice:

> *Burn, burn, you imps of hell,*
> *Once out, now in,*
> *Once in, soon out.*

"And with that he ran to the camp door, opened it wide, and with the rush of wind that followed came a whole deck of cards that fluttered across the floor near where the men were sitting. Then Smoky-Joe slammed-to the door, came back and said to the cook: 'Pick them up, lay them face-up on the table, and when you come to the Jack I'll tell you what you wrote on its back.' Then he turned his face away so he couldn't see what was going on.

"So the cook picked up all the cards, and stood by the table and dealt them out face-up while the rest of the crew crowded about him goggly-eyed. Finally he came to the Jack and said: 'I have it, Smoky-Joe.'

"And Smoky-Joe said: 'You wrote your own name and the figures two-one-six on the back of it. Turn it over for the others to see.'

"It was so. There was the cook's name and the numerals two-one-six.

"For a long minute no one spoke. Then the boss gave a sudden racking cough, and every man jumped, their faces pale as death, and backed away from Smoky-Joe as if he was the devil. As for him, he gave a low laugh, picked up the cards, put them in his pocket, walked over to the Deacon-seat, sat down and didn't say another word. About nine o'clock he went to his bunk and soon seemed sound asleep."

Harry paused in his tale, rose to his feet and threw more wood on the fire. A few rods below us a salmon leaped and fell back with a loud splash. "He'll be in the net before long," he said, then reseated himself beside me and continued:

"The cook and cookee were up first next morning to prepare breakfast; and the teamsters to feed the horses; and soon all the crew rolled out, dressed, and crowded to the bench to wash themselves. That is, all but Smoky-Joe, though for a time no one noticed his absence. Then some one said: 'Where's Smoky-Joe?' and no one knew.

"Well, Doctor, his pack and snow-shoes were gone from their accustomed place to the left of the door near where he slept...and he had vanished.

"It was now daylight, and several of the men crowded outdoors to see if they could see Smoky-Joe's tracks and which direction he'd took. But they soon came back and reported that, other than the tracks of the teamsters when they went to the hovel to feed the horses, there were no others—snowshoe or tracks of man or beast. They'd even looked in the hovel thinking he might be there. They all thought it mighty odd that he

Chapter X

could have got out of his bunk, dressed and opened the camp door without any of them waking. At any rate no man could reach the settlement unless he used snowshoes, so they thought he couldn't be human. Well, Doctor, what do you make of it?"

I shook my head, then said: "Of course, Harry, if it was snowing when he left it would have filled in his tracks."

"Of course. But, if you remember, I said the storm had stopped by the time the cook threw the potato peelings out. The wind gone down, and stars shining. And at that time Smoky-Joe was asleep—at least he seemed to be. Besides that, no tote-team had come in from the settlement for four days."

"Yes," I said. "I remember, now. You say he talked?"

"That's right, according to old Montgomery, the boss. It's said he was a religious Presbyterian, so he'd hardly be a liar."

"Like Long John Silver, in *Treasure Island*," I said. "I've never heard that ghosts talked, if Smoky-Joe *was a ghost*. But, Harry, what about the horses? Were they untied the morning Smoky-Joe disappeared?"

"No, Doctor. But the curious part of it is that they were untied for three mornings after; then the queer goings-on stopped—just like that!" and he snapped a thumb and finger together to emphasise his statement. "At any rate," he continued, "no one ever again heard anything of Smoky-Joe. He just vanished like…like smoke."

* * *

It is a singular coincidence that when I was a child my mother told me a tale about a man in a lumber camp on the Miramichi who, like Smoky-Joe, did a similar trick with cards. At that time lumber camps didn't have stoves; the only heat both for warmth and cooking being from a fire made on the ground in the centre of the camp around which, at a safe distance, was the log floor hewed flat with the adze. There was a hole in the roof through which the smoke billowed, and it was through this smoke-hole that the character she told about threw the pack of cards, and then, saying some foreign words, opened the camp door and the cards poured in. She said the crew were scared stiff and declared the man was the devil.

Two summers ago, while I was fishing Big Gulquac Pool, on the Tobique, my guide told me a story similar—in most particulars—to that imparted to me years before by Harry Dale, about horses being mysteriously untied in a hovel contiguous to a lumber shanty. He said that he had been one of the crew at the time of the strange proceedings, and stoutly averred that it was quite true and, although he and the other men took turns watching, no one had entered the hovel; consequently they had come to the conclusion that the untying of the horses was due to supernatural causes.

Is it possible that Smoky-Joe (or his ghost) travelled all over the province?

* * *

"Oh, Doctor," said Harry, "he's in." He meant the salmon we had heard jump previously. So I went with him in his boat to the net and he lifted out the twenty-pounder.

It was now late, and the moon had sunk below the horizon. So I thanked Harry for his entertaining story and told him I must start for home and snatch a few hour's sleep.

"Oh," he said, "it's early yet! I haven't told you about Peter Loler racing the stage coach from Fredericton to Woodstock."[50]

As a matter of fact I was already familiar with that bit of folklore, so I said that it must wait for another time.

He accompanied me up the path to my car and laid a salmon he had insisted I must take with me in the trunk. Then I thanked him again and drove slowly homeward.

---

50   In 1865. "After being told by a stagecoach driver that he would not be allowed to ride the stagecoach from Fredericton to Woodstock, a distance of about 60 miles, Loler made a vow to get to Woodstock before the stagecoach—and did! The four horses that he was racing against had to be changed four times with fresh horses during the trip." In "Food for Thought," by M.H.Salahshurian. [Facebook 2013]

CHAPTER XI

For a considerable distance the road was only a few rods from the river which—now that the moon had gone down—was dark and inexpressibly mysterious. Suddenly, rounding a bend of the road, I saw the light of a flambeau over the water, the dim outline of a canoe, and in it two men. I thought they could only be old Chief Polchies[51] and his brother, Noël. I stopped the car, turned off lights and ignition, leaned my head out of the window and watched their movements. They were quite near the shore, and so preoccupied with their business they evidently hadn't heard my coming.

It requires courage and poise to stand in a frail canoe and pole it upstream against a swift current racing over a rock-strewn bar; and keen eyesight and expert judgment on the part of him who, standing upright behind the flambeau, picks out a fish and drives the narrow jaws of his spear over its back.*(18b)*

As I watched I could clearly see them cruising, now to the right, now to the left, again moving forwards against the tumbling waters. Then I saw the Indian in the stern suddenly hold his craft almost stationary with his setting pole, and saw old Peter's long-handled spear cleave the water—down—down. Then he drew it up with a big fish and deposited it in the bottom of the canoe.

I leaned farther out of the window, and said in the Maliseet tongue: *"Ka-loo-ut!"* (good). And across the short, intervening space of water heard Peter's musical voice: "That you, Doc?"

"Yes," I answered. "How'd you guess?"

---

51 Peter Polchies (1865-1934) was younger than Noël (1860-1927).

He gave a low laugh, then said: "Me an' Noël go down river first. We see two men by Harry's net. We go to shore farther down. I walk up road, hide in bushes, look an' see you with him; not warden. Now I spear one salmon for Noël, then we go home."

"That's right," I said. "*Adio,*"[52] and starting the car sped along the highway towards Woodstock.

* * *

It is now illegal to catch salmon by drift or set-net[53] in the non-tidal waters of New Brunswick. But the fish formerly taken by net or spear comprised only a meagre few in comparison to the vast numbers which got by safely to reach the headwaters.

The serious diminution in their numbers at the present time, both in the St John and its branches and in our other great rivers, is due to improved methods of the drifters in the north Atlantic, in the bays and harbours along the deeply indented coasts, and in the mouths of rivers where stake nets reach out from both shores, in all of which vaster numbers are taken than ever before. Besides these, the seal, sea-otter, porpoises, whales and other predators take a heavy toll, so that it is a marvel that any fish escape to find their natal rivers to reproduce their kind. Even here only a small percentage of the nine or ten thousand eggs a twelve-pound female salmon deposits in the redds hatch out, and thousands of these become the prey of lampreys, large trout, merganser ducks and kingfishers. In addition to these, pollution from sewers and industrial plants, and the dams in the St John waters are all deterrents to the ambition of the noble fish to seek their ancient spawning grounds.

* * *

Noël often came to my office.*(17)* "Just to make little visit," he would say. If I were not busy, we sat and talked. It was he who told me that Taffa

---

52   "*Adio*" or "*Adiou*" is, or was, the Maliseet "Good-bye".

53   Set nets are anchored on both ends of the net, one end on shore, the other in the water. [Wikipedia]

Pond[54] held big trout. "Big—big," he assured me. "Two pounds...yes. Might be more, sometime. It good place for otter too. You go up to little island where brook it come in from northwest. Stay quiet: you see'm."

I later found that he had spoken the truth. There *were* big trout at Taffa Pond, but only to be caught shortly after the ice left. One evening, in late September, while paddling my birchbark canoe (perhaps the last of such craft made by the St John River Indians), I saw five otters close to the mouth of the brook he had mentioned. I was within one hundred yards of them when they saw me. They immediately dove. A few moments later they reached land and, their bodies rising and falling in wavelike undulations, disappeared among the long rushes which bordered the pond.

Perhaps the last time Noël visited me he was in his seventies[55] and much enfeebled in body. I asked him about his health, and he said: 'I not well, Fred; I got bad cough. I take medicine; it not do any good.'

I said: "Your two daughters died of tuberculosis, didn't they?"

"Ah-ha," he answered. "They had the sickness."

"And you live in the same house?"

"Ah-ha. Same place."

It was a miserable shack not fit for human habitation, as I well knew. So I said: "Have you asked the Indian agent to build you another house?"

"Ah-ha, I ask'm many time. He say government make one. But year and year go by and they not do it."

"Noël," I said, "you have a crooked knife; you have dry cedar; you know how to make shavings—well, make a good fire and burn it, then the government will have to build you a new house. And," I added, "if the government should happen to discover what you've done and make trouble for you, I'll go to Ottawa and make the ears of the Indian officials burn hotter than your house."

He gave a wan smile, coughed, then said: "That not bad idea, Fred."

---

54 GFC had a camp at Taffa Lake. I never heard him call Taffa a pond. He does so in his writing only here and in *Noël and Jimmy-Why*. In both cases he may have been remembering Noël's word for it.

55 He cannot have been in his seventies; he died on December 12, 1927, aged 67 or 68. (His tombstone says he was 68, but census records suggest that he was 67.)

Before he left I went to the nearby drug store, purchased a bottle of Scott's Emulsion and gave it to him. He wanted to pay me but I told him no. It was a gift—only a small one for the many things he had done for me.

* * *

A week later, as I was about to enter my office, I saw him coming up the sidewalk, and I waited until he was beside me. I shook his brown hand and said: "Well, Noël, how are you today?"

"Oh," he replied, "I not much better, Fred." Then: "You remember what you tell me about crooked knife an' cedar shavin's an' good fire? Well, next mornin', after you tell me, I make nice fire at end of my house. It burn good, make much smoke. But what you think? Well, all Indians in village see smoke, run with pails of water, put out fire. Next day I try again. Same thing happen. So I think I try once more. I make nice cedar shavin's with my crooked knife, pile on plenty wood. Oh, it fine fire. Shoot up side of house. I think: well, I get new one now for sure. But oh my! All the people come again, carry big pail water, throw it on, put it out like before. Too good neighbours, Fred." He paused, then, with that fatalism so characteristic of his race, he added: "No use, Fred."

A few days before Christmas he entered my office carrying a beautiful pair of child's snowshoes with gay red rosettes on the foresides of the frames. *(18a)* I admired them and he said: "You give them to your little girl for Christmas present."

"That's a bright idea, Noël," I said, and added: "How much shall I pay you, Noël?"

"Not anything," he answered. "I give them to you for young daughter."

"But, Noël," I protested, "I *must* pay you. You can't afford to make snowshoes and give them away."

He smiled and said: "You do things for me, an' not take money. So I make little present for you."

To argue longer would have been discourteous on my part, so I said: "Forgive me, Noël. You're quite right. Thank you. I'll tell my daughter that good Saint Noël Polchies gave them to her."

Chapter XI

His kind old face, pathetic in its thinness, lighted up with a pleased smile. *"Adio,* Fred," he said, and went slowly out the door and down the stairs.

* * *

Two years later (in the summer) I heard that Noël had passed away.[56] I drove down to the Indian village, knocked on the door of his home. A solemn-faced niece opened it and asked me to enter. The clean front room was almost bare of furniture. At one end stood the plain black coffin that contained all that was mortal of my old friend. Near by on a small table was a vase containing a few red paper flowers.

The niece went into another room and Mrs. Polchies entered—a tall, bony woman whose hair, although she was past seventy, was still almost wholly black. She carried herself straight, like a grenadier, and had a shawl about her shoulders. I took her hand, and she said, her voice low but distinct: "You want to see Noël?"

"Yes," I said. With stately tread she walked over to the coffin, drew back the black cloth that covered his face, and said: "Look—see'm." Then she walked back and seated herself in the one chair in the room.

I gazed for fully a minute on the placid face which death had robbed of all pain and suffering, so that it looked like that of the Noël I had known forty years before,[57] then I turned to where the wife sat. Unwilling to show her grief to a white man—even though he was the friend of her husband— she had covered her head and face with her shawl. But I could tell by the heaving of her shoulders that she was weeping. I laid a hand on her shoulder and said, my voice husky: "Noël was a good man." Then I added the futile words: "Have courage."

She half withdrew the shawl from her face and said: "Yes—Noël he good man. You him good friend."

* * *

---

56 GFC misremembered. Noel died on 12 December 1927, not in the summer.

57 This is a particularly dramatic example of GFC's impressionistic treatment of time. He met Noël Polchies in about 1907. Noël died in 1927. GFC knew him for twenty years, not forty.

I seldom give flowers to the dead, preferring rather to give the money to some charitable institution in memory of the departed. If in life the deceased is an Anglican I give the money to the Rector to forward to the secretary of Home Missions for use among the Indians of the far north. But in the present case I went to the local florist and purchased a dozen each of the most beautiful red roses and carnations he had, took them down and gave them to the widow.

Two weeks later on my way downriver I stopped at her home to see how she was making out. She was seated in a little shed off the kitchen skinning eels to dry and smoke. We talked for a few minutes then, as I was about to depart, she said: "You wait." She got up, went into the kitchen and came out holding a crooked knife in her hand. It was Noël's favourite knife. On the back of the thumb-piece of the long handle he had carved with consummate artistry the face of a woman. She held it out to me and said: "I think Noël he want you to have this."

Then I said something I have always regretted. I knew that it was a valuable thing—a museum piece—and not wanting to take advantage of emotions caused by her recent bereavement, I said: "Oh no, Mrs. Polchies, you mustn't give it to me."

She didn't say a word, but turned and set it carefully on the shelf behind her. She had no sooner done it than it struck me that in all probability she thought I had spurned her intended gift. But it was then too late for me to say I would gladly accept it.

Some five years ago her grandson casually mentioned to me that, the autumn following Noël's death, a noted American ethnologist had stopped at the Indian village and, among other objects of their material culture, had purchased the beautiful crooked knife and that it now reposes in a museum.

I regret that it does not hold an honoured place among my own collection of Indian stone implements and other objects at present in the Fisher Memorial Library in my native town. I'm sure Noël would have wished it there.

I am sorry that he was not interred close to the river beside which he was born and lived all his life. With his brother (who did even better carvings on wood, and also excelled any Indian I know in shaping little animals out of stone) he rests in the Roman Catholic cemetery overlooking the

Meduxnekeag stream, whose myriad pools were once filled with salmon from which, until seventy years ago, their ancestors had taken canoe-loads of fish.

Today it is very doubtful if more than two dozen salmon are yearly taken by spear along the St John and its tributaries. For the men who lived contemporary with Noël and Peter Polchies have also passed from the scene, and those few Indians of the present generation who own canoes have become ardent fly-fishermen.

CHAPTER XII

I had written to Bill Gillalpen[G], the same splendid and entertaining fellow who had guided me on a memorable trip two years before when, with my friend Larry, guided by Charlie, and a cook named Henry in a third canoe, we had run the Main Southwest Miramichi River to Boiestown.[58] Never did New Brunswick guide have a greater fund of quaint anecdotes and folklore than Bill. He was a remarkable mimic and had the true *raconteur's* gift of building up interest and suspense to the very end. Like Falstaff, he was not above "adding such embellishments and circumstances as he well knew how."[59] Moreover, he was one of the most cheerful men I have ever known, and, for some reason of his own, seemed to regard me with much the same devotion as that which Corporal Trim had for Uncle Toby.[60]

He had written that he would arrive at Juniper on the night train, bringing his own canoe, run the North Branch to the Forks, and when our trip ended would run the main river to his own home below Boiestown.

So here I was, my supper long since ended, seated on the verandah *(21b)* of the little camp overlooking the Forks Pool, *(21a)* smoking my pipe and

---

58 GFC recounts the trip in *Six Salmon Rivers*, dating it to 1925. So this trip was probably in 1927.

59 Augustine Birrell, "Falstaff," in *Obiter Dicta*, 1885.

60 Characters in Laurence Sterne's *Tristram Shandy*, 1767.

G For reasons that will later appear obvious [Bill's alcoholism] I haven't given Bill's correct surname, nor that of the village in which he was born. As for the yarns he spun, some of them are similar to legends my mother told me. Others may have been the product of his own remarkable imagination.

quite alone. About an hour since, I had heard the hoarse whistle of the locomotive as it approached Juniper, so Bill should arrive any moment.

The night was beautiful. High in the cold north hung that group of brilliant stars which form the constellation we know as the Big Dipper but from remote times has also been called *Ursa Major* (the Great Bear), of which Chaucer wrote in his enchanting mediaeval English: "The sterre y-clept 'the Bere' that enclyneth his ravisshinge courses abouten the soverein heighte of the worlde."[61]

Suddenly I heard the quacking of ducks and the beat of their wings as they sped down the Forks Pool to the main river. Then the thump of a setting-pole against the gunwale of a canoe, and around the bend I saw the dim, upright form of Bill. "Hullo, Bill," I called; and across the waters floated his cheery voice: "Hullo, Doctor." I hurried into the camp, took down the Coleman lantern, and in little more time than it takes to tell reached the shore.

He had already landed. I flashed the light on his face, glistening with fly-dope, took his hand. His grip was strong: that of a man you could depend on through thick and thin. He said: "Gosh, Doctor, I'm glad to be with you again. I almost ran into two deer at the mouth of the Bogan;[62] an' routed some ducks just around the bend."

"Good sentinels, Bill," I said. "They told me you were coming."

He shouldered his pack and bed-roll and followed me up to the camp.

I fried him bacon and eggs, made a pot of tea and sat beside him while he ate. He told me there was a good run of salmon in the lower pools waiting for a rise of water to come up. Then, with a merry twinkle in his eyes: "We'll have a good time—salmon or not."

"That's the boy!" I said. "A day off is a day gained."

"Right," he said.

The next morning, after breakfast, we loaded the canoe with a small tent, cooking utensils, enough food to last a week, and dropped downriver to

---

61 In *The Consolations of Philosophy*, by Boethius, trans. Chaucer. GFC may have found this quotation in a secondary source. The *Consolations* is a book-length theological/philosophical treatise, and Chaucer's translation, in Middle English, is heavy going.

62 In New Brunswick a bogan is a narrow stream winding through marshy land to a lake or river.

Chapter XII

the pool at the mouth of Biggar Brook. No one was fishing it, so we took a dozen nice pan-trout on the right below the brook, and from midriver a twelve-pound salmon that gave us a good fight before we landed it. Then we proceeded to a small camping-ground above the head of Crooked Rapids where we had decided to tent until the following day.

It didn't take long to set up the tent, peg it down, dig a trench around it, cut bundles of soft fir boughs, carry them back to the tent and make a mattress over which we laid our sleeping bags. "First things first," said Bill. "All we need now is firewood. He cut the wood: white birch, dry spruce and cedar; and I cut two forked stakes—four feet long—from maple saplings, sharpened the ends and forced them into the earth, about five feet apart, on the site where we proposed making our camp-fire. Then I cut a straight piece, called *chip-la-kwa-gun* by the Indians, and laid it within the forks of the two uprights. Thus, by lifting either end of the *chip-la-kwa-gun*, we could slip the handles of the boiling kettles over or off it without fear of upsetting the contents.

We carried the wood to the tent, piled some of it inside to keep dry in case of rain, and gathered boulders to form a circle in which to make and confine the campfire.

* * *

We had boiled potatoes, fried bacon and trout, and made a kettle of good strong tea for which Bill got water from a little spring at the foot of the Rapids. Then, for dessert, strawberry pie my wife had given me when I left home. What ho! good friends, have you ever eaten a whole quarter of strawberry pie in the out-of-doors? Nowhere does it taste better than beside a little river and no dull care within many miles to mar its flavour. And when we had quite finished we sprinkled plenty of bread crumbs a few feet distant for the birds, remembering that we had fared well, and that they are a part of our priceless heritage without which the world would not be quite the same.[63] While Bill washed the dishes, I got the canoe seat, set it against a tree, sat down, filled my pipe with my favourite tobacco and

---

63 An unobtrusive instance of GFC's environmentalism.

smoked contentedly. And the aroma of it mingled with the innumerable odours of earth and trees, especially that of the balsam fir. Across the river a sandpiper alighted on a big boulder and nodded and tipped its tail as though it were saying "How do you do?" Then it flew upstream uttering its plaintive: "Wet-feet! Wet-feet!" as, I think, Henry van Dyke has interpreted it.[64] The Indians call it *ne-ne-mek-tchus,* which describes its motions.

When Bill had scrubbed the frying pan with sand and small pebbles, rinsed it out, replaced it with the other things in the tent, we took my rod, and going back of the tent, fastened the leader to a sapling, unwound all the casting line and what backing was wet, from the reel, looped it around another sapling, left it to dry, and returned to the tent, where Bill seated himself with his back to a tree and I on the canoe seat.

* * *

There was silence for a few minutes, but I could feel Bill's mind working and knew that something was soon coming that would be of interest. A blue jay appeared like a phantom, perched on a tree only a few rods distant, and, like a ventriloquist gave us a brief sample of his mimicry of other birds, then flew across the river, its brilliant blue and white flashing in the sun while he shrieked his "Jay! Jay!" as though in derision of all other feathered creatures.

Bill turned his face to me, and there was a twinkle in his grey eyes as he said: "Did I ever tell you about Mrs J. who I guided on this same stretch of water, and of what a great talker she was? We hooked a thirty-pounder in the Salmon Hole and it led us below Biggar Brook just above where we are now."

"You mean the woman who had the set of camps near Push-And-Be-Damned Rapids, shot the bear, had it stuffed in New York and you canoed it to the Rapids?"[65]

"Oh no," he answered; "this was another, an' no relation." He paused, and after a low chuckle: "The only woman I ever met, before or since, who could beat her was my aunt Libby, mother's sister. Of course mother could talk

---

64   In van Dyke's *Little Rivers,* 1896.

65   The story is in *Six Salmon Rivers.*

Chapter XII

too, an' my grandmother... Perhaps I inherited their gift. But aunt Libby, well, she'd talk the legs off an iron pot. It didn't matter what is was: religion, sheepshearin', spinnin', cows, or how old some neighbour was when she died, an' who she was related to (as if that mattered a continental). An' argue! She always took the opposite side: John Jones wasn't born at Blackville, but at Boiestown, because his sister's cousin had told her that she was born there the same year; an' it was in 1883 because... Oh, well, the only time aunt Libby come near runnin' down was one day when I was only a little gaffer. We lived at Boiestown at that time. My uncle by marriage came to pay us a visit. After breakfast aunt Libby took him into the parlour, an' started talkin' about the family history from the time they came to the Miramichi back in 1815. She kept it up until noon when we had dinner, then she dragged him back to the parlour an' started in where she'd left off. But I think she was nettled because he wouldn't argue with her. He just set there, smoked his pipe, an' took what she had to say, with only a yawn oncet in a while, or sayin': 'Yes, Libby... Yes, Libby.' She told mother about it next day.

"Well, about four in the afternoon, I went into the parlour to borrow uncle's jacknife. At first I could hardly see them for tobacco smoke. Then I did. He was stretched out flat on his back on the floor, his pipe beside him, his eyes closed, an' lookin' awful pale around the gills. An' aunt Libby was on her knees beside him whisperin' in his ear. That's all she was capable of doin' at that stage, only able to whisper." Bill paused a few moments, then went on: "Now, Doctor, to get back to Mrs J. Three years after the First Great War,[66] when I was twenty-five, I got a job guidin' with Murdoch MacKenzie, at the Forks. As you know, he had quite an outfit at that time, used to send lots of parties through to Boiestown. Well, one Sunday evenin' I was just comin' outa Mac's house when a big car rolled into the yard, an' Mrs J. an' her husband got out. She was a short, dumpy two-hundred-pounder, her face as round as a berry, cheeks like a June rose, an' her mouth covered with the reddest lip-stick I'd ever seen. She'd plucked her eyebrows in the shape of a half-moon an' blacked 'em; but you could see between 'em they was the

---

66 In 1927 Bill would not have called World War I "the *First* Great War". GFC probably heard Bill's stories on fishing trips over many years, but tells them here, with a narrator's licence, as if he heard them all during the 1927 trip.

same colour as her yellow hair. She did have nice brown eyes, even if they was almost as big as a rabbit's." Bill paused again, and I said: "It seems to me, Bill, that you must have looked her over very carefully."

"Um," he said, "couldn't help it. There was so much of her. But you should have seen her husband: a little spindly, wrinkled critter that wouldn't make good bear-bait: not bigger'n a cup of tea. An' kind of scared-lookin'. It wasn't long before I knew the reason: she ordered him about just as though he was a servant. That night the five sports that had arrived drew cards, each card with the initials of the different guides on the back. It was just my hard luck that Mrs J. drew me.

"She an' her husband put up at Mac's house, an' the other men sports stayed in the big building Mac used to call the 'shop'. Us guides bunked in the cabin across the river. Next mornin' she come out rigged in shorts that come to her knees (I'd never seen 'em before on women). An' I thinks to myself: 'You'll be eat up today, my fine lady, or I don't known Miramichi mosquitoes.' But I was wrong, as you'll learn later. Gosh! She had on a wide-brimmed felt hat like western cowboys wear; an' all around the band was stuck the oddest menagerie I'd ever seen before or since: Big fly-hooks with long, yellow, red an' blue feathers; spoonhooks, plugs an' what-not. Well, we'd no sooner got to the canoes—where all the other guides waited for their sports—when she said to her husband: 'Run back to the house, Dearie, an' get my dark glasses.' So off he starts, lookin' for all the world like a little beetle runnin' on stilts. Then, when he'd returned, she says: 'Oh, Dearie, I forgot my box of chocolates. They're on the table by my bed.' So off he goes without a word, just like a trained puppy." Bill paused and said apologetically: "Want me to stop an' grease the line?"

"Oh, no, Bill," I answered. "Not for worlds. I believe this is going to be interesting. Your descriptions are perfect. Somerset Maugham[67] couldn't better them."

"Never knew him," said Bill. "He must have fished this river before *my* time, or while I was overseas."

---

67 An English popular novelist, who was in the 1930s the highest-earning writer in the world.

Chapter XII

To Bill almost every name mentioned meant some individual who had hunted or fished at one time or another on the Miramichi.

"I never heard he did," I said. "In fact I don't think he was ever in New Brunswick."

"Gosh!" he returned. "What a lot he's missed! Well, I finally got Mrs J. into the canoe, an' she sot down on the seat with such a thump I thought she'd gone through the bottom. An' I thinks to myself: 'This is the last trip for me on this river, or any other, because she'll drown me sure as thunder.' Anyways I got in, seated myself and started off downriver. She turned her head around an' called to her husband: 'Be sure an' have a good time, Dearie. An' *don't come back without a salmon.*' It was a *must*, if you get what I mean, Doctor. He didn't make any answer but: 'All right, Sweetie.' (In fact I didn't hear him say more'n a dozen words the whole week they was at the Forks.) Then she shifted her sights on me, an' hardly left off talkin' till we got back after one o'clock.

"She told me she'd never fished for salmon, but she had for tarpon off Florida an' Cuba: said she sat on a chair, had a short rod clamped in a sort of vise that moved like a universal joint, a reel as big as the gear-housin' on a model T Ford, an' a thousand feet of line hitched to a copper wire. They stuck some sort of bait on a big hook an' threw it overboard."

Bill took a breather, then went on: "So far as I'm concerned no sea fishin' for me. Oceans ain't friendly, an' the only person I ever heard of tryin' to talk to one was that English king, who had such a swelled head he tried to stop the tide comin' in. 'Course he didn't have no luck. Now you get close to a river an' a brook: they've got a hundred voices, if you get what I mean, Doctor."

"Yes, Bill," I said: "I understand."

He scratched his head a moment then: "Where was I—? Oh, yes, that Mrs J. She said she'd been born on the prairie, raised wheat an' kept a few cattle an' a couple of ponies. Then, when she was twenty, they struck an oil well on her place, an' sold it for a million dollars to B.A. or I.O.—I forgit which. Then they found a gusher, that was bigger, on the next section, where her present husband lived. 'I thought it'd be a good idea if I married him,' she said. 'So one afternoon I jumped on my bronco an' galloped bareback to his place. I told him I'd come to ask a straight-forward question, an' didn't want *no* for answer; because if he said it I'd abduct him anyway. We was married next day by a Justice of the Peace.'

* * *

"We hadn't gone very far when she took a big jar of some kind of cream and rubbed it all over her arms an' bare legs: a regular thick mess that would discourage the most ugly mosquito between the Forks and Boiestown.

"'You've tried it before?' I asked her.

"'Oh yes,' she says. 'It works. It softens their bills so they double up and can't get through.'

"'Softens their bills?' I says. 'That's a new one. P'raps you've got something there: like...like soap-lather does to a man's beard before he shaves.'

"'That's the idea,' she said. Then she started eatin' chocolates, but didn't stop talkin'. She asked me to have some, but I said, no thank you.

"'What are you eatin?' she asked.

"I told her I was chewin' tobacco.

"'Oh,' she said, 'what a nasty habit'; an' give a shudder that shook the canoe.

"'Well,' I said, 'it's all in the way of thinkin'. Each one to his likes.' Then I said: 'If you took a chew you'd like it.'

"She gave another shudder an' said: 'Thank you, William. I tried it once, when I was thirteen. My father chewed, so one day I snitched one of his plugs, took it out to the corral when I went to get my pony, an' just as I'd saddled him, I took a bite of the stuff, then swung myself up an' started off. I hadn't got far when my throat began to tighten, then my head started to spin, an' the whole sky an' prairie went round. My toes slipped out of the stirrups an' I tumbled to the grass. I was awful sick.'

"Then she started off on another tack: 'After I was married, I took Basil (her husband) to New York, then to England, then to Europe: Paris, Germany, Spain, Switzerland an' Venice—a place where the houses an' shops butt right up against canals, with gondolas rushin' here an' there sculled by black-haired young men in velvet jackets an' knee breeks, an' singin' tra-la-la with a lot of etceteras.'

"From what I gathered about them canals," said Bill, "they need an anti-pollution law, because no selfrespectin' salmon would live in them. Then

Chapter XII

she started in talkin' about shoes, an' lace an' hats an' new dresses an' other trinkets she'd bought. Quite a list, but for some reason or other she soon shifted her sights back to shoes.

"Well, we got to the Salmon Hole. I anchored at the head where we always begin. 'What are you goin' to do?' she asked, turnin' her head.

"'We fish here,' I answered, an' picked up her rod. It wasn't too bad, but I didn't like the reel. With all the drag on, a mouse could have run off with the line. So I asked her if I could put on mine. She gave me a crimson smile an' said: 'OK, that's all right with me.' So I put on my Hardy Perfect… When I'd done that she whipped off her hat an' chirped: 'Now, William, we can try some of these beautiful flies.'

"I didn't want to hurt her feelin's, so I said: 'Well, Ma'am, the salmon in this river was educated on flies like this an' I don't want to change their diet yet awhile. P'raps later.' So I opened my fly-box an' showed her a Jock Scott. 'Oh,' she says, 'what an uninterestin' lookin' fly! Say, brother, you ain't kiddin' me, are you?'

"'No,' I said. 'Not for a million.'

"'Dollars?' she says.

"'Yes.'

"'Holy Mike!' she said. 'I'd sell my husband for less than ten thousand, now that he's made his will in my favour, then I'd marry you.'

"Well, Doctor, I tied on the Jock an' handed her the rod. Oh, she could throw a pretty good line, but all the time she was castin' she rattled on about shoes. A twelve or fourteen pounder come twice, but she saw it comin' an' jerked away the fly. 'Holy Mike!' she squealed, 'I almost had it!'

"'Yes, Ma'am,' I said. But I didn't add the cuss words she did, but somethin' blazin' I don't often use before women. She didn't mind. She only said: 'You swear beautiful, William; but I bet my father could beat you. He had the biggest collection of swear words between Winnipeg an' the Rockies.'

"'Well,' I said, 'he must have been born on the Miramichi; or perhaps an ancestor was.'

"She said she didn't think so, then returned to shoes, chatterin' on so fast I couldn't hear myself think. However, I did my duty an' tried to inoculate her in the art of hookin' a fish. But it wasn't no use. I said: 'When he comes let him have the hook. Don't lift the rod till you feel him, then not too hard.'

Song of the Reel

She raised another fish an' took the fly right out of its mouth. Then I said: 'Do you mind if I take the rod, Mrs J.? P'raps I can hook one.'

"'Oh, by all means,' she says, as good-natured as pie. 'But, William, don't call me Mrs J. or Ma'am. My husband caller me Sweetie. How about you calling me Bertha?' But I didn't call her Bertha, an' I guess she forgot to remind me. So I took the rod she held back to me, an' hadn't made half a dozen casts when a big fish made a boil, took the fly an' went tearin' across the pool like the *Whooper*[H] on a down grade. 'Here, Ma'am,' I says, 'take the rod,' reached over her shoulder and give it to her. Just then the salmon flung itself straight into the air an' fell back in the water with a splash like as if you'd thrown in a four-foot pulp log.

"'Holy Mike!' she says. Then: 'I told the clerk I wanted size four double-A; not five-B. But he said the measurement says 5-B… Holy Mike! Where's the fish goin';' For it had swung about an' was headin' down the pool, an' the reel roarin' like a lawn mower. I told her not to touch the handle. She said: 'OK brother.' Then: 'He insisted I should have 5-B…as though I hadn't worn 4 double-A's all my life…or, well, since leavin' New York… Holy Mike! Where's the brute goin'?' she cried again; for the salmon was far down the pool an' I was paddlin' after him as fast as I could go.

"As you know, Doctor, the Salmon Hole is a long stretch of water. He navigated it to the very end, ran past Harry Murphy's camp, then stopped for a breather. So I moved down the right-hand shore, and told her to reel up. She was pantin' like a hound dog when it's ninety degrees in the shade. If you remember, Doctor, I said she was a husky two-hundred pounder, an' she now leaned so hard against the back of the seat it cracked like kindlin' wood, an' she tumbled back an' half over the cross-bar, so that the rod almost touched my head, an' the canoe almost upset. I tossed the anchor, got my hands under her arms, lifted her up onto the seat, then—I couldn't help it—laughed till the tears come to my eyes.

H *(Note)* The Whooper was the Canada Eastern train that formerly plied between Fredericton and Newcastle, and named after a mythical creature said to haunt the Dungarvon river (a tributary of the Miramichi) and startle rivermen and woodsmen by its diabolical screams. Hence, when the train made its very first run to Newcastle, and the people of the valley heard its hoarse whistle, they said: "That's the Dungarvon Whooper." Which was soon shortened to *The Whooper*.

Chapter XII

"'Holy Mike!' she cried. 'It's nothing to laugh about. I might've been drowned.'

"Sorry, Ma'am," I says. 'I beg your pardon. You can't swim?' I asked.

"'Like a stone,' she answered. 'I *told* you I was born on the prairie.'

"'Same with me,' I said. 'I mean I can't swim either.'

"She just said: 'And you've been on the river *all your life!*' (just as if she was a judge handin' out a jail sentence) when the salmon started off again. So I up with the anchor and started after it, tellin' her to reel in as fast as she could, because I was goin' to try an' get below it before it reached Rocky Bend. So she did, an' I managed to get below it along the far shore. Now the fish started to roll. I didn't like that because I was afraid it would work the hook out, or break the leader. Then sudden he stopped them dangerous tactics, an' bolted upstream a hundred yards, made a beautiful leap in the still water, fell back an' threw up showers of foam. Then back he come, roarin' past us with fifty yards of loose line trailin' behind him. Then he stopped. I was just about to tell her to reel in, when the reel began to spin again. Well, that fish continued right around the bend, cavorted a bit in the deep pool below, then began navigatin' the nest of sunken an' raised rocks at Rocky Bend. I was now polin', an' snubbin' pretty frequent because, as you know, the water is swift there, an' I didn't want to dump Mrs J. I told her to hold the rod high, an' I must say she did well, reelin' in when I told her, an' stoppin' when I said so. Well, we got through safe enough, an' reached the wide, more quiet pool just below the mouth of Biggar Brook, where we had a better chance to land the fish, if we ever was to. He was far towards the left shore when a log of pulp-wood floated into the pool, and just then that fish took it into his noodle to make a sudden turn, leaped out of the water and clean over that confounded log. I could see the line spinnin' over the bark, then it stopped sudden. 'Gone!' I groaned.

"'Holy Mike!' said Mrs J. 'That was a beautiful leap!'

"I drove the canoe across the pool to where the piece of pulp was floatin' downstream, an' told her to reel in. Then I saw that the line was caught under a scale of the bark, so I lifted it out an' the log went on its way. I didn't blame her; she'd done well, but I thought I'd gladly give a day's pay if we could have landed that fish. I only said: 'Reel in now, Mrs J.', which she did. But she'd only made a few turns when the rod top began to bend. 'Stop!' I said, 'it's caught on a rock. Take your hand off the reel or you'll break the rod!' an' dropped the anchor. Then everything began to happen at once. The line moved upstream; the drum revolved like mad. 'Holy Piscator!' I cried, 'he's still on!' He ran upriver a hundred yards past Biggar Brook, swung to the right, rose to the surface, made a side-splurge that parted the water same as a ploughshare turns a furrow. Then he sank to the bottom, or near it, an' ran down the pool like somethin' crazy. Said Mrs J.: 'How about cuttin' the line, an' let the critter go? I'm all in.'

"'Oh no,' I said. 'We can't do *that* after all we've gone through. We want to get that fish. It'd never do to go back to camp an' tell the others we cut the line: they'd have a great laugh on us. How about *me* takin' the rod?'

"'Thank God!' she said, an' handed it back to me.

"Well, Doc, all that fish wanted was a little rough handlin' like a scoldin' woman. So I gave him the butt—not too hard, an' pressed my finger on the line. He made a few rushes to the opposite shore; but each time I brought him back. Finally he edged up past the canoe not more'n twenty feet distant, rolled over on his side, but still wagglin' his tail. I reached for the gaff, picked it up, an' laid the business end across the gunwale of the canoe. Then, reelin' slowly, an' puttin' on only a little pressure, I let him slip backwards within reach of me. Now I held the rod in my left hand, with the line between my fingers, seized the handle of the gaff, reached out an' clipped him through the shoulder. I dropped the butt of the rod into the canoe, grabbed the gaff-handle with both hands, and hove the fish into the bottom of the boat, dropped on my knees atop it, pulled out the priest from my hip pocket an' clipped it over the nose three or four times. That did it.

"Mrs J. had turned her head to watch me. 'Holy Mike!' she said. 'That's a small critter to give us so much trouble!'

"'Yes,' I said. 'He gave lots of trouble, but he'll go thirty pounds.' (It did, as we learned later. I only know of two as big taken *this* far up the river.)

"'You know,' she said. 'I got the better of that clerk: I told him the size 4 double-A or nothin'. At first I thought he was goin' to keep on buckin' me—like a ornery bronco—but finally he said he'd send them to my hotel.'

"I pulled up the anchor and began polin' back to the Forks. An' all the way she talked an' ate chocolates, so that I was heartily glad when we got there.

Chapter XII

We found her husband had returned from his trip up the North Branch, an' had two three-pound grilse.

* * *

"After lunch she decided she'd take a rest, so she anointed her legs with a thick layer of cream, an' stretched out on a settee with a magazine an' another box of chocolates. Later I was just ready to have a nap when MacKenzie opened the door an' said: 'Bill, Sweetie wants you to come over right away—an' not maybe.'

"'Oh,' I groaned, 'I thought she didn't want to fish this afternoon.'

"'She don't,' he said, an' grinned. 'But she wants you.'

"So I got up, got my canoe an' poled over to where she was, with her cowboy hat pulled half over her eyes. I says: 'Here I am, Ma'am.'

"'Oh, William,' she says, lookin' up at me with a bright smile, 'I'm so glad you've come. I'm frightfully bored. Pull over that stool, sit down an' talk to me.'

"Talk to her, Doctor! She meant she wanted to do the talkin'. So I takes a chew of tobacco, sits down an' she begins. But it wasn't too bad. She shifted her sights to her ranch an' talked about horses an' wheat, an' cattle, an' oil, an' finally says: 'Look here, William, how about you comin' out west with me an' my husband? I'll give you a good job on the ranch, an' build you a nice house. Better say yes.'

"Then I told her about Mary. 'Besides,' I says, 'I wouldn't leave the Miramichi if I was given all the rest of Canada, an' the United States of America thrown in to boot.'

"She gave me a quick look with her big brown eyes, then shifted her sights to wheat an' stock raisin', pausin' every so often to pop a chocolate into her mouth. An' that was that, Doctor. But I tell you a feller needed to be encased in boiler-plate to resist her.

* * *

"Well, the next mornin' we dropped down here to Biggar Brook. She wanted to catch some trout, so I put on a *Queen of the Water* an' she landed twenty. She wanted to take more, but I said that accordin' to the law twenty was the limit for one day. That set her up: she said laws was meant to be broke. Then we had quite a argument. She said she'd gladly pay any fine; but I said that wouldn't take care of me—I'd lose my guide licence. With that she shut up. I mean she changed the subject.

So I took off the fly, tied on a Silver Doctor, and we fished at the big rock where I'd seen a grilse break water. But it wouldn't take, so about eleven o'clock she said she wanted to go to shore an' stretch her legs. So I landed her below the brook. She walked up an' down a few minutes, then entered the woods, an' I lighted my pipe for a change of tobacco, an' waited for her to come back.

"After a bit I felt drowsy, closed my eyes an' fell asleep. Then something woke me up. I looked about. No Mrs J. I glanced at my watch. She'd been gone more'n a half hour. Then, from far off, I heard a faint 'Whoohoo' repeated six or eight times. I says to myself: 'My God, she's lost!' I gets out of the canoe pretty quick, climbed the bank into the woods an' starts in the direction I'd heard the shoutin' that had begun again but sounded farther away than before. So I gave several whoops an' started runnin' fast as I could go to where I'd heard her. I crossed the tote-road an' swung to the right. (As you know, Doctor, that woods is thick an' hard goin'.) Finally I came to the brook an' saw her foot prints in the mud; they led along the brook, then I lost them. Then I saw some ferns she'd tramped down, an' where she'd stepped over a fallen log and brushed off a bit of the moss. I shouted again, listened, an' soon heard a faint answer from the depths of the woods away on the left. She'd swung in a half circle and crossed the brook. So I gave another shout, an' started that way. Well, Doc, to make a long story shorter, I finally come on her seated on the stump of a tree, that had fallen down years past, an' smokin' a cigarette.

"'Oh, hullo, William,' she says, as chipper as you please. 'I thought I'd take a little walk. Ain't the woods nice an' cool?'

"She had me dumb for a bit. Then I said: 'But I heard you shout, I thought you was lost.'

"'Me! Lost?' she says as calm as pie. 'Oh, no, William; not on your life! Why, I've travelled for half a day on the prairie when there was only a ranch

Chapter XII

house every dozen miles or so... But p'raps we'd better go back to the canoe an' have another try for that grilse.'

"'Yes,' I said. 'We'll foller the brook down to the tote-road.'

"'Now,' she said, 'that's a bright idea!' An' she didn't even blush.

* * *

"Well, we was together all that day, an' at the end of it my head was goin' round like it does when I'm off the waggon an' imbibed too much of the hearty. So the next mornin' I played sick, an' MacKenzie gave her Sam Henry for guide, an' he took her out.

"Early after lunch, when we guides was all in our shanty, I saw Sam whittlin' at a piece of cedar wood. He was always cuttin' out something: frogs or lizards or beavers or other little animals. Quite an artist he was. So I said to him: 'What's it now, Sam?'

"If looks could kill, you wouldn't have me here today, Doctor. Then he said: 'Ear-plugs, you blasted fool!'

* * *

"About five o'clock Sam started off up the North Branch with Sweetie. He had his ear-plugs in, over them a thick rubber bathin' cap, an' over that his felt hat.

"Well, Doctor, that night, after she and Sam had come back, me and MacKenzie was seated on the verandah, when she walks up to Mac, points a finger at him an' says: 'Look here, Mr. MacKenzie, what's the big idea sendin' me out with a deaf-mute? He doesn't even know how to talk with his fingers, which I do, because we had to learn home on account of havin' a deaf an' dumb cowhand. An' I tried sign language I got from a tribe of Injuns that lived near our ranch. Now, sir, *I want William back*. When we cut the cards for guides I drew him, an' I don't cal'ate to be cheated out of *my property.*'

"*Her property*, Doc! Think of it! Just as if I was a pair of boots, or a sports shirt!

"'All right, all right, Mrs J.' says MacKenzie. 'Of course you know Bill was sick today; that's why I gave you Sam. But, as you say, Bill's yours.'

"She gave him a painted smile, opened her box of chocolates an' asked him to help himself. So peace was restored. Then she turned to me, linked her arm in mine and says: 'Poor dear, what *you* need is a little drink of the joyful,' an' started me off to her room. But we'd only gone a few steps when she turned an' said to MacKenzie: 'Mr. MacKenzie, have lunch put up for William an' me in the mornin'. We'll stay out all day.'

"Well, Doctor, that was that. By the end of the week we took two more salmon—twelve-pounders—an' a couple of grilse. Sunday mornin', as we was all sayin' goodbye to the sports, she says to me: 'William,' she says, 'come here.' So I goes to where she stood beside her husband. An' what do you think she did, Doc?"

I shook my head. "She didn't kiss you?" I asked.

"Worse'n that," moaned Bill. "She flung both fat arms about my neck, drew me to her ample bosom, gave me a bear hug that almost took my breath away, an' a smack with her lips on mine that sounded like a whizz-bang. Then she drew back, pressed a fifty-dollar bill into my hand an' whispered: 'William, I've got a confession to make. I *was* lost that day! Goodbye, William.' She turned, grabbed her husband by the shoulders, pushed him into the car, took the wheel an' off they went.

"Of course when I got back to where the boys, an' the cook, an' the table girl stood, they was laughin' their heads off. No wonder—I had enough lipstick on my mouth to last the average small-size woman a week... I guess we can grease that line now, Doc."[68]

---

68   Ian Bernard says that GFC "would often wind his fly line onto a line winder to dry it overnight, then add grease from Hardy's [the great English outfitter] to the line in the morning so it would float." In about 1990 the Clarke estate donated GFC's line winder to the Atlantic Salmon Museum in Doaktown.

CHAPTER XIII

"In the old days," said Bill, "I've taken salmon in set-nets, driftin' for 'em, spearin', an' every other possible way except dynamitin'. Ever tickle a salmon, Doctor?"

I told him I had heard and read of it being done, and he said: "An old Scot named Angus Bruce showed me how. So one day, late in the season, when I was thirteen, I was up Rocky Brook an' some of the pools was filled with salmon. I could see a big one—a twenty-pounder—restin' beside a big boulder close to shore. So I got on it, reached down till my hand was just ahead of his tail. He moved off, but soon came back. I was lyin' flat on the rock with my hand still in the water close to the bottom, so I began scratchin' his belly with my finger-tips. He seemed to like it, just as a cat does when you scratch its head. So finally I moved my hand backwards till it was just ahead of its tail. Then I grabbed him. He gave a mighty rush, I lost my balance an' went head-first into the water. I was so scared I let go my grip. Lucky the water was low or I'd been drowned." Bill gave a low chuckle, then said: "An' oncet, when I was about twelve, me an' my brothers went up Clearwater, where a bunch of salmon was in a deep pool, an' couldn't get out because the water was too low above an' below them. We could see them plain, because the water was as clear as glass. So we put a big hook on a length of cord—used for makin' nets—tied it to a short stout alder pole, then threw out, an' when the line an' hook was over the back of one of the fish we gave a yank and jigged it: then we threw the pole in the water. The fish rushed here and there, jumped until it was tuckered out an' come to the top; then we waded out, grabbed the pole an' pulled the fish to shore. We caught six big salmon that day, an' thought it was great fun. But when father heard what we'd done he gave us a lickin' we didn't forget for many a day.

"Once't I saw a bear catch a salmon. *(20a)* I'd been up Clearwater with a sport, fishin' the pool below the second falls, an' we'd just returned to the river where I'd left my canoe, when we saw the bear an' stopped to watch him. He was crouched on his belly on a rock just below the mouth of the brook. You know, Doctor, no animal is quicker than a bear. Well, sudden its long arm shot like a torpedo into the water, an' he whipped a big salmon out, and ate it before our eyes. We could hear his jaws champin', an' a sort of slobberin' sound as when a pig is eatin' bran mash. Then he laid himself down again on the rock: Might-be hopin' another fish would come along. We didn't wait, because we had to get to Boiestown before dark, so began pullin' the canoe out of the bushes. When he heard that he gave one quick look, then jumped into the water and made it fly as he run towards the opposite shore. Then, when he couldn't get footin', he started to swim. We watched until he sprang up the bank an' disappeared in the woods." Bill paused a few moments then said: "I've heard that in the old days the Indians laid rocks across the mouth of Clearwater, leavin' just a narrow openin' for salmon to get through, an' above the openin' set a bag-net to catch them. Of course they camped on both sides of Clearwater, even hundreds of years ago, because I've heard tell of people findin' stone arrowheads an' other things. One man dug up hundreds of objects they'd made."

"Yes, Bill," I said. "I know that man."

"Do you, now?" he asked eagerly.

"His name was Clarke," I said, smiling.

"You?"

"Yes, Bill. But, to be exact, it was only one hundred and fifty pieces: arrowheads, knives, scrapers, stone gouges and some broken pottery. I also found such things right behind where we're sitting: but not so many as at Big Clearwater. On my first trip here, I had with me a young chap named Levi Grant whose parents live at the Forks."

"Oh, yes, Fred Grant and his wife, Dora. I know them. If you don't mind, I'd like to hear about your trip to Clearwater. I'm interested in them things. If you remember, when we run the river two years ago, I told you about findin' a stone axe an' some Injun bones at Rocky Brook when I was a kid.

Chapter XIII

But I didn't tell you that one day, in France, when I was helpin' dig a trench, I come on four or five—yes, five it was—long stone knives or darts about eight or ten inches long. They was pointed at both ends. I laid them aside, thinkin' to bring them home with me (because I had a hunch I wouldn't git killed). But the Jerries started a bombardment a half hour later an' we had to pull back. Then, that night, just as we was goin' back to take over our position, a big mortar shell landed where we'd been workin', threw up a ton of earth an' buried my find... Yes, Doctor?"

"You're sure they were pointed at both ends?"

"Yes, Doctor. Anything odd about that?"

"Yes, Bill," I answered, "because I dug up several of the same type at Bristol, on the St John River.*(18c)* And the type is quite rare. Eighty or more years ago quite a number were excavated near the village of Soloutré, in France. The same type has also been found at one station in England, in Northern Spain and several places in Germany, Hungary and north of Kiev. Archaeologists say they're from 20,000 to 25,000 years old. But I don't claim that my Bristol blades are that old because, if the geologists are correct, twelve thousand years ago this part of the country was covered with ice, just as parts of Greenland are now."

"I see," said Bill. He remained silent a few moments, then: "You mentioned Levi Grant a while back. Will you tell me something about that time he was with you?"

"Certainly—at least one humorous incident. I'd known for some years that there was an old Indian campsite at the mouth of Big Clearwater, so I hired Levi to go with me. He was only sixteen at the time, but an expert canoeman, had lived all his life in the woods and along the river. When we had arrived at Clearwater, set up our tent and had lunch, I did some exploring along the beach, and at one place found a great number of white quartz chippings that had been washed out of the bank above by the spring freshet. The ice had also torn off a large portion of the bank that now lay close to the place I wanted to dig. But there was a hole in the top twice the diameter of my thumb, and scores of bees were both entering it and coming out.

"I told Levi that there was a nest inside that lump of earth and that I didn't like the thought of being stung.

"'Oh,' he said, 'them's tame bees; they won't hurt you.'

"'Tame or not,' I said, 'I'll give them a wide berth.'

"He laughed. 'Want me to plug the hole?' he asked.

"'No—no, Levi,' I answered. 'You'll be wise to let them be.'

"He didn't heed me, but with another laugh walked down the shore to a clump of alders, cut off about eight inches of one big enough in circumference to fill the hole, came back and thrust one end in, completely plugging it. 'Now,' he said, 'you can dig in peace; but they're tame bees.'

"So we began digging, and in a few minutes uncovered a deposit of fire-stones, ashes, flint chippings and the usual assortment of finished stone tools. All the while the bees that had been gathering nectar from the innumerable flowers along the shore, were flying about their home trying to enter it, and since they didn't bother us Levi reiterated that they were perfectly harmless.

"Later in the day, mid-afternoon, I came on a lot of pottery fragments near the bees' home; at a fourteen-inch depth a long brownish-coloured knife, and a beautiful agate skinning knife. Then I dug farther inland. Finally I said: 'You know, Levi, it's rather a shame, the bees that are out cannot get in, and those in cannot get out.'

"'I'll pull the plug,' he said.

"'Better not, Levi: you'll get stung,'" I warned.

"'They're tame,' he repeated. 'If they wasn't we'd have been stung by the outers long ago.' And without another word he approached the big clod of earth.

"I walked hastily backwards towards the line of trees, then stopped. I saw him stretch out a hand and draw the plug. Immediately the bees inside poured out like smoke. Levi turned, ran towards the river. A bee shot past me with a sound like a stuka-bomber. Then, as Levi's heavy boots clattered over the cobbles, I heard him cry out: 'I'm stabbed!' and saw his hand clasp the back of his neck. Of course I couldn't help laughing. In fancy I can still hear his boots thudding over the rocks and his sudden cry: 'I'm stabbed!'

"He went a few yards more, then sat down on a big boulder and rocked back and forth while he roared with laughter. Never have I known anyone with a greater sense of risibility. Finally he rose to his feet and came towards me. Said I: 'I thought you said they were *tame* bees!' He gave a foolish grin, walked past me and vanished into the woods. In a few minutes he returned with a handful of black earth he had found at the margin of a spring-hole frequented by deer. He put some of this earth on the back of his neck and said: 'It'll take the sting out.'"

I ended my story. Bill chuckled and said: "I've had experiences with Levi's tame bees: hunted for their honey in the woods more'n once. He paused. I glanced at my watch and said: "It's about time to fish the Rapids, isn't it?"

* * *

We fished them and about sundown took a grilse and a two-pound sea-trout, then called it a day, and Bill began poling back to our little camp-site. Rounding the bend we saw a couple of deer standing in the shallow water along the left-hand shore. Suddenly they heard the canoe, stood gazing at us a few moments then, with necks straight out, waded to shore, made magnificent leaps to the bank above and vanished into the forest. A few canoe-lengths farther on we saw a musquash. Bill snubbed the canoe, held it against the current, and with lips compressed gave the mating call of the little creature. It turned and came straight towards the canoe until, seeing us, it dove and we saw it no more. And I remembered that God had said unto Noah and his sons: "And the fear of you and the dread of you shall be upon every beast of the earth, and upon every fowl of the air, upon all that move upon the earth, and upon all the fishes of the seas."

* * *

The sun had sunk below the tops of the trees when we reached our landing, disembarked, pulled up the canoe, then stood and feasted our eyes on the rose-pink afterglow that had mounted into the heavens, like a magic carpet unrolled for the feet of a deity, and was reflected on the river as far as the eye could reach. Then—from a tree near by—came the vesper hymn of the wood thrush, its links of music rising bell-like above the lilt of the rapids below as clear and sweet as the chime-notes "of an organ in some vast cathedral".[69]

---

69   Frank Chapman, *Bird Life, 1897.*

Song of the Reel

We waited, and again and again, for perhaps fifteen minutes, came the crystal-clear notes as the bird sang its benedictus. And I thought of those words of the Koran: "That bells hang in the trees of Paradise, and are set in motion by wind from the Throne of God, as often as the blessed wish for music."[70]

Again we waited, hoping for more, but the shy bird had finished its evensong.

A flock of half-grown black ducks, one behind the other, followed their mother down the opposite shore. Just above the head of the rapids the quickened current sped them faster. With their heads thrust upward and forward, they looked like a fleet of tiny, high-prowed dragon ships hastening to some safe port before darkness wholly settled over the river.

The colour in sky and water faded, and twilight, that mysterious harbinger of night, drew her grey cloak over the wilderness.

* * *

And so we returned to our little camp-site, made a new fire within the circle of boulders, brewed a kettle of tea and fried two slices of salmon.

It is difficult to describe the feeling of contentment that fills the angler or the hunter when he sits beside a little fire in the out-of-doors and partakes of his well-earned meal in the woods, either near a musical brook or a little river. I thought of the crowded cities: cars rushing hither and thither, the raucous notes of the horns, the huge electric signs, people hastening to theatres and movie palaces, the roar of traffic; while here Bill and I sat in the quiet of this vast wilderness eating our simple fare. Neither of us would have exchanged what we had for all that the fairest city gives to its teeming millions.

The moon, in its last quarter, bathed its reflection in the hurrying river, and from within the vast solitude of the forest behind us came the "Whoo!—hoo!" of an owl, which, a few moments later, was answered by another from the farther shore.

---

70 R.R. Madden, *Travels in Turkey, Egypt, Nubia, and Palestine, in 1824, 1825, 1826, and 1827*. London, 1829.

Chapter XIII

Bill gave a low chuckle, then said: "Years ago, Jack Murphy was drivin' tote-team with supplies to Mick Welch's lumber shanty on McBean Brook, an' I took passage with him one day to work with the crew. It was a long haul, an' we tipped the bottle of rum quite often. Dark comin', Jack fell asleep, so I took the reins; but the horses didn't need no guidin', they knew that woods-road as well as we did. About ten o'clock, just as we was climbin' the hill to the little clearin' where the shanty stood, an owl, quite handy, yopped his whoops from the top of one of the trees: 'Whop! hoo! whoo! hoo!' it called. Jack jerked up his head from his chest an' cried out: 'I'm Jack Murphy, goin' in to Mick Welch's camp with a load of oats. Who the hell are you?'"

Oh Bill, Bill! What a fund of quaint tales you treasured!

* * *

Now, for we had finished the last cup of tea and the mosquitoes were annoying, we dashed water on the fire, putting it out so that, should a wind spring up, it wouldn't carry sparks to the dry forest, we sought refuge within the tent, drew the netting across the opening to keep out the pests, lighted the Coleman lantern we had brought with us, then reclined comfortably on our sleeping bags. Said Bill: "I think I'll change my diet," and taking out his pipe, filled, lighted it, and we smoked in silence for a few minutes. Then Bill ceased smoking and began talking about fishing. He held my opinion that a salmon, if in the mood to take at all, will rise to almost any fly of suitable size, whatever pattern you use. "Of course," he added, "later in the season, when the water is lower than now, an' the sun blazin' on the pool, they get lazy, an' less inclined to take. Still, I've got 'em under them conditions. But there's certain windy days, when the canoe swings about like the pendulum on a clock, you might as well pull up anchor an' go to shore (hopin' it'll calm down), or return to camp. But I've found they take best from eight o'clock in the mornin' to twelve noon, an' after six in the evenin', an' even long after dark. Of course, Doc, this is all cold potatoes to you. But I want to tell you about one night I fished with Alex Scot. We'd fished the pool careful to the very end without gettin' a rise; it was dark an' the moon had come up. Then Alex said: 'How about goin' back to the "hot-spot" at the head of the pool and have another try?'

"I said: 'OK'. So back we goes, dropped the anchor and I began castin'. I raised five fish. They didn't make a boil—just bobbed up with their heads half out of water but didn't take the fly. Finally I cast a little to the left of them an' one come just as the others did, give a straight pounce at the fly, took it an' was hooked. It was a good fish, made some long runs, an' I couldn't see where it was. But we went to the left-hand shore an' sudden it come in just like a lamb. Two or three times Alex tried to net it, but he couldn't see it no more than I could. Each time it made short rushes an' made my reel hum; each time I brought it back. The last time Alex had his net down low, an' as it turned over on its side, close to his feet, he made a quick shift with his net, had it, an' stumbled back up the beach. I've caught 'em, too, drawin' the fly over the surface of the water same as we do trout fishin'. But in low water there's nothin' like a good heavy rain to wake them up. In fact, I like to fish when it's pourin' down so hard the drops bounce up like little dinner-bells." He paused, gave vent to one of his quiet chuckles, then went on: "As the water is now, I prefer to fish with greased line same as we did today. Then the fly sinks closer to the fish; an' if it's fished natural he's more apt to be interested. I noticed you mendin' your line this evenin' whenever it bagged below the swingin' fly. I cal'ate a baggin' line distracts 'em and keeps 'em down. The trouble with lots of anglers fishin' in glassy water, they pull the split-second they see the fish comin', instead of waitin' till they feel the tug. I used to pull myself when I first began fishin'. You have to with trout because they're faster takers. Then I'd close my eyes so I wouldn't pull, but I thought that was weakness on my part, so I got to countin' three, an' found that worked first-rate, because when I got to three the fish was on. But after a while I give up countin'. I've seen men, as soon as they 'felt' the fish, give the rod one heck of a jerk. to set the hook, they said. But when a fish has taken he's already made the turn, I mean is goin' back; the weight of its body sets the hook, an' no need to yank. Then it's time to lift the rod-tip. But what am I talkin' about? You've fished longer than me, so it's all cold potatoes."

"There's always something to learn," I said. "And it's always comforting to know that your own theories are shared and have been proved by someone else. But I've found that the only way to catch salmon, or trout, is to fish for them: never give up until it's time to leave the pool. And, above all, never think that we know it all: no one does. We can read every book on fishing that has ever been written, and yet find that on certain occasions the fish will upset all the theories of the experts, such as Hewitt,[71] who declared that, if there was a salmon in a pool, he could take it during the hottest day in summer."

"Yes," said Bill. "That's what he said. I knew him; an' he had a lot to learn!"

"And," I continued, "I've never yet seen a salmon rise for a fly that's bowling along the top of the water like a loose umbrella in a wind-storm. When such happens, I've found that there's either been a fault in tying it to the leader or some grease or oil has got on it. In the first case, the only thing to do is to retie it, in the second, to put on another fly."

* * *

This "mending of the line", of which Bill had previously spoken, is something I learned from Bill Ferguson and Jock Ogilvy: from the first on the Kedgwick, from the second on the Restigouche. It is a quite simple trick that needs only a little practice to do expertly. As Bill said, sometimes the line is carried by the current faster than the fly moves. To mend it, you lift the rod upwards and to the right or left, as the need may be, and the line rolls (much as a cowboy rolls his lariat) without disturbing the curve of the fly. By the same rolling movement you can (when you become proficient) raise the fly from the water and throw it wherever you want it. The first is a most interesting and satisfactory method of mending your line, and the second of making a new cast.

* * *

Where do fish lie? I have seen them all over the pool: to the right or left of boulders: in rapid water beside submerged ledges or ledges projecting at the sides of pools, and in low, swift, glassy water just where it glides over a bar. Generally they prefer four or five feet of water. But I have seen them breaking or leaping from deep, dark pools, although these are seldom taken. Above the run or No. 1 Pool on the Government reserved water on the Restigouche, they often lie in ten or twelve feet of water close to the

---

71   Edward R. Hewitt, author of several early-twentieth-century angling classics.

ledge on the right. But I have also seen numbers of them near the left-hand shore in about five feet of water, cruising back and forth close together. Seemingly they like company. It is quite possible that towards evening they drop back into the swift, more shallow waters or go on to the pool above. Numerous times, when I have landed a fish from the Forks Pool, on the Main Southwest Miramichi, I have hooked another a few minutes later, both females: this leading me to think that they were travelling together.

Once, on the Upsalquitch, a dozen or more fish, some of them side by side, others head to tail, passed so close to my anchored canoe on their way upriver I could have touched them with the paddle.

One evening, several years ago, just about dark, I was standing with my friends Doctor Grant and Charlie Clark on the verandah of our camp at the Forks, and suddenly we saw the wakes made by two fish, one just behind the first, that had come from some pool below. Our camp is on the southeast side of the South Branch of the Miramichi and, directly opposite, the North Branch swings around a sharp bend, mingles with the waters of the South Branch, and they form the Main Southwest Miramichi. *(21a)*

The two salmon proceeded perhaps one hundred feet up the South Branch as though their purpose was to seek one of the pools above. But suddenly the fish in the lead made a wide half-circle to the right, followed by the other and, both swimming close to the surface (for their wakes were plainly visible), reached the water right off the sandy bar that flanks the midsection of the North Branch Pool, and we saw them no more that night.

There would seem to be no doubt that both fish knew by the smell of the water in the South Branch that it was not the same *stream* in which they had lived as parr, smolt and grilse. To me it was the most interesting and irrecusable example of salmon instinct or sense of smell I have ever witnessed; although recently I read in *The Daily Gleaner* an article in which an American scientist quite emphatically stated that salmon *do not* have the sense of smell: but that, if they do return to the same river in which they evolved from the egg, or were deposited in it in the form of fry from a hatchery, it is only by accident. I wish the eminent scientist could have been present that night at the Forks and witnessed what I and my friends saw!

* * *

Chapter XIII

I asked Bill what he thought about the custom, on the Miramichi, of fishing for black salmon, also known as kelts, slinks, racers or spent fish.

"Well," he answered, "I fished for 'em when I was nine or ten years of age: but I didn't enjoy bein' hunched up in a canoe just after the ice left the river an' snow still in the woods. You had to be rigged up like an Eskimo to keep from freezin' to death. Then, when I got acquainted with old Angus Bruce, he cured me. 'Nae, laddie,' says he, 'you wouldna eat a sick coo, would you? Aye, laddie, to catch one of them slinks is as bad as beatin' up a mon that's been bed-ridden an' only up a few days.' An' he give a snort of disgust.

"You know, Doctor, them salmon's been in the river all winter, an' when they come down in the spring they're so thin their heads is bigger than their bodies; an' they're so hungry they'll take a red rag tied to a hook. Once late September, just before the season closed, I was fishin' with an Injun (there was a late run of bright fish),[72] an' he hooked a salmon that had been in the water all summer. It was as red as a smoked herrin'. He was disgusted. He took the hook careful from its mouth, dropped it back in the river an' said: 'You go down to salt water, make yourself clean, eat plenty smelts, get fat; come back next June, then, if I catch you, I eat'm.'... Now, if the anglers who come in droves in the early spring waited a few weeks, they'd catch fish as bright as a new silver dollar."

"That's right," I said. "But I met a lady last spring who had been fishing black salmon at the mouth of Cains. It was her fifth trip to the river. I asked her if she ate the fish, and if they were good. She assured me she did and that they were delicious."

"God pity her!" was Bill's comment. It sounded like a prayer.

"Of course," I went on, "those visiting anglers leave a lot of money in the province besides the license-fee that goes to the government."

Bill slowly shook his head. "I know, Doctor," he said. "I know. Money—money—money. They might build a few hundred yards of new highway with it, but I repeat that fishin' black salmon ain't sportin'."

"Thank you, Bill," I said. "I just wanted to get your opinion on the matter."

---

72   One that has not been long in the river. After a salmon has been in the river a couple of weeks, its skin starts to darken.

Song of the Reel

"You got it!" he said with a brevity that startled me. Taking out his plug of chewing tobacco he bit off a chunk with a snap of his strong teeth as though, by the act, he were further emphasising his remark.

CHAPTER XIV

After a few moments of silence he told me a nerve-creeping story of the were-wolf or *loup-garou*—that legendary creature of inherited superstition whose origin is shrouded in the mists of antiquity. Sometimes it is in the form of a dog, at others a goat, but more often a wolf, all of which are half-man and devour helpless children. It is a superstition that still lingers among several nations. Indeed, in the fifteenth century, a council of theologians, convoked by the emperor Sigismund, gravely decided that the *loup-garou* was a reality.

And so Bill told me the story as related by an Acadian-French woodsman to whom it had descended from his forebears, when this province of New Brunswick was a part of Acadia and first settled by people from Normandy.

It seems that one late summer three or four *coureurs de bois* or woods-rangers, had gone in a canoe to the headwaters of the Restigouche to net and spear salmon. Finally, the evening before starting for home, they had a big carousal, finished the last of four gallons of brandy they had brought with them, and danced half the night. One of them swore by the Virgin Mother of Christ, and even the others were shocked and reproved him as much as their drunken speech would allow them.

The next morning, just as they had passed through a dangerous rapids, they heard a great barking and wailing that came from the air above them. The man who had sworn by the Holy Virgin was seated in the middle of the canoe. They all looked up and saw a strange creature descending with the swiftness of a hawk. Its upper parts were like those of a man, the rest of it like a dog or wolf. It came closer, reached down with its long arms and, clutching the blasphemer by the shoulders, lifted him bodily out of the canoe, rose again into the air, and carried him, all in the fraction of a few moments, over the tops of the trees. And that was the last his comrades saw of him. The following autumn some moose hunters came on a lot of bones cross-piled in the form of a cairn. On the top was a skull, and between the teeth a wedge of wood about eight inches long held firm by a withe of basket-ash passed under the jaws and tied on the top of the skull.

* * *

A shudder passed over me. Bill lighted his pipe, smoked a few minutes in silence, then said: "I can tell you one that happened on the Miramichi back in the old days. Want to hear it?"

"Yes, Bill, I'm interested in folklore. My Scottish ancestors had a great fund of it."

"Well," he said, "this is a bit gruesome, but…"

"I thought the first was gruesome enough," I broke in. "Pardon me, Bill."

—"But I don't think that one was true," he went on. "For why? Well, the porcupines an' other woods critters would have ate those bones. But this other—you know, Doctor, I do believe in the devil. Well, years ago, after the first settlers come from Nashwaak to Boiestown, a most awful man got a big grant of land between Boiestown an' Doaktown. He had a lot of pine an' spruce on his place, employed crews to cut'm an' rafted'm downriver to Newcastle, an' made a heap of money. Then he opened a store an' sold all kinds of merchandise to the other settlers. An' if any other man attempted to start in the like business he'd go to him an' offer to buy him out. If the feller refused, he'd say: 'All right, I'll drive you out of business.'

An' he did: he'd drop his prices, an' of course, since the people could get things cheaper from him, they gave him their trade. He also let out money on mortgages at such high rates of interest they couldn't meet the payments. Then he'd foreclose the mortgage, an' the farm, with all its timber, was his. Besides all this he was cruel to his wife an' children, would beat them unmerciful. He never went to church an' wouldn't let his wife an' children go; said there wasn't any god an' mocked at religion. Once a minister of the gospel went to his home an' tried to reason with him, but he told him he could manage his own life without help from any damn parson, an' drove him off.

Chapter XIV

"So things went on for some years, an' everybody hated an' feared him; then he disappeared. Yes, his wife woke up one mornin' an' he was gone. Of course she figured he'd gone to a tavern down the road to get some rum. But when night come he wasn't back. Then she thought he might have taken crazy an' drowned himself in the river. So she went to the nearest neighbour an' told him her fears. He said: 'Don't worry, he'll be back. Every hog knows his own wallow.'

"But he didn't, an' next day the people decided to organise a search-party. They went to the barn, looked in the hayloft, but no sign of him. Then they come out, an' as they was roundin' the barn to go to the river to see if his boat was there, they saw a bundle on top of the manure-pile. So they clambered up it and there was his clothes an' boots, all in a hundred pieces; an' there was his bones, but not a scrap of flesh on 'em. They looked around, an' at the other side, at the foot of the manure-pile, they saw the marks of a clove-hoof in the soft soil that didn't belong to no beast on the farm or anywhere else. Queer, wasn't it?" Bill paused a few moments then continued: "The neighbours figgered that the devil had come for him and shook him all to pieces. Nothin' else could have done it. What do you think, Doctor?"

"Just another folk-tale, Bill." But I didn't tell him that when I was a lad my mother had told me the same yarn, with slight differences. Instead, I told him about the giants of Dundee, and the one at Edinburgh that had three heads, and that there are fairy dogs, fairy mice, fairy men; and that at one place, in Inverness, there is a well into which, on the first day of May, people drop coins, still perpetuating an ancient custom. And in prehistoric times certain North American tribes threw arrowheads into springs to bring them good luck in fishing, hunting, and before going on the warpath.

When I had finished Bill shook his head solemnly and said: "But *that* last story I told you about was different. The old people on the Miramichi said it was true. You know the devil is most powerful."

"Yes," I admitted. "But a bear could have disposed of him. That would explain the torn clothes, would it not?"

He scratched his head, lighted his pipe, took a few puffs, then said: "You know I never thought of *that*." He took a few more puffs, blew out the smoke, and said, with a note of triumph: "But that don't explain the clove-hoof, does it? At any rate I believe it was the devil. You can believe what you want. Anyhow, the settlement was well rid of the old sinner."

Doubtless the settlers also preferred to believe that the devil had done the mischief.

* * *

"An'," said Bill, "can you explain how certain people have the power to stop nose-bleed or any caused by the cut of an axe or other accident? There was a feller in our village who could do that. All you had to do was telephone him you were bleedin', and he'd say, 'OK, it'll stop in five minutes.' An' it would. An' when my mother was a girl, about seventeen, she had ugly warts on her hands. One day an old Irish pedlar came along with his pack filled with ribbons, thread, combs, bootlaces, pins, jew's-harps an' what-not. An' seeing her hands, he said: 'Miss Pretty-face, 'tis a shame to see such nice hands covered with warts. Hold out your hands,' says he. So she held out her hands. He took first one then the other in his, an said: 'I'll charm them. They'll all be gone at the end of seven days.' Then he touched one of his forefingers with the tip of his tongue, an' touched every wart, an' said somethin' in Irish she couldn't understand. Then he said: 'Give me a penny, Miss.' So she went to her room where she kept her savin's an' brought him out a dozen pennies. But he said: 'Only one, Miss Pretty-face,' an' he wouldn't take no more.

"Well, the days went by, an' every day she'd look at the warts an' they hadn't shrunk one bit. An' she felt what a fool she'd been to part with her penny. So she went to bed at nine o'clock on the seventh day with the warts still on her hands. But when she woke in the mornin' an' started to wash her face an' hands she saw that every wart had disappeared. After that she never had no more. Now wasn't that odd?" said Bill, and, without waiting for my answer, went on: "I know it happened just as she said, because mother was a Christian woman an' never lied....that is, only a few times if she thought it would save anyone's character when they was gossiped about. Want me to put out the light an' turn in, Doctor?"

* * *

Chapter XIV

I had heard the same story from my mother, who had had the same experience.

I got into my sleeping bag; Bill didn't immediately follow my example. Presently I glanced towards him and dimly saw him on his knees, hands clasped in front of him, and thought I heard the whispered words: "An' please give me strength to keep away from the bottle. Amen." A few moments later he was in his sleeping bag. Then, remembering the little ritual my family always observed before departing for sleep, I put out my hand, touched him on the shoulder, and said: "Goodnight, Bill, and God bless you." Never shall I forget the quick touch of his hand on mine, and his voice, a little husky: "God bless you. Goodnight, Doctor."

Good old Bill! One of the best canoemen and comrades I have ever known on the Miramichi. As I write this I can conjure up the image of him, feet braced against the cedar ribs of the canoe as he guided the frail craft between granite boulders, or with his great strength holding it with his setting-pole while his quick eye picked out the most suitable channel.

* * *

I lay awake for some time thinking over the events of the day, then dropped off to sleep, but awakened some time later to hear one of our tin pails, beyond our campfire site, topple over. Slipping out of my sleeping bag, I seized the flashlight, and, even as I pressed the button, I thought (so much are we inheritors of superstition) of the story Bill had told of the *loup-garou* and a chill ran up my spine. I heard a heavy body strike the water near the canoe landing. Quickly I pulled back the tent flap, centred the golden beam of light on the river and saw a large bear swimming towards the opposite shore.

Bill roused himself. "What is it?" he asked.

I told him. He said: "I bet the critter got our salmon," got up, and we went out and found that both salmon, grilse and sea trout were gone. Luckily the dumping over of the cooking kettle and my sudden awakening had saved our smaller trout from a like fate.

* * *

Song of the Reel

Once again I was awakened by the hoarse whistle of the night express announcing its approach to the bridge at Half-Moon Cove; in a few minutes heard the rush and clatter of the wheels along the rails beyond the moonlit palisade of trees across the river; then, until distance swallowed the sounds, the clickety! clack! clickety! clack! over the track joints.

I imagined the passengers, some asleep in the swaying coaches while more wakeful spirits smoked or talked of world or local affairs; the engineer with ready hand near the throttle, and the fireman shovelling coal into the glowing maw of the huge monster that carried its human freight to distant towns and cities. And I was glad to be in my little tent (with Bill beside me) knowing that on the morrow we would be running the lovely river. And so I again drifted into sleep—a sleep so profound I didn't awaken until eight o'clock, and saw Bill place his black boiling kettle over the *chip-la-kwa-gun* and swing it over the fire. So I called out goodmorning to him; and his cheery voice repeated the salutation. Then I got up and dressed, and, going to the river, cupped the cold water in my hands, washed myself, brushed my hair, returned and helped Bill prepare breakfast.

* * *

Bacon and eggs, toast and coffee. Oh, it was good! And as we ate we heard, far back of us on the ridge a cock partridge drum his reveille: "Rump! Rump! Rump! Rup! Rup! Rup" like mild thunder.

Said Bill: "I've seen them old drummers performin' more than once. They stand on a log, stretch their bodies upright an' clap their wings so fast you can't see them move. Then they prance around a bit as though proud of themselves, an' perhaps, after a few minutes, repeat their drummin'."

We heard a splash in the pool across the river, saw a belted kingfisher emerge with a small fish in its mouth and fly up-stream a few rods to a big spruce. And I remembered that Halcyon is the Greek name for the kingfisher, that the ancient Sicilians believed that the bird laid its eggs and incubated them for fourteen days before the winter solstice on the surface of the sea, during which time the waves of the sea were always unruffled. Hence the term—"Halcyon Days".

Chapter XIV

*Amidst our arms as quiet you shall be
As Halcyon brooding on a winter's sea.*

Dryden[73]

We ate slowly. We were in no hurry. Hurry, as I've always maintained, is one of the curses of our civilisation. Everything is tuned to high-gear. The train leaves for the city at a certain hour, so we bolt our breakfast, swallow a cup of coffee and rush to the station. "All aboard!" Before we reach our destination we are on our feet crowding forward against others to reach the door, and are crowded by those behind. The train comes to a stop, we dash out, down the steps, and along the platform to reach the exit, then to the avenue, rush along the sidewalk, jostle and in turn are jostled by the hurrying crowds coming and going. We reach the building with its numerous floors, dash to the elevator, press the "up" button, are impatient if the elevator doesn't arrive on the instant. If we chance to be late for work we chase the hours trying to catch up with Time. But, although Time has for centuries been depicted as an aged man with flowing beard, no one has ever been able to overtake him. It is he who turns the tables on us and catches us up in the end: and only then, if we are vouchsafed a moment's consciousness, do we recognise his face.

---

73 From his play *The Indian Emperor*, Act IV, Scene IV. I don't think GFC had read the play; the couplet is much quoted.

PHOTOGRAPHS

Part Two

14 a. Earl Cole, back view, with salmon

14 b. Earl Cole, silhouette

14 c. Keith Wright, Pattersons Pool

14 d. GFC as a bridegroom, 1912

Photographs 14 a., b. and c. are by Mike Saunders

15. Northampton Church steeple, summer 1967

A few years after I photographed this church, its onion dome was struck by lightning. It was not rebuilt, but replaced with a squat pyramidal cap. The same fate has befallen most of the 19th-century churches I photographed in central New Brunswick between the 1960s and 1990s.

16. The St John River at twilight, 1967
below Mactaquac

17. Noel Polchies

18 a. Child's snowshoes made by Noel Polchies in about 1921

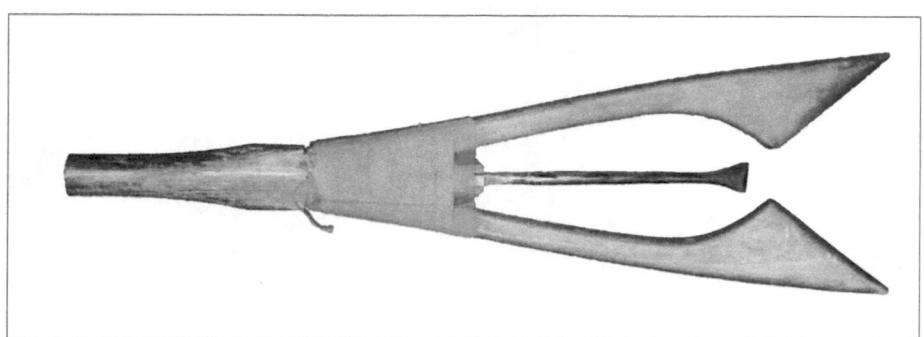

18 b. Salmon spear owned by GFC

18 c. Double-pointed blades excavated by GFC at Shiktehawk, 1932

19 a. GFC, Murdoch Mackenzie, Dr Grant and unknown, beside the GFC-Grant-Clark camp, c. 1925

19 b. George Greer and GFC with trout, c. 1919

19 c. Dr Grant in dugout canoe with trout.

19 d. Henry Wilson with trout, 1916

GFC, and friends, at the Forks of the Main Southwest Miramichi between 1916 and about 1925

20 a. Bear catching salmon, by H. E. M. Sellen

20 b. Beaver gnawing birch stump, by Fred Grant

21 a. The Forks pool, 1997

21 b. The camp at the Forks in 2012.

The first camp was built in 1907; GFC, Dr Grant and Charlie Clark bought the lease in 1921. GFC's grandson Ian Bernard rebuilt it in 1992, closely matching the original.

22. Bull moose, by H. E. M. Sellen

23. Mist on the Miramichi, 1972

24 a. Ian Bernard poling at the Forks, 1971

24 b. Still water at the Forks, 2012

25. Song of the Reel

GFC's grandson Ian Bernard now owns the lease of the camp at the Forks. He put this sign above the door when he rebuilt the camp in 1992.

CHAPTER XV

We sprinkled more crumbs for the birds, and, the canoe loaded with our effects, I seated myself near the bow, Bill got in, with his setting-pole pushed out a few yards, then held it until the current had swung the bow pointing downstream, and we were off.

The channel through Crooked Rapids is close to the righthand shore between big boulders. Only once did Bill have to snub the downward rush of the canoe, swing the stern leftwards, ease it gently past a nasty boulder; then we reached the basin below, swung around the bend on the left, where occasionally there is a good cast, and went on. We could see the railroad tracks on the high bank above, and before we had passed them a long freight train thundered past us and disappeared between the line of trees to Half Moon and beyond. A heron—the great blue heron—its long legs strung out behind it, sailed majestically high over the waters and skimmed the treetops, possibly bound for Napadogan Lake and good fishing.

Ahead of us we could hear the wild cacophony of Black Rapids, and see the ranks of charging waves upon whose foam-tipped helmets the sun shimmered like molten silver that, but for our dark glasses, would have been intolerable. They dashed against projecting boulders, swept around them on either side and galloped on to join their ever-advancing comrades.

At this season of the year (unless there has been a rise of water) the only canoeable channel is on the left. You who have run this portion of the river will remember the hog-backed ledge of rock that projects several feet above the surface of the water; how the current strikes it with tremendous force and is hurled sideways in an angry wave that rushes like a mill-race between it and the northern shore. You will recall how your guide, with his setting-pole, eased the canoe straight towards the upper or right angle of the ledge, then, holding with all his strength while you thought it would strike and be dashed to pieces, he gave a mighty shove forwards, and, as the bow struck the heaped-up wave he straightened out the canoe, which sped like an arrow down the narrow passage.

This Bill did, his sturdy form one with all the motions of the canoe; and, out of danger for the present, he gave a low chuckle as we met the short, choppy waves below. I could feel and hear their slapping, plump! plump! against the frail bottom of the canoe as the bow rose and fell in rhythmic undulations. Then, in a few moments, we were in quieter water and Bill began singing one of his favourite hymns; for, drunk or sober, there was in him an abiding religious trait that, as he once said to me: "fought the devil an' all his imps."

I glimpsed occasional clumps of the Canada lily with its yellow-orange bells, and the blue-flag, nodding on their long stalks. And among the varied species of trees (which make of this river a paradise of green) an occasional white birch—the *mas-kwe-mus* or canoe-birch of the Maliseet Indians: and here and there a lordly pine rearing its height far above the others.

* * *

And as we went I thought of some of the anglers and guides, especially the latter, I had known in the past: Angus MacCormack, Harvey Biggar, Joe Nixon, Bill and Larry Sweet, Charlie Grey, Alex Lyons, Murdoch MacKenzie and Turney Gray, all of whom used to run the river from the Forks to Boiestown in long dugout canoes of pine. Thirty feet long those canoes, and much better able to withstand the punishment dealt by boulders and shallow bars than the present canvas-covered canoes shod with birch strips. Moreover, the river seemed to love the dugout; *(7b, 19c)* when you pushed it against the rapids and withdrew the setting-pole it did not lose headway but continued its momentum until you had made another push. Not so the canvas-covered canoe. It is as though the river said: "You must fight for every yard!"

Turney Gray made dugout canoes. In style and symmetry they far transcended any others I have ever seen. For Turney was an artist. Once, he felled a suitable pine, far up McKeel Brook (fourteen miles below the

Chapter XV

Forks) floated it to its confluence with the Miramichi, laid a series of skids and manhandled it to the bank above. Here, with axe and adze and spokeshave he fashioned it into a thing of beauty and utility, then poled it upriver to his little camp a couple of miles below Juniper Station.

The dugout belongs to the past, at least on the upper reaches of the Main Southwest Miramichi: its place is taken by the canvas-covered canoe.

For a dozen years following my first trip to the Forks, Murdoch MacKenzie *(19a)* had half a dozen dugouts. He gave names to all of them. One he christened *Sally-Ann McCann*. And, to a lap-streak[74] craft that didn't belong to him, *The Drunkard's Doom*.

* * *

How one memory evokes another! Doctor Grant and I had reached our camp at the Forks one evening in July twenty-seven years ago.[75] About midnight, as we sat with Joe Nixon, the fish warden, on the verandah, MacKenzie entered the camp and told Joe he had received a telephone message from Glassville informing him that three men had gone to the North Branch to "spear the pools". MacKenzie was a magistrate, and he now told Joe to go up the Branch and apprehend the poachers.

Joe was now seventy years of age, and didn't like the prospect of poling up the crooked stream. The Doctor, who was always ready for adventure, said: "We'll go with you, Joe. Come on, Fred."

I was tired after the long drive to the Forks, and as reluctant as Joe to make the journey, but after a little coaxing on the Doctor's part, I consented to go. I noticed that Joe carried his rifle with him and laid it in the centre of the dugout where I seated myself. Then, Joe poling stern and the Doctor bow, we proceeded up the tortuous stream walled in by palisades of spruce, elm and birch trees. There was no moon. It was an ideal night for spearing fish. Save for the thud of the setting-poles and the swish of the water against the bow of the canoe all was silent and ghostly.

---

74 In the lap-streak method of hull planking each plank overlaps the next by a short distance.

75 About 1934, if GFC wrote this passage in 1961.

We had gone a little better than a mile and had reached a wide, deep pool when, just around a sharp bend, we saw a reddish flare that mounted above the tree tops. Then the Drunkard's Doom swung into view, an iron noggin, filled with flaming pitch-pine, projecting over the bow. Behind this I saw a tall, dark figure standing upright, a long-handled spear poised for action. Back of him, seated in the middle, was another, and a third stood in the stern guiding the craft with a setting pole.

We were in shadow close to the left-hand shore, and they hadn't seen us. Joe and the Doctor pushed our boat towards the Drunkard's Doom. Only then were they aware of us. The man in the stern roared out: "Holy smoke, Jim! Dump the noggin!"[76]

Quick as a flash Jim thrust his spear beneath the thing, swung it downside up, the flaming pitch-pine struck the water with a loud hiss, and the river was plunged in darkness.

The bow of our craft struck the poachers' boat amidship; the Doctor, now on his knees, reached out and seized the gunwale with both hands. But Jim whacked him over the fingers with the handle of his salmon-spear and he had to let go. Then, poling as fast as they could work their arms, they sped down the pool and we after them. The Doctor called out: "You might as well stop, boys, or if we have to we'll follow you to Boiestown!"

We were gaining on them, and the man I call Jim warned us: "If you come closer we'll dump you in the river!"

I had no desire to take a midnight bath—especially since both banks were high. Impulsively my hand reached for and picked up Joe's rifle, and injecting a shell into the barrel I pointed the muzzle into the air and pulled the trigger. Then came a chorus of voices from the other boat: "We give up! We give up!"

More quickly than it takes to tell we were beside them, and found that all three were near neighbours of Joe Nixon's; and, save for a disposition to indulge in an occasional bit of poaching, good citizens. Moreover, they had all been loyal patients of Doctor Grant's. (We learned later that it had

---

76   In rural North American English a noggin could be a small tub or bucket. The OED describes this usage as "now rare".

Chapter XV

been their intention to take what fish they could in the Branch, then pass the Forks, while Joe was asleep, and spear the Salmon Hole.)

We had a talk with them. The Doctor, not because he feared to lose them or their relatives as patients (he was above that) but because he was one of the kindest and most generous of men, said that he and I would help pay a portion of their fine; and, for of course the Drunkard's Doom would be confiscated, purchase and return it to them. We suggested that they come down to our camp, stay there the rest of the night. In the morning we'd take them before MacKenzie, and doubtless he'd impose only a light fine on them. But Joe, who was in a state bordering on a nervous break-down, said he'd have to consult his "little book".

As for the men, they were perfectly agreeable to go with us; and even had a laugh over the affair. They'd been caught and that was their hard luck. So, singing merrily, they preceded us downriver.

At the camp they were treated to a hefty drink of gin. We made a fire in the stove, brewed tea, had a good lunch, then sat on the verandah and chatted until daybreak. (All except Joe, who went to his cabin to consult his little book.)

To shorten my tale, Joe decided he couldn't take his neighbours before MacKenzie without first telephoning the Fishery Overseer at Woodstock. In the meantime his neighbours could depart to their homes. The Doctor and I stayed two days at the Forks.

A few days later the Sheriff of Carleton County served papers on the three men demanding that they appear before the magistrate at Woodstock the following Friday. They were fined fifty dollars each and the boat confiscated. The Doctor and I paid the fishery department five dollars for it, and we notified the owners. Actually it wasn't worth that much: a leaky thing that had seen its best days. They didn't bother getting it, and for five years it remained beneath the camp where we had stored it. Then it disappeared. Thus passed the Drunkard's Doom.

Perhaps old Joe Nixon had taken the correct course. At any rate I never heard afterwards of anyone spearing the North Branch.

* * *

One day, the following summer, Joe's nearest neighbour came into my office, shook hands with me, whispered that he had a bottle of whisky and would I have a drink with him. I thanked him but said I never drank during office hours. However, I led him into another room, got a glass and told him to have one for me too. He understood.

Two years ago I went to the village of Andover to attend a political rally. After it was over I was standing chatting with some of the people, when a middle-aged man came rushing up one of the aisles, leaped over a settee, threw both arms about me and gave me a bear hug that bent my ribs. Then he said: "You don't remember me. But I'm sure you haven't forgotten the night, twenty-seven years ago, on the North Branch." Then I knew him. He was another of Joe Nixon's neighbours!

* * *

We slipped under the railroad bridge at Half-Moon Cove whence we could see Lewey Mountain a mile beyond, Its riverside is flanked by a wide barren with the usual stunted spruce, tamarack, alders and various species of shrubs. Lewey Mountain and the rapids below it were named after an old Micmac Indian who had his wigwam on the flat terrace above the falls. There is a mound, in the shape of a grave, and here someone—if not Lewey—was buried long years past within the shadow of the mountain and beside the fast-flowing river.

Lewey Mountain is covered from base to summit with huge flat granite boulders, so that one can make the ascent on them without touching bare earth. I climbed it one early October day, and from the top could see Miramichi and Napadogan lakes, jewels set within a symphony of scarlet and gold maples, like a tapestry wrought in the exotic East, while on the horizon the purple haze of mid-day formed a background and spread upwards towards the zenith.

* * *

If the spirits of anglers who have fished the Miramichi have any rendezvous on this earth, they must frequent Half-Moon Cove. For here, ever since the railroad was constructed, they and their guides have come

Chapter XV

year after year, stayed the night, and in the morning embarked in canoes to fish the river as far as Boiestown.

It is only about two miles from Half-Moon to Lake Brook, which leads from Miramichi Lake, which Baptiste Louis Franquelin, the young French engineer-cartographer, had seen and mapped in 1686. But long before that, Indians had camped below the mouth of the brook, and had left their finished and broken artifacts which succeeding centuries have covered with sandy loam. Perchance they had come here to net gaspereau, which, as soon as the ice leaves the river, still speed up the brook in thousands. And after the Indians, white settlers near the St John, waters made seasonal trips to this place in dugout canoes and took away big sacks filled with the fish.

We landed at the old camping ground, unloaded our duffle, set up the tent, dug a trench about it, then cut a plentiful supply of fir boughs for our mattress. Fir boughs are best, for the needles lie flat on the branches, and, if they are laid with care, the ends of the branches concealed beneath each succeeding layer, the bed is soft and springy.

Bill is as finicky in his choice of boughs, never large ones, and in placing them just right, as is a woman in selecting her lipstick and perfume. Then, after we had cut wood for our camp-fire, and a new *chip-la-kwa-gun* for the kettles, I set up my light trout rod and tied on a small Queen of the Water.

* * *

Just below our camping ground there are two flat-topped granite boulders a few feet from the shore, and opposite them a resting place for trout. I waded out, clambered up on the first boulder, and had made only two or three casts when a quarter-pound trout took the fly, bent the frail tip in a half circle and the small reel spun its gentle song. Here let me say, that ounce for ounce and pound for pound trout will equal the play of salmon. True, they don't leap after being hooked, but they rush hither and thither, come to the surface, slap the water with their tails and struggle by every manoeuvre they know to break free. Finally Bill, who was beside me, scooped it up in the net, killed it, released the fly and I made another cast; another trout made a beautiful curve out of the water, took the fly going down, and after a brief struggle was safely landed. Then, remembering that Bill enjoyed catching trout, I insisted that he take the rod in spite of his protests that he liked to see me fish.

So I lighted my pipe and watched his efforts. He cast a beautiful line and soon hooked a fish bigger than either of mine. When he had exhausted it I did the netting. Then he hooked another, lost it, and tried again. In fifteen minutes we had seven trout, then went to shore and cleaned them while I started a fire within a circle of stones some previous campers had laid and used.

There is a little ice-cold spring, just over the bank near the beach, which at the present low water was uncovered. So, the trout ready, Bill cupped up enough to fill the boiling kettle, for he is as particular about using spring-water for making tea as is the famous Chinese author, Lin Yutang;[77] although I question whether Mr. Yutang would tolerate Bill's stout brew.

The seven trout completely filled the big frying pan into which Bill had first put a generous lump of butter. Then, the handle wired in a cleft stick, he held the pan over the fire and carefully cooked them. We didn't bother cooking potatoes but, when the fish were done and the tea brewed, seated ourselves and ate bread with the fish. No need to say they were delicious, as trout are when cooked soon after caught. We ate every morsel, picking the bones clean, ate more bread, drank more tea, finally finished off with the remainder of the strawberry pie, and called it a meal. Then, after washing the few tin plates and cups, Bill filled his pipe, and I mine, lighted them with the glowing end of a cedar-stick plucked from the fire, and drew in the fragrant smoke: more fragrant since the brand contained that distilled essence that nature imparts to wood. Yes, anyone who chooses may use matches or lighter-fluid to light his pipe, but I maintain (although everyone to his choice, as Bill says) that tobacco is more satisfying, more fragrant, when fired with a lighted brand, be it cedar, birch or maple.

* * *

---

77 1895-1976: novelist, translator, and populariser of Chinese philosophy. GFC owned his *The Importance of Living*, 1937.

Chapter XV

About sundown we saw a host of cave swallows darting hither and thither over the river, picking up a late hatch of water-born ephemera, those tiny insects that, because of imperfect development of their mouths, are unable to eat, and so live a few hours only, or at most a day or two. Those that had struggled into the air were caught by the swallows who swung about on banked wings and darted in pursuit of others. Nothing could be more graceful than their flight as, looking like miniature feathered aerial torpedoes, they evaded by quick twists and turns their ever advancing or wheeling comrades. Or some of them swooped so close to the surface of the water to pick up other prey, whose frail wings struggled to lift them airborne, that their breasts touched the water for a split-second leaving innumerable tiny bubbles, as small fish do when they break the surface.

We watched with fascinated interest until dusk began to settle over forest and river, when they left as suddenly as they had appeared.

"Well," said Bill, "you can learn a lot if you have eyes to see, and take the time to look."

While we smoked, half a dozen birds raised their voices in rapturous litanies. Among them I recognised the notes of the veery or Wilson's thrush (the little *tà-n-é-li-âin* of the Micmac and Maliseet Indians); the song sparrow and the white-throat. They kept it up for four or five minutes, singing alternately, each seemingly trying to excel the others, then ceased. And there was profound silence save for the occasional snapping of our woodfire that sent up a shower of miniature stars. Then, as though he had but waited for this magic moment, a hermit thrush, hidden in the dense clump of alders along the shore, sent out his enchanting melody: "O spheral, spheral! O holy, holy!—sweet!"

* * *

Only last evening a friend told me that, some years ago, he, with other friends, tented one night at *Long Stump* Bar (a famous grilse pool on the North Branch of the Main Southwest Miramichi) and that in the morning, a little after sunrise, they heard several hundred birds singing all at once: silver threads of melody that vibrated on the still air like the notes of as many string instruments. Nothing, he told me, had ever so impressed him with the divinity of Nature.

Hundreds of birds singing at once? Yes, I believed him; for up the valley of the St John River, at my daughter's farm, I have heard at least fifty birds singing at the same time.

Before ever the ancient Vikings had followed the Pole Star and found their way to Iceland and Greenland and the continent of North America; before ever the mariner's compass had been invented, or a timepiece to determine longitude, the birds had charted all the sky lanes, had pinpointed the most distant corners of the globe. Think of it, you scientists whose inventive genius has split the atom to devastate a Hiroshima and a Nagasaki, that those tiny birds (who can balance themselves on a twig little bigger than the pencil-point with which I now write) have come year after year to this bit of land that constitutes my garden plot, only a few rods out of all the vast universe, and built their nests and reared their young, and sang their madrigals without the slightest variation from those self-same notes they used in the time of Chaucer and Francis Bacon!

Are birds only creatures of instinct? "We too are creatures of instinct. We breathe and act by instinct; but we talk and build houses by reason. And so do the birds. It is more philosophical, surely, to attribute actions in them to the same causes to which we attribute them, from actual experience, in ourselves. 'But if so,' some will say, 'birds must have souls.' We must define what kind of soul or no-soul a bird may or may not have... What we are, we are by the grace of God. Our own powers and the burden of them we know full well. It does not lessen their dignity or their beauty in our eyes to hear that the birds of the air partake, even a little, of the same gifts of God as we."[1]

* * *

Where were we? Oh, yes, Bill and I were smoking our pipes beside the little camp-fire below Lake Brook, a hermit thrush had finished his evensong, dusk was settling over forest and river, and a quiet, so profound you could feel it, like that which precedes a benediction, pervaded the scene. Then a salmon leaped beyond the big rock and fell back with a resounding splash.

---

[1] Charles Kingsley: "A Charm of Birds" [in *Prose Idylls*, 1877].

Chapter XV

"He'll likely be there in the mornin'," said Bill.

A few stars winked in the sky. The little camp-fire was dying. Bill rose and laid on some small logs of white birch; soon they burst into glorious flame, and he said: "It gives you a comfortable feelin', doesn't it?"

"Yes," I answered.

A little later, as we were about to enter the tent for the night, we heard, far overhead, the steady drumming of a big air-liner winging its course along the darkened skyway towards Gander, and looking up saw the tail-light, like a star that had abandoned its orbit, winking an accompaniment to the throbbing of the engines until it was lost to view beyond the far horizon. And I remembered that, during the Great War,[78] Charlie, the Doctor and I had sat so many times on the verandah of our little camp at the Forks, and had seen the big B47s[79] on their way overseas to augment the fighting strength of the British Isles.

---

78 World War II, not I: airplanes did not cross the Atlantic in World War I.

79 GFC is mistaken. B-47s were developed between 1945 and 1947 and did not enter regular service till 1952.

CHAPTER XVI

We reclined on the soft bed of fir boughs we had covered with our sleeping bags, our bodies filled with that sense of free-from-care comfort which few but fishermen experience. And Bill told me a story about Angus Bruce, his parrot and his tame crow. Angus had been a pipe-major in the Royal 42nd or Black Watch, served with his regiment during the South African War and had come to New Brunswick after the end of that affair. He drank a quart of Scotch whisky every week of the year except Christmas, when he purchased five quarts: not only for the refreshment of visitors, but to give an extra wee drappie to his parrot and crow, both of whom, according to Bill, were confirmed alcoholics. "But," said Bill, "though Angus drank whisky every day of his life, he never got tight. He told father that when a man couldn't tiptoe along a chalk line laid on the floor, it was time for him to stop drinkin' for the night."

He was a tall, raw-boned man with the chest of a prize fighter, sandy hair, smiling blue eyes and a few freckles on the cheek bones. He lived on the interest of some investments he had judiciously made after coming to Canada. One evening, when Bill's father was paying him a visit, and the bottle had passed around quite freely, Angus confided to him that, during his last year in Africa, he one day came upon a dead Kaffir lying on the sand. Beside him was a little bag or wallet made from the skin of some animal. So he opened it and found that it contained more than a handful of stones he knew were diamonds. How the Kaffir had came by them Angus neither knew nor cared, but he supposed that he had either worked in a diamond mine and filched them, or had found them himself.

Angus said that maybe the stones were treasure trove and belonged to the government. But, since the Boers also claimed South Africa, which party—British or Boers—had a just claim to the stones presented a problem too recondite to bother even a Scotsman. "Moreover," Angus said to his visitor: "the Bruces hae gie more than enough bluid to the crown without it takin' my wee stanes, so I decided to keepit them mysel'."

When Angus had returned to Scotland, he made a journey to London, and after much haggling with a diamond merchant, who didn't bother to ask their origin, sold him the stones for five thousand pounds.

Angus was an ardent fly-fisherman and knew all the tricks. While in Africa he had met a Canadian gunner, named Ben Harris,[80] who told him about the splendid salmon fishing on the Miramichi. So he bought a draft on a Canadian bank for five thousand pounds, sailed to Montreal, and shortly afterward found his way to Ludlow on the Miramichi. Here, according to Bill's yarn (the beginning of which I have shortened, for he had gone into every detail of the finding of the diamonds and their subsequent sale), Angus built himself a small house, did no work save to cut a little wood for his needs, and, as soon as the June run of salmon began, fished almost every day.

Said Bill: "He was the same Angus that showed me how to tickle an' take a salmon with my hand. He tied his own flies: not many, because he said a few were enough. When I was quite a young lad I often went with him to the river, an' he showed me the best of all I know about fishin'. Durin' the September run he generally caught a barrel of bright fish, then dried an' smoked 'em. He called it kipperin'."

"Well," continued Bill, "one day Angus went down to Newcastle, at the mouth of the Miramichi, to transact some business, an' met a sailor who'd come into port on a schooner that was then loadin' pine lumber for Aberdeen. He was a Scot named MacLeod. Angus first saw him in a boardin' house, an' hearin' him speak broad Scots, walks up to him an' starts talkin'. Then Angus took him to a room he'd hired for the night. Soon they

---

80 This may have been GFC's maternal uncle Benjamin Harris, who lived on the Miramichi and served in the Royal Canadian Regiment of Infantry in the Boer War—though, if so, it is odd that GFC didn't say so, since he knew his uncle.

Chapter XVI

was gettin' on the outside of a bottle of whisky, an' exchangin' gossip about Taymouth, where Angus had been born, an' what place what-not.

"Later in the evenin' they both went on board the schooner, an' MacLeod showed Angus his parrot that could talk an' swear in several languages. Angus was so delighted with Roddy (as MacLeod called him, though his full name was Roderick Dhu) that when he heard him swearin' in Gaelic he asked MacLeod if he'd sell him. So after much hagglin', because they was both hard-bargainin' Scots, Angus got the bird as well as the cage, for seventy-five dollars and fifty cents. But MacLeod cautioned Angus that he'd have to give him a daily ration of whisky or he'd raise the roof.

"Well, Angus brought Roddy back with him to Ludlow, an' he lived for another thirty years. Sort of a rusty-crimson, the parrot was, an' God alone knowed how old. MacLeod had told Angus it was at least seventy an' would probably live to be a hundred or more. Angus taught it some extra swear words, such as only Miramichi lumbermen an' guides know: not words like takin' the Lord's name in vain; 'cause Angus, though he seldom went to church, was a God-fearin' man. After a bit he let Roddy outa the cage, an' everything went all right until Angus picked up a crow that had banged into a telephone wire an' broke its leg. He took it in the house, made a couple of splints from a piece of cedar wood, put them around the critter's leg, an' fastened it tight with some tape he had. Then he gave it some bread crumbs an' a teaspoonful of whisky to pep up its spirits, because it seemed quite low. Seeing the crow so well treated, Roddy flew over, perched on Angus's shoulder an' croaked: 'Whisky! Whisky! Roddy wants whisky!' So Angus had to give him some, or he'd never let up yappin'. Then he put him in the cage that hung near the window.

"Well, the crow's leg healed all right; but the bone was set wrong, an' ever after that it limped. Angus called it Matilda after his dead wife; but whether it was male or female, he didn't know. It was awful jealous of Roddy, had a vile temper, an' as soon as it learned a few swear words (you know, Doctor, crows can learn to talk a bit too), it would limp over beneath the cage an' cuss at Roddy, an' cuss at Angus's cat an' dog, and fly at them an' jump on their backs an' give 'em a sample of its sharp beak an' claws. They was scared stiff an' never fought back.

"Angus said he hated to beat a cripple, so he never give Matilda a cuff, which it needed. But Roddy was most awful miserable bein' kept in his cage, so at last Angus let him out. But no sooner done than Matilda flew at Roddy in a rage, jumped on his back and give him some unmerciful blows on the head with her beak, an' pulled some of the fine feathers outa his top-knot. Angus had a hard job separatin' them, but at last he got Roddy back in his cage an' shut the door. Then, for half an hour, you couldn't hear yourself think because of them two critters swearin' at each other somethin' awful.

"In no time after this, some of the neighbours used to drop in Sunday evenin's to see the birds an' teach them new cuss words. One day, John Harris, from Blackville, came to visit Angus. He had follered the sea in his younger days, an' could speak seven different languages. But after hearin' Roddy goin' through his vocabulary of cuss words an' other words, he said the bird had him beat.

"The parson heard of all this, came to Angus, an' told him he'd have to get rid of Roddy an' Matilda, 'cause they was corruptin' the settlement when the members oughter be at church. But Angus refused, said birds nor nothin' else could corrupt anyone on the Miramichi worse than he was already. Then the parson got a bit angry at Angus, an' told him that if he didn't mend his ways he'd end up in the fiery pit along with millions of other sinners. So Angus told him, that if he made his sermons more interestin' his people wouldn't come to visit Roddy an' Matilda. Just then Roddy piped up: 'Whisky! Whisky! Roddy wants whisky, damn you!'

"'There,' said the parson, 'I've heard with my own ears! An' *you* taught him *that*?'

"'Nae,' said Angus, 'I didna. He learned them worrds, an' a lot more, before I got him. But let me tell you, parson, I've tried to do right by Roddy an' save his soul. He knows his "down-I-lay-me's" an' says them every night before I put the wee rug over his cage. An' I believe that's more'n a lot of your kirk members do.'

"Well, at that the parson left in a huff, an' Angus give both Roddy an' Matilda a teaspoonful of whisky; as he later told father, to get the bad taste of the parson outa their systems. Then he took a drink himself, lifted down his bagpipes, put his lips to the mouthpiece, blowed up the bag, an' began playin' *Bonnie Dundee* or some such thing. I used to hear him often when

I was a lad. Well, no sooner had the dronin' started than Roddy cried out: 'Stop! Stop that damn noise!' An' Matilda swore. Angus later said to my father: 'I told Roddy he certainly wasna born in Scotland, or he'd never object to the pipes, because they give out the bonniest music in all the worrld'. But he kept on playin', even though Roddy croaked for him to go outdoors, an' Matilda limped into a corner an' turned her back on him.

"Well, Doctor," continued Bill, "Angus finally decided to marry again. She was an old maid—sixty, if a day—an' wanted most awful to have *Missus* on her tombstone when she died. She'd lived at Upper Blackville, an' was so religious she wouldn't even say 'darn' or 'drat it' if an iron fell on her toes. Anyways she married Angus. Some people said it was for his money; but she said because she thought she could mend his drinkin' habits. Oh, she was a good housekeeper—always scrubbin, sweepin' an' dustin'. An' on rainy days she wouldn't let Angus's dog an' cat in the house until she'd washed an' dried their feet. Angus told father that if she ever got inter heaven she'd spend most of her time lookin' for cobwebs an' dust, an' make all the other angels miserable. But the marriage didn't last long because of Roddy an' Matilda swearin', an' the whisky Roddy called for, an' never let up 'till he got it, an' Angus playin the pipes. So at the end of three months she said to Angus: 'It's either me, or the birds that's got to go. As for the pipes, I can't abide them, an' you'll have to give over playin' them. So speak up, man.'

"It didn't take Angus a second to make up his mind. 'As for the birds,' he said, 'I winna pairt with them for all the siller in Boiestown, nor for all the lassies an' wimmen. As for the pipes—they're a bonny comfort to me, an' I winna let them be. Why, woman, they'd greet somethin' awfu' if I dinna play them at least two or three times a week. An' so, it's you for packin' your trunk, my good woman, an' that's that, an' no more.'

"So she packs her things an' goes. Then Angus rigs himself out in his kilt an' sporran, sticks a long bowie knife in his stockin-leg, flings his plaid over his shoulder, gets down his pipes an' plays for half an hour, even though Roddy croaked for him to stop, an' Matilda sulked in her favourite sulkin' corner.

"Well, Doctor, years passed. An' one July day, after dinner, Angus takes his salmon rod an' gaff an' goes down where his boat was on the beach to catch a salmon for his supper. He left Roddy in his cage with the rug throwed over it, an' Matilda perched as peaceful as you please on the high top of the rockin'-chair, swingin' her body backwards an' forwards an' makin' it rock. She always liked that. P'raps thought she was back in the woods an' the wind blowin'.

"It was well on in late afternoon when Angus came back luggin' a sixteen-pounder. Everything was quiet till he opened the door, when he heard Roddy pipe up: 'I killed her! I killed her! Whisky! Whisky! Roddy wants whisky!'

He was perched on the back of the rockin-chair where Matilda had been, his head an' body minus a lot of feathers. Matilda was lyin' on the floor stone dead. Angus said it must have been an awful fight, because there was red an' black feathers all over the floor. Said Angus to my father: 'I dinna want to wrang the memory of Matilda, but I canna help thinkin' that she started the fecht.'

"Poor Angus was in an awful stew, because he loved Matilda almost as much as he did Roddy. So after he'd scolded the parrot, he picked up Matilda, wrapped her careful in an old shawl, took her outside an' give her decent burial. Then he goes back an' puts Roddy in his cage. How he had got out, Angus didn't know, but he told father that the latch on the cage door couldn't have been caught right. Anyways, he got his pipes an' started playin' some kind of a lament, I think he called it. An' all the time Roddy was croakin': 'I killed her! Stop that noise! Whisky! Whisky! Whisky! Roddy wants whisky!' So finally Angus had to give him a spoonful, an' that quieted him.

* * *

"Shortly after that an Englishman come on a visit to his daughter, who'd married a Canadian. Somehow Angus learned that he could play chess, so he called on him an' invited him down to his house. An' most of that autumn, an' the followin' winter an' until spring come they played chess. Angus had wanted to show me how to play, but it was too quiet a game for me, an' my tongue wanted to wag. P'raps, Doctor, you know the game; but if you don't it's something like checkers. So there the old Englishman an' Angus would set in Angus's kitchen, their shoulders hunched up like a couple of groundhogs, an' the knights an' dukes an' the rooks an' what-not

Chapter XVI

where checkers would be if they was playin' that game. They'd sit for hours, an' hardly speak a word. But one night they had an argument about some rule or other; an' they both got hot. At last the Englishman says—stiff as you please: 'You don't know what you're talkin' about, Mr. Bruce. I never yet knew a Scot who could play chess.'

"At that Angus flared up an' said: 'Weel, mon, if I dinna ken it, my ancestors kent enough to beat yours at Bannockburn.'

"'An' mine yours at Culloden,' says the Englishman.

"'Aye,' says Angus; 'but they wouldna if the dommed MacDonalds had fecht, instead of mowin' up the heather with their broadswords.'

"'As for Bannockburn,' says the other, 'your people didn't play fair. They dug holes in the ground, an' our horses fell in them. It was a dirty trick, Mr. Bruce.'

"Says Angus: 'All's fair in luve an' war.' Then he stops, puts out his hand, an' says: 'I dinna like to have hot words with a guest, so let's call it off an' get on with the game.' So the Englishman takes Angus's hand, an' says: 'I accept your apology, Mr. Bruce... You admit, then, that you was wrong in the first place?'

"'Na—Na,' says Angus, 'it was aboot throwin' Bannockburn in your teeth. I dinna admit I was wrang aboot the rule we was at odds aboot. But let that flea stick on the wa.'[J] So he gets up, pours two drinks of whisky, sets one in front of the Englishman, sets down himself an' says: 'Weel, let's hae a wee drappie, then get on with the game. Your health, mon,' he says, an' lifts his glass.

"The Englishman smiles, then gives a good-natured laugh an' says: 'Whoever is as stubborn as a Scot!'

"Angus set down his glass on the table an' says, says he:' Noo, my friend, you've made a false move just like you done with the wee chess. Weel, the only mon that's as stubborn as a Scot is an Englishman.' An' with that he picks up his glass, gives a nod to his guest; an' he gives a laugh an' says: 'Well, Angus, you've checkmated me.' So they both drinks to each other, an' started the game again.

J   *Let bygones be bygones.*

* * *

"When June come, an' the first run of silver salmon began, Angus took his friend fishin', an' he soon learned to cast a good line an' caught several fish. Indeed, he told Angus that it was next best to playin' chess. But Angus said it was better. At any rate, he and Angus fished all that summer, until it was time for the Englishman to go back to England.

"Two years after that Angus died; an' Angus's brother—who had come out the year before—and had a small farm below Boiestown, took Roddy to *his* place. He was a most religious man, an' never drank any hard liquor. But he did drink rivers of black tea sweetened with molasses. He was awful shocked when people come in an' Roddy started to swear and call for whisky; then he'd have to throw a cloth over the cage so Roddy would think it was night an' go to sleep. Well, in a short time Roddy gave up the ghost. Might-be he missed his ration of whisky; but I think he was lonesome for Angus." Bill ceased, filled his pipe and smoked in silence for several moments. Finally he said: "I 'spose birds do get lonesome for their friends." He paused, then: "That salmon we heard jump tonight oughter take in the mornin' if he doesn't go upstream. Want me to turn down the lantern?"

I told him yes, and soon heard his gentle breathing and knew he had dropped off to sleep.

* * *

Oh Bill! Bill! As in an earlier age people clustered at the feet of a minnesinger and listened enraptured to his songs, so I can imagine you, seated by some murmuring brook or little river meandering through Elysian field, surrounded by erstwhile brothers of the angle while they chuckle or rock with laughter at your quaint tales. You, pausing only between the periods, or to recall some half-forgotten phrase. As when a spinner stays the busy hum of wheel and spindle to add another length of filmy wool, and sets them whirling yet again to twist it into close-spun yarn. Thus, Bill, I fancy you, with ever-ready wit and twinkling eye, spinning your various tales of fish and men.

CHAPTER XVII

After breakfast Bill poled me to the head of the pool where the water drops over ripply shallows, let down his anchor and I began casting. My objective was a boulder around one side of which the water curled in a smooth glide. I fished carefully, letting out line after each cast until finally, when the fly swung into the top of the glide, a good-sized salmon made a swirl and hit it. Then I tightened, and it struck off downstream, leaped three or four feet out of the water, fell back with a splash, ran towards the left-hand shore and leaped again.

"A twelve-pounder!" cried Bill, as he lifted the anchor and with his paddle swung the canoe to the right until he got slightly below the fish. It now bore upstream against the current, where we wanted it. As every angler knows, a fish drowns more quickly if held against the current.[81] This one was a fighter; although, as Bill had said, not above a twelve-pounder. But a twelve-pounder, althought it doesn't feel and give one the sensation of weight as a twenty or thirty-pound fish, is, if fresh run, more often than not more active; and I have often found them to take longer to land than much larger fish. As for having them ready for the net or the gaff one minute to the pound, that is as may be. I have taken them in less and more. I have had big fish ready to net or gaff in five minutes.

---

81 Ian Bernard says that "drown" is probably a colloquialism. "Suffocate" is more accurate. Salmon prefer to face upstream so that the oxygen-rich water goes into their mouths and exits through their gills, which absorb oxygen as the water passes over them. If an angler forces a salmon to point downstream towards the end of a fight, the water forces its gills open, so that it tires faster and eventually suffocates.

The salmon was boring steadily upstream towards its resting rock, but suddenly made a dart to its left and sped downriver again while I reeled in to take up any slack line. For a slack line can be dangerous; one must always keep a tight line and "feel" the fish. Now it stopped its mad career, sank to the bottom of the river and started the jigging tactics so nerve-racking to anglers. So Bill reached over my shoulder and gave the rod, above the reel, a few sharp blows with the back of his jack-knife. That did the trick and the fish started off again; not fast, but with a determined heavy pull that bent tip and middle joint in a bow. So I eased the strain and let it take out line. It went close to the opposite shore, rose to the surface in a big boil and gave a smash with its tail at the leader. Happily I had dropped my rod-tip almost to the level of the water. So, although it struck the leader and caused the reel to spin with a shriek, no damage was done, and the fish turned and again bored upstream.

"He's a fighter," said Bill; "an' we want him for dinner."

We did, for, if you remember, the bear had stolen the grilse and the remainder of the salmon we had taken, the salmon at the mouth of Biggar Brook, and the grilse at the foot of Crooked Rapids.

"He's well hooked," I said. I had no sooner spoken than the fish made a sudden turn and darted straight for the canoe. A trick (if it is one) they more often than not execute; probably because too much pressure is put on their mouths. At any rate I reeled in quickly. It came within a few yards of the canoe, and doubtless seeing it, swung off into deeper water downstream. I let it go, maintaining only slight pressure. Suddenly it rose to the surface and showed a portion of its silvery side.

"He's about tired out," said Bill, and reached for the long-handled net behind him. But he had no sooner said the words when the fish again disappeared, bore steadily downstream; and again he had to paddle hard to get below it.

"This is taking too long," I said. And no sooner were the words uttered than the fish turned over on its side and floated motionless on top of the water.

Bill paddled over below it, dropped his lead, shook out the folds of the mesh and dipped it. I applied just a little pressure with the rod, let the fish drop over the mouth of the net and Bill lifted it into the canoe.

Chapter XVII

It was firmly hooked on the outside of the mouth in the thick gristle and, as Bill said, we could have fought it to Boiestown. It went a couple of ounces over twelve pounds—the average weight of fish taken so far up the river. But no wonder it had fought so hard—with its mouth closed!

"Do you want to try for another?" asked Bill.

"No," I answered. "This is enough for one day."

When we reached shore in front of our tent, Bill asked me if I minded if he fished for trout from the big rock.

I told him he could fish as long as he liked, but he'd have to net them himself, because I wanted to do some digging to the left of the tent.

"OK," he said. "But I'll clean the salmon first, then take the little trout rod." So saying, he bit off a chew of tobacco and began gutting the salmon. Really it was a beauty, fresh run and bright as a newly minted coin.

* * *

It is no wonder that Miramichi salmon are such good fighters. They have fought their way up innumerable rapids from the head of tide-water and, like athletes who have trained for some competition, have acquired amazing agility and strength.

Little has been said or written about the habits of salmon, their lies and the manner of fishing them, that is not contained in publications of one hundred years ago; notably *Ephemera*, who edited the 1853 edition of *The Compleat Angler* (which contains Cotton's portion on fly fishing) and I have found his notes at the bottom of some of the pages extremely interesting and informative; especially because they conform with the knowledge of many of the older guides I have fished with: knowledge acquired from a life-time spent on the most famous salmon waters of New Brunswick.

* * *

While Bill fished, I took my spade and hand-trowel (I always carry both with me on my fishing trips), selected a bit of terrain a few rods back of his stand, began digging, and soon discovered a medley of flint chippings struck off by some aboriginal craftsman while he manufactured his arrowheads and other artifacts. There were flakes of milky quartz, of reddish-brown slate, and of grey-coloured chert. But the white quartz predominated. Now I sank a trench some six feet in length and carefully working down the sides with my trowel, heard, at a four-inch depth, the unmistakable 'clink' that warns the worker that he has touched some flint-like rock. This was a small snub-nose scraper of red jasper, beautifully chipped. Soon I heard another clinking sound, worked around the object until I could grasp it with my fingers, and found I had a skinning knife I thought was milky quartz. It was four and one-half inches wide at the base, gradually tapering to a needle-like point. If the artificer had taken a beech leaf for his model (which perhaps he did) it could not have been more like. So I left my digging for the present, and going to the river washed the sandy loam from its almost flat surface, then held it up between my eyes and the sun and saw that, far from being milky quartz, it was like a piece of crystal—so transparent I could see my thumb held back of it. Delighted, I walked down to where Bill stood on his rock. "What luck?" I asked.

"Four nice trout," he replied, and held up the largest for me to see. It was a beauty, more than half a pound, I thought. Then I showed him my find.

He reeled in his line, laid the rod on the big boulder, came to shore, took the knife, held it in the palm of his hand and gazed at it, his eyes expressing his amazement. Then he said: "The feller that made this was an artist! An artist! I wish I could have seen him doin' it." (How many times, finding pieces of equal workmanship, I have wished the same thing.) "When I've caught two more trout," he added, "I'll help you dig, if you don't mind."

"I'd like that," I said. He smiled his thanks, returned the knife to me, clambered back on his boulder, picked up the rod, released the hook from the reel and renewed his casting.

He got his two trout, which made six in all, came to shore, took out his jack-knife, cleaned and prepared them for the frying pan. Then he glanced up at me and said: "You can have salmon for dinner if you want to, but it's trout for Bill."

"Trout for me also," I said.

It was still only mid-morning, so we both went to the place I'd been digging. I gave him my trowel, showed him how to work. He soon caught on and, after a half hour, unearthed a perfect red-jasper arrowhead. He was as pleased as a child who had been given a new toy, took it down to the river, washed it off, came back and held it out to me, saying I could add it to my collection.

"No, no," I said. "It's yours. Keep it to remember this trip. I have plenty more like it."

"What!" he almost gasped. "Me! Mine?" Then: "I don't need this to make me remember our trip—or the other I took with you. And say, Doctor, if you think I'm worth takin', an' ever want me to go with you again, I'll do it an' no pay."

He meant it. Bill was like that. I said: "Bill, old chap, there's no guide in the world I'd rather have."

"Thanks," he said. "I enjoy being with you," and carefully placed the arrowhead in his breast pocket. "Think of it," he said, "hundreds of anglers an' hunters have camped here, an' didn't know what was under the ground!"

As we worked he paused two or three times, took the arrowhead from his pocket and holding it in the palm of his hand gazed at it with awe and admiration.

* * *

Later we went some little distance back of the tent to get firewood. Bill limbed the dead branches from a fallen spruce, chopped them into suitable lengths, split these into quarters and even smaller pieces, which I carried to the fire-place. From a dry cedar he split several sixteen-inch lengths into kindling. Some of these we put inside the tent so that, if it chanced to rain, we would have dry wood to start our fire. Finally he found a white birch that had been felled by a beaver the previous autumn.*(20b)* Doubtless (before he could use it) the small creature had met its fate at the hands of some trapper; and its hide later had been incorporated with others to fashion a woman's coat or jacket.

No wood makes a more pleasing fire than dry birch. Bill cut it into short sections, split it and, when he had added it to our pile, he gave a contented smile, then made a fire, put one of the kettles, filled with water, over the *chip-la-kwa-gun*, swung it over the blaze, and put in half a dozen potatoes. No peeled potatoes for Bill or me; for boiled in their "jackets", they retain all their flavour, all their nourishment, which otherwise would be extracted by the water. Now he half-filled another kettle with spring-water to make a brew of tea and suspended it from the *chip-la-kwa-gun* over the fire.

When the potatoes were ready and the trout fried, we fell to; and, after we had finished, had our dessert of tinned pears and little cakes filled with dates my wife had given me before I left home. And there were no sounds save the occasional song of a bird, the chatter of a squirrel, and the staccato notes of a woodpecker as it hammered at a dead tree and made the chips fly in its search for woodworms and larvae. Once a deer mouse (sometimes called the kangaroo mouse because of very short forelegs) visited us, and from a few feet distant looked us over with its beady eyes, then stole away as silently as it had come.

* * *

After the dishes were washed and dried, I lighted my pipe; Bill took a chew of tobacco, seated himself beside me, and, while the sunlit river flowed on as it had ever since the glaciers had carved out the valley untold ages ago, we talked of fish.

"You know," said Bill, "I never used a greased line until I was twelve, an' old Angus taught me. I'd gone up to his home to pay him a visit an' see the birds. He was out at the side of the house with his fish-line strung between two posts, rubbin' it with a bit of rag. So I asked what he was doin'. 'I've greased the line, laddie,' he says. Noo I'm rubbin' it in. Ye ken, Willie, after a line's been fished, it takes up water, an' doesna shoot well through the rings. A greased line doesna sink, an' is more liker to tak a fish at this height of water.'

"After he had rubbed it some more he wound it on his reel, took me to the shore where his boat was an' asked me to get in the stern an' pole him to midriver well above a couple of rocks where salmon often rested. So I did as he asked; an' when he'd dropped the anchor he picked up his rod, slipped the fly from the reel and begins castin'. It was a long rod, Doctor, much longer than we use, an' heavier. If he wanted to he could cast almost to both shores. In no time he raised a fish that didn't take. So after restin' it he tried again; but no luck. I said: 'Why not change flies, Angus?'

"'Nae, nae, Willie,' he said, 'if her ladyship winna tak the Jock, she'll tak no other. I'll no pamper her. Nae—nae. Somethin's wrang.' He reeled in his line an' said: 'Set the boat above an' to the left, laddie.' So he lifted the anchor, an I poled until he told me to stop, then he dropped the lead. He waited a few minutes, picked up his rod an' began castin' downstream (away from where he'd raised the fish) till he had a good length of line out, with several coils at his feet in the bottom of the boat. Then, when he'd cast, all the line would shoot out to where he wanted it. At last he half-turned his body, an' sent the fly just to the right of the two rocks an' a bit above them. Then he takes hold of the line above the reel-seat an' pulls the fly at an angle. Say, Doctor, that fish made a swirl that hove up the water, the tip bent an' I knowed it was on. Then, still holdin' the line atween his finger an' thumb, Angus wound up the coils at his feet, the salmon bolted down-river, an' he played it from the reel.

"'That's what her ladyship wanted,' said Angus. 'In the other position the fly wasna swingin' fast enough to suit her.'"

I told Bill that one of my old guides, Jock Ogilvy, had used the same trick one day I was with him on the Tobique. "Did Angus land the fish?" I asked.

"Sure," replied Bill. "We had it in the boat within ten minutes: a fourteen-pounder it was. Yes, Old Angus was one of the best fishermen I've ever known."

* * *

"Once," said Bill, "father decided to take a trip for trout to the headwaters of the Little Sou'west, asked Angus to go along, an' took me too. At that time I was fourteen. Father an' Angus poled up to Big Clearwater an' up to a place where there was a set of lumber camps; then we follered an old trapline for three or four miles, an' camped for the night.

"Angus had a mighty heavy pack filled with grub, blankets an' three bottles of whisky. He wouldn't go nowhere without whisky. An' say, Doctor, what else do you think he had?"

I couldn't guess, so he enlightened me. "A five-pound bag of oatmeal. I mean *oatmeal*, not rolled oats. So after we'd set up a little lean-to of poles an' boughs, an' made a fire to boil the kettle, Angus looked around an' found a thin flat stone bigger across the top than a fryin' pan, an' set it close to the fire. 'Just a wee bannock stane,' he told us. So he mixed some of the oatmeal with water to a thick paste, an' when the stone was hot, made a rounded lump of the mix, laid it on the stone an' patted it until it was about three-quarters of an inch thick. When one side was cooked he turned it over. By the time father had a panful of pork fried the cake was done. After Angus and father each had a drink of whisky we began eatin'. An' wasn't that bannock good covered with homemade butter! (Once, years later, when I was at Burnt Hill Brook, I found I'd left my fryin pan at the Sisters Brook where I'd dinnered. I didn't want to pole back two miles for it, so rememberin' Angus's bannock stone, I found a flat slate stone an' used it for my fryin'-pan to cook some bacon. Couldn't have been better.) Well, next day we started off again. As p'raps you know, Doctor, that country is all wilderness, with a snarl of lakes, deadwaters an' brooks that go on to Bay Chaleur. An' there's mountains two thousand feet high. Angus loved them, said they reminded him of Scotland but without the bonny heather. As I've said before, he was a big, raw-boned man, an' strong as a moose. It was a sight to see him trampin' over ridges an' hills as easy as if he was walkin' on a made road. An' his pack—although it must have weighed eighty pounds—didn't bother him more than if it had been ten.

"Bye-an'-bye we climbed a mountain more than sixteen hundred feet above sea-level, an' come to Moose Lake, the head of Rocky Brook. There's no higher body of water like it in New Brunswick. Here we stopped an' set up a lean-to of poles an' birch-bark. After we'd dinnered, we found some old dry cedar rampikes an' made a raft big enough to hold the three of us. Say, Doctor, I never saw so many trout or as big, except at a place I'll tell you about later. In no time we caught two dozen that would go a pound each an' three or four two-pounders. So we landed, gutted 'em, then goes back to our lean-to. We'd just got there when we saw a big bear rummagin' at our packs. Angus gives a roar you could hear a half-mile. But that bear didn't scare. It stood up on its hind legs, bared its teeth an' growled somethin' fierce. Angus had his double-bitted axe, started for the brute, an' it starts for him. Father yelled for Angus to stop. He did, but didn't back up. He held his axe high above his head, an' when the bear rushed him he made a swipe at it with all his strength. But his nibs stepped to one side, just like a boxer, made a swipe with his paw an' knocked the axe out of Angus's hands. Then, as Angus pulled out his long knife, the bear reached out an' gives him a claw that ripped his shirt open an' brought the blood. Then, as

Chapter XVII

Angus staggered back, bruin threw both arms about him an' hugged him so hard it would have broke the ribs of any ordinary man—which Angus wasn't. So they went whirlin' round an' round with Angus's arm against the bear's throat, an' it tryin' to get at his face with its long teeth.

"Father, who was no mean hand with an axe, had got his axe where it stood by a tree. But he was afraid to hit at the bear because he was afraid he'd strike Angus.

"I was 'most scared stiff, but picked up a long pole, reached out an' managed to give the bear a clip over the head. He was so surprised he thought father had hit him, so with a roar he let go of Angus an' started for father. Then father gives him a swipe with the axe, an' Angus rushed in an' snapped his knife up to the hilt in the bear's neck, drew it out an' quick as a flash gives him another stab, an' father brought his double-bitter down on its head. It went through it as if it was a rotten log. It fell over on its side an' give up the ghost.

"Angus's chest was bleedin' bad where the bear's claws had ripped through his shirt, but he walks over to his pack, calm as you please, lifted out one of the bottles of whisky, took out the cork, half-filled a tin cup, an' handed it to father. 'Here, William,' he says, 'tak it a.' Father did, then Angus poured out one for himself. Father said: 'You'd better rub some of that on your chest, Angus; them claws might have pizon on 'em.' Says Angus: 'Na, na', William, it'd be a waste of good whisky.' However, after he'd drunk it he did wipe off the blood, then got the bag of salt, took a handful an' rubbed it into the wounds, like he was kipperin' a fish. The sight of him doin' that made my teeth chitter like when you're half froze. But I remembered what a young Injun friend had once told me about fir balsam, so I peeled off a piece of the thin outer bark that held the balsam, and collected enough to cover Angus's scratches. Then I comes to where he an' father was cuttin' off the bear's snout (to turn in to the government an' get the bounty), an' asked Angus to let me put the balsam on his wounds.

"'Oh-aye, laddie,' he said. 'I dinna think the wee scratches will do ony hurt, but I'll try your preescription.'

"So I put the sticky stuff on his hairy chest, an' it stuck closer than a brother. Then he said: 'My thanks to ye, Willie. It's too bad your father didna bring ye up on the bottle, or I'd gie ye a wee drappie of the good whisky. But I'll gie one to him with your thanks, an' tak a sma' one myself for quid luck to all of us.'

"Well, Doctor, them wounds healed in three or four days, but the scars stayed as long as he lived. Often, when he had visitors, he'd bare his chest, that looked as if a spring-tooth harrow had gouged it, then tell the whole story. He was a great hand at tellin' a story.

* * *

"The next mornin' we travelled over to Injun Lake, the head of the Little Sou'west, where we caught some nice trout. Could have filled a barrel but we wanted to see more of the country. From Injun Lake we follered the woods until we come to a three-mile-long deadwater, an' then along the shore to Sou-west Lake. Its Injun name is *tu-a-dook*. There we camped. At the inlet is a trout pool that is the best in New Brunswick. All we had to do was stand on some big rocks and cast. I never fished where the trout were so hungry. We caught two or three dozen. Some would go a pound each, but there were others two an' three pounds. Father told Angus (as he had told me many times) that once he had gone there with a party of surveyors runnin' lines for the government, an' they caught trout that went six pounds.

"Father an' I fished with bait. But Angus had brought along a trout rod an' used a fly. It was great fun seein' the big fellows fling themselves outa the water, take it and fight like furies, slappin' the water with their tails, runnin' here an' there with the reel hummin' like mad. Talk about salmon fightin'! They've got nothin' on trout. We had no landin' net, so Angus had to play them dead, bring them in close to his rock, then reach down with his hand an' lift 'em out.

"When we'd done fishin', father an' Angus split them down the back, rubbed them with salt, dried 'em, then smoked 'em on a little platform of saplin's over a slow fire.

"That night we saw a big bull moose walk along the shore.*(22)* It had a mighty spread of antlers, I'd say sixty inches, an' a foot an' a half wide. Of course they was in the velvet. Angus had never before seen a moose. 'Aye,' he said, 'yon's a bonny animal.'

"It came along as proud as you please until it scented the smoke from the campfire, then turned an' glided like a ghost into the woods.

Chapter XVII

"In the mornin' we started back for the head of Rocky Brook, then went on to Clearwater. Angus said he'd never enjoyed a trip so much in all his life. Of course, Doctor, I've been there since that time, an' travelled clear to the Tobique waters; but I think I liked that experience with father an' Angus more than any other. I often wonder why more sports don't go there to fish trout. Of course it means long tramps, an' few of them like to walk so far. But if they want trout fishin', well, there it is. Want to try for another salmon, Doctor?"

CHAPTER XVIII

I remember hearing fifty years ago that some of the visiting anglers on the Restigouche objected to the guides using iron-shod setting-poles while going up or downriver. Their argument was that the thud of the iron against the rocky bottom disturbed the salmon and kept them down.

Now there is no doubt that the salmon is capable of receiving vibrations from a considerable distance, just as a man with his head under water can hear another who holds two rocks submerged and strikes them sharply together. The water not only conveys the sounds but accentuates them to such an extent that they hurt the eardrums. But I do not believe that the salmon is unduly disturbed by the iron-shod setting-pole. At any rate the guides now on the Restigouche not only use them on occasion but also employ out-board motors on the canoes. Indeed, as I've said before, I have good reason to believe that the sound of the motor often rouses the fish from the lethargy which a very hot day seems to induce. I have known anglers who (after a fish has risen and refused or missed the fly) have immediately tied on another of different pattern; and, that not proving effective, tried others without the fish rising again. Personally I do not like changing flies. The fact that the fish has risen once would seem to indicate that it is interested, but that the fly had not been presented just right or was not moving fast enough.

A man must learn to catch fish by trial and error: by observing how his guide fishes, and following his advice. As for flies (as I think I have said before), any good fly of standard pattern will get results if it is *presented right and the fish is in the mood to take*. Above all, if we do not kill a fish today, we must not blame the guide and say he is no good. The fault is doubtless our own, not his. Of course we have come on a fishing trip and hope to catch one or more salmon before we return home; but let us remember that we are having a day off. Surely it is something to be alive and in good health: we can add to both by absorbing some of the beauty that environs our little river wheresoever it may be. Happiness, like good health, is not fully appreciated until we have lost it; and, like good health, often depends on a contented mind. I know of no better way of achieving this than by taking a day off and going fishing…quite often.

* * *

"You know," said Bill, breaking what for him had been an unusually long silence, "except for the years I was overseas, I've been guidin' since I was thirteen, and I've seldom had any angry words with my sports. We usually got along fine. But there was one fellow I just couldn't take. He might have had lots of money, cars an' what-not, but he was the most selfish cuss I ever knew, an' the worst fish-hog. Once he had a friend with him who was one of the best salmon anglers I've ever known, an' a gentleman to boot. How he ever ganged up with the other critter I couldn't make out. One day this nice guy (I'll call Mr. A.) was fishin' a certain pool and raised a big fish that didn't take. At that pool you could fish by wadin'. So what did Mr. B. do? Well, Doctor, he picks up his rod, wades out an' casts right where Mr. A. had got the rise. Mr. A. didn't say nothin', be just reeled in his line an' went to shore. Well, Mr. B. hooked the fish, played it, an' I netted it for him. But from that time I despised him worse'n pizon.

"The next mornin' he said he wanted to fish a pool three miles upriver, so I took him in my canoe. He caught two salmon an' a grilse before noon, then said he wanted to stay an' fish later in the day. I told him we had no lunch; an' he said he'd brought some with him in his knapsack. So I put him to shore. He sat down under a tree, took out his sandwiches an' began eatin' them; never asked me if I had a stomach or not. I was sittin' close by, an' gettin' madder every minute. Finally, I couldn't take it no longer, so I got up, went down to the canoe, lifted it into the water, picked up my settin'-pole, got in an' gave it a shove off.

"'Say you,' he bawls out, just as if I was dirt, 'where you goin'?'

"'Back to home to get my dinner,' I says. 'I'll be back here in three hours; might be four.'

"'You can't do that!' he bellers. 'You can't leave me alone in this God-forsaken place. There might be bears around.'

"I snubbed the canoe. Says I: 'One of the *best places* for 'em on the Miramichi. This is their crossin'-place to get to the mountain back there. But,' says I, 'you needn't be scared if one or more comes, because they'd have to be devil-awful hungry to eat you, Mr. B.' An' with that I poled away from the critter.

"Well, Doctor, I was back just under four hours. An' I hadn't hurried: just poled along steady so's I could keep my promise. But when I landed, an' walked up the bank where I'd left him, he wasn't there that I could see. An' I wondered if a bear *had* carried him off, or he'd gone for a walk in the woods an' got lost. It wouldn't have mattered to me one way or the other.

"Presently I heard a scramblin' in a big birch tree near by, an' there he was comin' down, just as awkward as a cow. I didn't laugh, but felt like it.

"He never said a word when he got to ground. He took out his pipe, filled, lighted it and raised such a cloud of smoke, it made me think of the train we call the *Dungarvon Whooper* makin' an up-grade.

"That cured him. Next day he put in enough grub to do both of us. But I'd brought my own. So when he asked me to have some hard-boiled eggs I said: 'No, thank you, Mr. B. Hardboiled eggs don't set well on my stomach.'

* * *

"Well, Doctor, that feller knowed about everything there was to know about fishin' salmon. I mean he thought he did. Bless you, he'd discovered this method an' that method, when I knowed darn well he'd got most all he knowed from me an' other guides he'd fished with. If you suggested he tie on a Silver Wilkinson he'd say a Silver Doctor was best; as though whichever it was mattered a continental damn. No use to argue with him 'cause he'd git mad as a wet hen an' cuss you. It's the truth, Doctor, that a man can buy a licence to fish salmon, but he can't buy what it takes to make a gentleman—if you get what I mean."

I couldn't help smiling at Bill's philosophical remark: but he had hit it right on the button. "Yes, Bill," I said. "I quite understand. Robin Hood never shot a better shaft."

He grinned, then said: "Oh yes, I read about him in one of my school books. He lived a long time ago, didn't he?"

"Yes, Bill."

"An' the prince filled his bugle with pennies… Yes…yes, it all comes back now."

* * *

Said Bill: "Speakin' of cows a few moments ago, makes me think of a cow old Angus had. Did you ever hear of a cow gettin' drunk, Doctor?"

"No, Bill, I answered; and wondered what was now coming from his fertile brain, and whether it was fact or fiction.'

He went on: "I've seen bees get so drunk sippin' nectar from flowers that they finally fell to the ground an' stayed there for a while. Well, old Angus had one devil of a cow he called Bessie. He kept her in a bit of pasture fenced in with cedar rails. But she'd jump over them, or lift the top rails off with her horns an' get out. She was always in trouble an' gettin' caught by the cow-reeve an' put in the pound. Then Angus had to pay a dollar to get her out. Or she was swallowin' her cud, an' then he had to roll up a fist-full of grass an' stuff it into her throat. But like everything else he owned—like Roddy an' Matilda—he wouldn't part with her. Not because she was a good milker, an' she was, but because he liked her.

"But as matter of fact I don't believe he could have give her away, let alone sell her, because every farmer from Blackville to Hayes' Bar knew what she was like.

"Finally he bought some wire fencin', an' put that up in place of the cedar rail fence. But Bessie made light of that. She'd make a run an' go over it slick as a whistle, an' Angus had to bail her out of pound again. He thought she might be bewitched or have the devil in her.

"One day, in September, when there was a big run of salmon, Angus sent word for me to come up to his place an' we'd catch some of the fish to kipper. So I goes up about eight in the mornin', an' there was Angus holdin' up Bessie an' tryin' to make her walk. But she'd only go a few steps then tumble over on the off-side of Angus.

"'What's wrong with Bessie?' I asked.

"'Wrang?' he says. 'She's druken, Willie; druken as a fool.'

"So I looked at her; her sides were all puffed out like a pizoned pup's. 'Praps she's goin' to have a calf,' I said.

"'Calf?' he snorted. 'I wish it was that. Na—na, she's druken, as I said.'

"I began to laugh, thinkin' to myself that he had given Bessie a drink of whisky as he often did Roddy an' Matilda. Then I said: 'On whisky, Angus?'

"'Na', na', laddie,' says he, 'I wouldna waste good whisky on Bessie. It wad tak too much. It's apples.'

"'Apples?' I says.

"'Yes, Willie. You ken that apple tree, the wild one doon by the river? Weel, last night's wind blew half of the apples to the ground. Bessie got out, an' only the good Lord kens how many she ate. When I got up this mornin' she was just beyond the fence, staggerin' like a druken sailor. So I brought her inside, an' was just tryin' to walk her up an' doon a wee bit to sober her up. But she got worse an' tumbled owre.'

"'But apples, Angus?' says I. 'I never thought *they* would make a cow drunk.'

"'This coo is different, laddie, there's some sort of acid in her stomach that mixes with the apples an' makes alcohol in just a few hours. So, laddie, you stand on the other side of her. I'll lift her up, an' between us we'll balance her an' help her walk it off.'

"Well, Doctor, I was then a hefty lad comin' on sixteen, so when Angus (who was a strong as a moose, as I said before) got Bessie to her feet, I pressed with all my strength on my side of her, an' Angus on his side. At first she wouldn't budge a foot, but Angus reached out with one hand, gives her tail a twist, an' off she goes, staggerin' from one side to the other. Said Angus: 'She couldna walk the chalk-line, Willie!'

"Every so often she'd tumble over again an' it was a chore to get her on her feet again. But we kept at it, an' bye'n-bye she got so she could go under her own power. So Angus said: 'We'll let her bide, laddie, an' I'll gie her a dose of salts.' So he did, an' she swallowed a handful as nice as you please. Then we led her to the pasture, left her, an' Angus got his fishin' rod an' gaff an' we went to the river. Said Angus: 'Some men get druken on too muckle whisky, others on too muckle food, an' some on too muckle religion. But I think too muckle food is the worst; though of course the parsons, being prejudiced against strong drink, claim whisky is. Aye, Willie, it's a thin horse for a long race, an' a mon that sets too muckle store on his stomach had better mak his will an' order his coffin.'

* * *

"As soon as Angus had caught, and I gaffed one salmon, he handed me the rod, an' said: 'Noo, laddie, let's see if you've profited from my last lesson. Dinna cast too long a line. As I said before, a short line taks more fish than a lang one.' (For, Doctor, it was one of my faults to throw a long line—a matter of pride, I suppose.)

"Between us we took eight salmon: all but one fresh-run hookbills, an' it was as red as a smoked herrin' from bein' a long time in the fresh water. So Angus took the hook careful out of his mouth and let it go.

"You know, Doctor, in some respects a salmon is like the man who's livin' in sin. I'm talkin' about the fish that stays in fresh water all winter. Then he's thin; the scales sunk into his body. He's sick an' ain't fit for food. So in the spring, after the ice goes out, he runs down to salt water to get his health back. An' the man that's a sinner has to make his peace with God to be put right again. An' no man ever bought religion with hard cash. He's got to give something of himself first, an' get the rest from the Almighty. I know. I've had to many a time.

* * *

"Well, Doctor, when we got back to Angus's home Bessie seemed in fair condition. So Angus put a halter on her neck, tied on a long rope, an' tethered her to a stake he drove in his bit of pasture. 'I dinna think she'll break away noo,' he said. So we went up near the house, slit each fish down the back, took out the bones, and rubbed the insides with a little whisky, then some salt, dried, then put them on a wooden frame over a slow fire to kipper. Before I left for home, Angus asked me if I'd like to go fishin' the followin' day. Of course I said yes.

Chapter XVIII

"So next mornin' I goes up, an' there was Bessie rollin' around on the ground outside the fence an' Angus tryin' to get her on her feet.

"'You don't mean to tell me she broke the halter?' I asked him.

"'Yes, Willie,' he said, 'an' noo druken as a fiddler's bitch!'

"I helped get her on her feet, an' we walked her up an' down. She was in worse condition than the day before. She'd roll her eyes, an' open her mouth, an' give little bellers like as if she was havin' a joke all to herself.

"It took a couple of valuable hours from fishin' to bring her around a bit, then we led her to the pasture, put her inside, Angus got a basket, an' we went down to the apple tree, picked up all that was on the ground an' dumped them in the river. After we'd got through fishin', Angus made a new halter from a piece of hamestrap, put it on Bessie's neck, an' tethered her solid. An' that was that. Except for swallowin' her cud every week or so, she didn't give no more trouble."

"Oh Bill, Bill!" I said. "What a yarn!"

He looked hurt. "It's true as true," he protested. "Bessie was drunk on somethin'. As Angus said: 'There's different kinds of intoxication, Willie... Some get druken on religion, some on strong drink, an' others on too much food.'"

CHAPTER XIX

About ten o'clock that night we heard thunder in the distance. Said Bill: "I thought we'd get rain when I saw the smoke from the campfire hangin' low in the air." He got to his feet, went down to the river, pulled the canoe well up on the little beach, turned it bottom up, then came back.

The thunder continued, rolled nearer, reverberated against Lewey Mountain in prolonged rumblings, while flashes of forked lightning came with awe-inspiring frequency, lighting up the interior of our little tent. Then the rain began: not a few drops, but in a perfect deluge, as though the heavens had suddenly opened. It beat against the roof of the tent with a continuous tattoo that Bill said was like the thumping of numerous finger-tips on a drumhead. "This'll raise the headwaters," he added.

Across the river a jagged streak of lightning tore out of the sky and struck a tree, for we heard a terrific crash as it plunged to earth, tearing its own branches and those of other trees.

"Passchendaele," said Bill. "It was awful when the guns let loose." And lighted his pipe. Then, back of us, we heard other mutterings of thunder that gradually grew louder and approached nearer. Another storm from the southwards was approaching. Soon it seemed as if each were trying to outdo the other in a tremendous artillery duel. A wind sprang up; we could hear the groaning and creaking of the trees as they swayed back and forth. It shook the tent and I feared that it would collapse or be blown away. And above the roar of the wind and the lashing of the rain came the deafening salvoes of thunder and lightning that seemed to be right in the camp yard.

I thought of the Indians who, in the old days, had camped on this very spot, and wondered with what superstitious emotions they had endured what we were hearing and witnessing. And of the forest creatures on ridge and in the swampy areas—did they cower in fear? Or did they accept with indifference what man, no matter who he is, cannot help but dread?

For two hours or more the thunder and lightning kept up without abatement then, like a disgruntled monster, retreated with low mutterings eastwards… But the rain continued all night long. Lucky for us that Bill had dug a trench around the outside of the tent, otherwise our bedding would have been drenched. As it was we slept peacefully after the electric storm had passed on until after daylight, then found the sky clear, the sun drinking up the moisture on ground and shrub, and the birds singing.

* * *

The river was in spate, a brown flood on which floated branches of trees, pieces of lumber, short pulp-logs, and a few alders whose bark had been peeled by beavers and set adrift by the rise of water. Such a rise would, we knew, bring up fish from the pools many miles below us, as well as activate those already up.

We had intended to break camp and drop downriver to McKiel, but since the river was rising and would continue for the next twenty-four hours, we decided to remain where we were until the following morning. So, after a hearty breakfast of bacon and fried salmon, we did a little digging at the site I had already discovered.

Bill found another stone arrowhead, and a spearhead of iron that had doubtless been traded by the early French in return for a beaver pelt. Extending our trench, we uncovered at a lower level a firehole that contained some pottery sherds, and a seven-inch stone gouge that had been badly marred by the heat of successive campfires. But it was an interesting piece, for the groove extended from one end to the other, and is the only one exhibiting this feature that I possess.

CHAPTER XX

Next morning we had barely completed stowing our tent and other things in the canoe, when three canoes passed us on their way downriver, which, although still mud-coloured, was beginning to ease off. Two of the canoes each contained an angler and his guide; the third was the cook's, loaded with supplies covered with a tarpaulin. Fishermen who would doubtless fish the available pools before finally reaching Boiestown forty miles distant. The guides called out "Hullo" to Bill, who later told me they were the Munn brothers and two of the best river-men and guides on the Miramichi.

We followed in their wake, threaded the narrow channel on the right of Lewey Island, and a little later caught up with the three canoes "holding" just above Lewey Rapids. The guides and the cook were looking over the situation before attempting the descent.

At this place the river is contracted by two huge slate ledges that push out from either shore, and between them the accumulated waters pour like a mill-race down a declivity only about twenty-five feet in width. At the bottom, slightly to the right of centre, is a big granite boulder. At the present height of water the whole force of the current struck against it and curled off its left side in a big wave that finally smoothed out in the basin below. It is a passage that requires the utmost skill to navigate safely.

Bill was "holding" our canoe a little above those of the Munns. To the left the cook stood upright in the stern of his craft. Suddenly I saw him give his shoulders a slight upsurge, as though he were saying to himself: "Well, here goes, whatever the outcome." Shipping his setting-pole he seized his paddle, drove it into the water and the canoe shot like an arrow down the declivity of raging foam. The bow struck the curled-up wave, was tossed a little to the left of the boulder, and swung the stern to the right. But the cook knew his business. He swung the stern to the left, straightened out and, the water lapping the gunwales, was safely past the danger spot into the basin, sped around the sharp bend and, more quickly than it takes to tell, was lost to view.

Next the Munn boys (as Bill called them) navigated the rapids: then we followed... Several times I had shot Lewey Rapids, but never at this height of water. I cast a hasty glance backwards at Bill, saw his broad shoulders slightly stooped, his eyes filled with joyous excitement, then I turned and looked before me. As with the other canoes the big wave struck our bow a resounding slap; the spray dashed into my face, then we were past it and speeding around the bend.

A few years ago a cook—an expert canoeman—taking supplies to one of the camps downriver, upset at the Narrows. Luckily he was able to cling to the bottom of his upturned canoe and eventually got it to shore farther down. But he had to pole back to Half-Moon Cove, catch the train to Boiestown, purchase new supplies, come back on the next train, and make another attempt to run the Narrows. He did it safely. But one has to run the Narrows in high water to appreciate how difficult they are.

* * *

We shot past Lewey Pool where in lower water there is a good cast; then the three Boyce's Rocks. From these is a long comparatively straight stretch to and beyond the *Perdue* (a back water) to Otter Brook, then a sharp left-hand turn leads to the Old Hen and Chickens—a series of five boulders running as straight as a plumb line. At the foot is a good fishing stand. Thus, turning and twisting between shores covered with evergreens, maples, white, yellow birches, and other trees, breath-taking in their primitive setting, we came to McKiel Pond, entered the Narrows, navigated them without mishap, and then, on our left, saw McKiel Brook mingling its brown-coloured waters with those of the Miramichi.

In low water it is difficult to reach the camp-ground below the brook, but this day we glided easily to shore. Then we carried the tent and dunnage to the high flat terrace, where, for unnumbered years, explorers, river-drivers, anglers and hunters had camped. Here, two hundred and seventy-five years

Chapter XX

ago, when New Brunswick (then a part of Acadia) was under the sway of France, came the young engineer-cartographer, Baptiste Louis Franquelin with his Micmac canoemen. He mapped the river and its tributaries and handed down to us their Indian names. That of McKiel Brook and Lake is *Too-a-gan-ech*. The name McKiel is that of an old lumberman who for many years operated in this region of the Miramichi.

The lake is a beautiful sheet of water, long famous for its excellent trout fishing; and the surrounding terrain, while still the habitat of deer, was formerly famous for its numerous moose. The brook, during its last three miles, until it vents into the Miramichi, "flows through a glacier-cut valley or ravine across a projection from the highlands on the east, thereby isolating the striking and conspicuous Lewey's Mountain."[K]

For many years after Franquelin's time we hear nothing about McKiel; then, in 1844, Sir James Alexander visited the place; in 1862 Sir Arthur Gordon, Governor of New Brunswick; in 1879 A. Pendarves Vivian;[82] and in 1897 our own Frank Risteen[83] and Professor Ganong, all of whom wrote about the brook and its lake in glowing terms.

River Miramichi, daughter of ice and snow: if you could speak, what tales you could tell: sagas of rivermen tumbling millions of feet of logs into your swollen current: of breaking log-jams piled twenty or more feet high and, when the key-logs gave way, rushing to safety over the plunging mass. Down through the years would come unrecorded tales of anglers, in pine dugouts or canvas-covered canoes, fishing the myriad pools and rapids from Juniper to Boiestown and beyond; of nights spent in tent or lean-to of spruce-bark while they recounted the day's good-luck or ill-luck, and the camp-fire cast its golden shadows against the encircling trees. There would be word pictures of winter days and nights when imprisoned air beneath the ice rushed back and forth with the speed of a torpedo, squealing and groaning like some prehistoric monster in travail, with only the silent hills to hear.

---

82 British industrialist and travel writer, 1834-1926.

83 Author of *Fredericton, New Brunswick and the St. John River for the Tourist and Sportsman*, 1909.

K   W.F. Ganong. [Canadian botanist, historian and cartographer, 1864-1941. (Wikipedia)]

Then the spring break-up, and millions of tons of ice carried tumultuously past lowland and highland to give up its life in the distant sea. And then... then, you could relate that, from that same sea, the female silver salmon had sped in their thousands up your numerous rapids; and later, when the males arrived, conjoined with them in the task of reproducing their kind.

You could sing of deciduous trees unfolding their young buds to bedeck lowland and upland in a symphony of leaves of various greens; of the return of the migrant birds; and along your shores marsh marigolds lifting their golden faces to greet the sun. And then, in their season, of the dome-like clusters of the mountain laurel, the white umbels of the dogwood, the blue flag and the bell-shaped reddish-yellow Canada lily nodding on its long stalk; the magenta-pink of the Joe Pye weed, and the wild rose half hiding its beauty among the alders and tall grasses.

These the contemplative angler has seen, and absorbed of their loveliness without which you, my river, would have less of intimacy and charm...

Not yet (and we hope it never will be) has man attempted to dam your swift-flowing waters. Nor does pollution from sewer or pulp-mill sully your purity between Boiestown and the most remote sources of your many tributaries which have their origin in the mountainous highlands whose jagged peaks form a barrier between them and the Tobique waters. I pray you remain thus for the enjoyment and heart's-ease of all future generations...

* * *

Barely had we made our camp-fire when, as though they had been awaiting the smoke-signal, we were visited by two of those feathered creatures variously known as the Canada jay, moosebird, woodsman's friend, whisky-jack and gorby. We threw them some scraps of bread. Each picked up a piece, flew away with it and almost immediately returned for more. This they did until none was left. We saw and heard other birds: the little veery and the white-throat; and a red-winged blackbird that flew upriver—evidently in search of some marsh, for I have seldom seen them anywhere else.

Chapter XX

As I saw these birds I remembered Longfellow's poem *The Birds of Killingworth*.[84]

The poet tells how the birds stole the settlers' seed corn, and the seeds of other vegetables, and their cherries when ripe, and the deacons and magistrates met in solemn conclave and decided to exterminate the birds. Only one member of the community—the young schoolmaster, who was engaged to marry the fair Almira, protested. But without avail, for they hired men and boys, supplied them with guns, powder and shot and offered them a bounty for each bird killed.

> *And so the dreadful massacre began;*
> *O'er fields and orchards, and o'er woodland crests,*
> *The ceaseless fusillade of terror ran...*
> *A slaughter to be told in groans, not words,*
> *The very St. Bartholomew of birds.*

The result was that all the birds were killed and:

> *...in the orchards fed*
> *Myriads of caterpillars, and around*
> *The cultivated fields and garden beds*
> *Hosts of devouring insects crawled, and found*
> *No foe to check their march till they had made*
> *The land a desert without leaf or shade.*

Then the terrible decree had to be rescinded; birds were brought in from other places and set free to mingle their songs with the wedding service of the schoolmaster and his Almira.

> *And a new heaven bent over a new earth*
> *Amid the sunny farms of Killingworth.*

The afternoon passed, and the long grey twilight, and mysterious, awe-inspiring night enfolded river and hills. We were alone in a vast wilderness

---

84 In *Tales of a Wayside Inn*, 1863.

as primitive as when the glaciers retreated centuries ago. The brook tinkled and sang over its rocky bed: the river swirled against half-submerged boulders and along the shores and chuckled and gurgled its age-old litany. Back of us, among the trees, we heard that shy bird we seldom see. Its strange notes which we have interpreted *whip-poor-will*, and the Indians *hu-wip-o-lis*, fell on our ears with insistent repetition. Then, from the black solitude beyond the hurrying waters, came the raucous *who!—hoo!—augh!* of the great horned owl. Only one who has heard that startling cry breaking through the still atmosphere with the explosive suddenness of a bomb, can appreciate how weird and diabolic it sounds. It is as though some maniacal denizen of the nether regions had broken its bonds and was hurling its derision of all other creatures on the earth and in the heavens. Twice more the clarion cacophony rent the night, then, as though satisfied that it had heaped sufficient contumely on its hearers, the bird ceased as suddenly as it had begun.

The stars swung into orbit: constellations that, in the remote past, were named by Chaldean astronomers, desert nomads, Phoenician sailors, Greeks, Romans and Scandinavian peoples. I pointed out to Bill the constellations the Greeks had named the Great Bear and the Little Bear (more commonly recognised by us as the Big and the Little Dipper). Then told him the old fable that has come down to us of how Callisto, through the jealousy of Juno (the ox-eyed wife of Jupiter and queen of heaven), was changed by Jupiter into a she-bear: of how Callisto's son, Arcas, while out hunting, would have killed her, but that Jupiter (the all-powerful) turned him into a he-bear and transferred both mother and son to the heavens as the magnificent constellations the Great and the Little Bear. And I said how remarkable it was that, long before the white man saw the shores of North America, our Micmac Indians called the four main stars of the greater constellation *Mooin—their* name for the bear. But, well knowing that that animal has little or no tail, they named the three stars that form the preternaturally long appendage of the Greek bear the *Three Hunters;* a small star near one of the hunters the *Kettle* which he carries, and Berenice's hair the *Bear's Den*. A much more interesting as well as a more true-to-nature conception than that embodied in the Greek fable.

Chapter XX

"Of course," said Bill, "trust an Indian to know his animals. But who was this Berenice? It's a pretty name."

Then I told him that, in the remote past, Berenice, the wife of Ptolemy III—who had gone to make war against Asia—vowed that, if he returned the victor over his enemies, she would sacrifice her beautiful hair to the gods. So she cut it off and hung it in the temple of the war-god. But it was stolen the first night, and Conon of Samos told the king that the winds had wafted it to heaven, where it still forms the seven stars near the tail of Leo the Lion.

When I had ended, Bill said: "Of course it's a fairy story; but a nice one." He was silent for a few moments then said: "I just know the Big Dipper and the Little Dipper, an' of course the Milky Way, an' the North Star. Old Angus told me how to locate it. Him tellin' me about the North Star came in handy once. I was sixteen, and took Silas Calhoun with me to the headwaters of the Little Sou'west Miramichi to fish for trout. Comin' back we got turned around in that big snarl of lakes, dead-waters an' wilderness that stretches from the Miramichi waters to the Tobique. Neither of us had a compass. So finally we put up a lean-to of poles an' spruce bark. Course you're never lost till you think you are, if you get what I mean. It clouded over that night an' rained for two days. We had nothin' to eat but trout and a bit of bread. Then the sky cleared during the third night, an' I began lookin' up an' around trying to locate the North Star; an' when I did I couldn't believe my eyes, because I thought it and the Big Dipper and Little Dipper must have shifted. I was like a man who thinks his compass is wrong. An' Silas was like me: thought north was in another direction. But finally I come to my senses when I remembered that Angus had told me that the North Star doesn't move its position—or only a little. So I cut a stick, set it in the ground, made a cleft in the top, and put in another stick pointin' in the direction of that star. When daylight come we took our course and in no time reached the outlet of Rocky Brook Lake. Then all was easy goin'. The trouble with so many of us is we don't use our heads. When we come to a brook we oughter remember that it's sure to lead to some other body of water, and follow it. No, Doctor, I was often lost in London an' other cities, but only that once in the woods, an' that once taught me a lesson I've never forgot."

"Even the longest river flows somewhere safe to sea,"[85] I said.
"Exactly," said Bill.

* * *

The night was chilly, as July nights often are in the valley of the Miramichi, but we were warm in our sleeping bags. I am usually a light sleeper, and on this night awakened to hear a gnawing sound outside the tent. Getting quietly out of my nest (for I did not want to arouse Bill) I opened the tentflap, stepped outside, and saw the dim form of a porcupine waddling into the dark. It had been busy at Bill's axe-handle which, through long use, had absorbed salt from his hands. The porcupine is a lover of salt.

I reached inside the tent, got my mackinaw, put more wood on the red coals of the camp-fire then, as it broke into flame, sat down on the seat I had earlier removed from the canoe, filled and lighted my pipe, and, with mind serene, picked out the various constellations that, for untold ages, had kept their strange formation.

Across the hurrying river the trees formed a dark mass: only a few distinguishable one from the other. But on the crest of the ridge the symmetrical tops of the sombre spruces (like bell-shaped pagodas of China and Siam) stood out in bold relief against the lighter horizon.

How lovely the night! I sat entranced. And after a short time Dawn, immortal goddess garbed in vestments gray, and taper lit, with silent, measured step stole down the valley slopes. But for yet a little while proud Venus held her flaming beacon in that huge immensity we call the sky, then faded like a dream. And objects near and far took on vague form; but finally, as though a curtain were being slowly withdrawn, the ever-increasing light revealed in sharper outline the trees, the rocks, the bushes on the shores, and the low spirals of mist that raced the hurrying waters. *(23)*

Back of the tent the enchanting notes of a swamp sparrow rose in matutinal praise to the ever-recurring miracle. The grass and shrubs and ferns and flowering weeds were strung with globes of dew. A doe deer, and twin fawns in coats of red with spots of white, appeared like phantoms on

---

85   Swinburne, "The Garden of Proserpine". GFC has adapted the line to the context: in the original it is the "weariest" river that "winds" to sea.

Chapter XX

the farther shore. Far overhead a crow drew a black line above the pinnacles of spruce and pine. Then in the east the sky was flushed with rosy-gold; and soon, in regal splendour, the sun walked his old pathway beneath the inverted bowl of azure space.

So, in my younger days, in darkened room on winter nights, I had seen the lamps lighted; at first the wicks turned low until the heat had warmed the cold, glass globes, and in the faint glow all things were indistinct. Then, with the wicks turned higher, the furniture and ornaments and books and pictures on the walls stood revealed in all their homely loveliness.

* * *

Behind me I heard Bill's voice: "How long have you been up?"

I told him, and he said: "You should have woken me."

He came outside, stood a few moments looking at the fire, then picked up his axe and muttered: "Porcupine, eh! Was it the little critter that roused you?"

"Yes," I answered. "But I wouldn't have missed sitting here and watching the day dawn for much gold."

"Yes," he said, "I understand. It's as though God had talked to you."

The river had dropped another foot and cleared itself of silt, so after breakfast we got into the canoe and Bill dropped me down to the first of the two best casts below the mouth of the brook.

I had tied on a double No. 4 thunder and lightning. Personally I prefer the double to the single hook; and in all of my experience on half a dozen salmon rivers the guides have preferred it. Most of them have fished all their lives since their early teens, and I bow to their judgment in most things pertaining to the sport.

We didn't get a rise at the first drop, so Bill upped anchor, allowed the canoe to slip its length below, again anchored it, and I resumed casting, gradually lengthening line until I had about fifty feet out. The fly had only swung a couple of yards down-stream, and was sunk deep, when I noticed a small "boil" that could have been made by sea trout or grilse. Then there was a tug that bent the tip and the second joint of my rod in a beautiful curve. The reel screamed, an electric thrill passed over me as I raised the rod: a thrill that few if any but the angler experience. Nothing I know can equal it. You know you are in for a battle which either you or the fish will win. And it has always a good chance of winning.

A man may win large sums on a sweepstake, but except for buying the ticket he has done nothing else. He merely waits, goes about his daily task and then, one day, receives notice that he has won on a certain horse he has never seen. The angler, by his own skill, hooks a fish and enjoys the thrill of landing or losing it. Personally I would rather land a fighting Atlantic salmon than win a sweepstake. "The more fool you!" I can hear someone say.

Where were we? Oh yes, I had hooked a salmon on the second drop below McKiel Brook. Evidently it had been given new life by the rise of water. It raced like a torpedo close to the right hand shore, leaped, then ran downstream, taking out all my casting line and half of the backing before Bill had time to pull up anchor, fasten the rope, seize his setting-pole and follow it. I do not like to play a fish on a long line, because then it has a better chance of getting the leader, if not a considerable length of line, around a boulder and breaking away. Bill knew this as well as I did, so he got even with the fish on the off side while I reeled in until there was no further drag by the water and I could *feel* the fish. At this it darted upstream where we wanted it, because a fish is more easily killed in that position.

There was little talk between us. Bill knew what to do and did it without any fuss. Nor did he shout instructions, any one of which might be outdated the next moment. For, as I have said before, the salmon is the most unpredictable of the finny tribe. We may decide to reel in the very moment *it* decides to make a furious run in any direction. Then we must take our fingers off the reel-handle, for to attempt to stop the dynamic creature may well mean disaster for us. If it is going upstream the only thing to do is to hold the rod high until the pressure on its mouth causes it to stop its mad career. This one did, and Bill slowly backed the canoe up-stream until we were just a little below it. Then I knew by the quick run it now made that it was going to make another leap. It did, falling back on its side with a resounding smack. I liked that, because I knew it was equal to a body-blow a boxer gives his opponent.

Bill gave a low chuckle. "That'll take some of the wind out of him. He's well hooked."

Chapter XX

The salmon sank to the bottom and swam around in short circles, at the same time shaking its head. I didn't like that, so eased up on the pressure. Almost immediately the circling and jigging ceased, and the fish bore upriver away from centre. Then, with a long run that made my reel screech in protest, it leaped again and struck the water head first, cleaving the surface with such velocity there was scarcely a ripple left. I had, as before, dropped the rod-tip so that, if it chanced to fall on the cast, it would only have the pressure of the reel drum which would, of course, spin off a few more yards of line. I thought the fish would go downstream again; but it didn't: instead it raced straight for the canoe while I reeled in as fast as my fingers could turn the reel-handle to take up the slack line, and Bill drove the canoe close to the shore. Then "feeling" the fish and fearing that it would come too close to handle easily while it was still so full of fight, I swung the tip of the rod to the left, put a finger on the line above the reel-seat, and had the satisfaction of seeing it turn and again make off to the middle of the river, where it rose to the surface and churned the water with its broad tail. Neither did I like that, so I eased the strain on its mouth; it ceased its dangerous antics, wholly submerged, swam slowly up-stream a few rods, again came to the surface and made a boil.

"He's gettin' tired," said Bill, then made the only suggestion during the whole battle: "Don't give'm the butt too hard, Doctor." Just then the salmon turned and came slowly towards us. We could plainly see its long body and small head. Now Bill shipped his setting-pole, let down the anchor, and picking up the big landing net, stepped carefully into the water and waded out a few yards. Then, as the fish came closer, he gently dipped the net while I reeled in very slowly, and held the rod not too high. The fish was only a couple of yards above Bill when, with a sudden swirl that made the reel hum like a gang-saw, it darted to midstream, then headed towards the mouth of the brook.

Bill laughed and said: "There's many a slip between the net and the fish, Doctor." And lifted the net out of the water.

Again the struggle went on. The fish worked its way back and forth, then slowly backed downstream, made another boil, showed part of its white belly, and all the while I was reeling in. It led like a lamb, and once more

Bill put his long-handled net into the water. Nearer and nearer it came until it was over the net. With the quickness of an adder Bill lifted it high into the air, waded back to the canoe, and taking his priest from his hip pocket gave it two or three blows on the head that quieted it for all time. Then he looked at me, grinned, and said: "As old Angus would say: 'it's a bonny fish!' A fifteen-pounder—p'raps seventeen. Want to try for another?"

"No, Bill," I answered, "all we want is enough to eat."

"OK," he said, got into the canoe, poled back to the mouth of the brook, landed, and I climbed the bank to our camping-place, while he remained at the river until he had gutted the fish and removed the gills.

* * *

Before we cooked dinner Bill took the big tin water-kettle, crossed the river, and returned with spring-water. No rare crystal goblet blown by Venetian or Florentine craftsman can reflect the sparkle of spring-water as does the polished inner surface of a tin kettle. I dipped my cup and drank... And here, oh, Spring Water, let me speak your praise: no drink from still or wine-press can compare with you to quench the thirst. In desert wastes weary travellers have clamoured for one cup of your life-giving nectar. And men on shipboard (the water casks empty), their lips cracked, throats parched, and bodies sapped of fluid, have steered to distant coasts to find you and, like worshippers at a shrine, knelt, and drank, then filled their casks.

I have come upon you cupped in moss in shaded dell where erstwhile the shy arbutus bloomed on tangled stems. Or, halfway up the slope of ridge, couched at the base of birch or maple tree. And here, with sigh of thanksgiving, set down my pack, and lying flat, lowered my face, to where your cool depths bubbled translucent globes as clear as any diamond that ever bedecked the crown of king or emperor. With half-held breath I drank, paused, and drank again. Then sated, rose to my feet, blessed you. put on my pack (now lighter) and went my way refreshed, my steps no longer lagging... A draught of cold water... Men have been willing to barter their hopes of paradise for one cup, one thimbleful of you!

* * *

Chapter XX

I do not know of any food better than boiled salmon, and potatoes in their jackets, and tender green peas (at the present time from the tin). Then—not forgetting to feed the birds and a friendly squirrel—to relax with a pipe of good tobacco and peace in our hearts... I will share my rivers but not divorce myself from them so long as I have strength to visit them. Then, while memory remains, try to recapture in fancy the old days and dear companions. Finally, when my earthly substance is no more, I would ask no other bliss than to find in the other world some comparable little river, on whose banks will be the hemlock, the spruce, the white birch, and the lordly pine high above all the others; each bough strung with countless needles set apart like harp strings, for the wind to touch with whispered runes. And last, but not least, innumerable wild flowers and birds... And then, I pray, the kindly shades of Walton, and Wotton, Jo Davers, Cotton and (although he was not a fisherman) the gentle "Elia";[86] and all my old angling friends and the guides I have known and loved.

---

86   Izaak Walton wrote a life of Henry Wotton; quoted Jo Davers; and used to visit Charles Cotton. Charles Lamb's *The Essays of Elia* was one of GFC's favourite books.

CHAPTER XXI

"Do you mind," asked Bill, "if I try for some trout at the mouth of the brook?"

"Not at all," I said. "I'll sit here and watch you. Perhaps later take a nap, or later I may walk up the tote-road and look for raspberries."

"You won't be going far enough to see Jim J.'s ghost," he said, "because it only hangs around Dead Man's Camp. That's eight miles from here."

I smiled and said: "Not that far today. But I'm not afraid of ghosts. Who was Jim J?"

"Well," he answered, "he was an old feller who used to stay summers at the depot-camp an' look after the supplies so bears wouldn't get in an' eat 'em... There was always sugar an' a puncheon of molasses, a barrel of salt pork and other things left over after the winter's lumberin' operations. You know bears like sweets. At any rate Jim J. took sick an' died, an' when some fishermen was goin' up to the lake, they stopped an' found him stretched out on the floor. An' what do you think he'd done?"

I shook my head and said: "I couldn't guess, Bill."

"No," he said, "nor anyone else. Well, before he died he took a lot of plugs of smokin' tobacco, an' cut 'em all up fine with his jack-knife, an' spread it in a circle on the floor. Then he laid himself down in the circle, an' that's how they found him—all surrounded with tobacco. Odd, wasn't it? Would you know why he did that?"

"No, Bill."

"Nor anyone else," he said. "But some think that because he was a great hand to smoke, he'd cut it up so he'd have some until he croaked. But, Doctor, his pipe an' matches was on the window-sill several feet distant.

Anyway, one of the guides went back to Boiestown an' told the police. They come up an' buried him just off the tote-road, an' put up a board with his name on it. Then, the next year, a priest come all the way from Boiestown, said the burial service an' sprinkled some holy water over the grave... Good of him, wasn't it?"

"Yes, Bill, especially considering the distance he came... You say Jim J.'s ghost has been seen?"

"Oh yes," he answered. "Lumbermen an' river-drivers an' fishermen have seen it. It was settin' on the side of the grave holdin' out a pipe in its hand just as if it was beggin' for tobacco. Once my chum Silas Calhoun an' his brother was goin' in to the lake, an' just as dusk come on they saw it. Like you he wasn't scared of ghosts, so he tossed a plug of tobacco to Jim J.'s ghost where it was sittin' near the grave. Then he an' his brother went on. They stayed a day and a half at the lake, caught a lot of trout, then started back to the river where they'd left their canoe. Well, when they come to the grave the plug of tobacco was gone. As Silas later said to me: 'No bear or any other animal would take tobacco, so it must have been Jim J.' After that, whenever Silas was goin' that way he left a plug of tobacco. You wouldn't believe, Doctor, that a ghost could smoke?"

"No, Bill," I answered. "But did you ever see Jim J.'s ghost?"

He shook his head. "No, Doctor, you've got to believe in ghosts to see 'em."

* * *

So Bill took my trout rod, tied a Parmachenee Belle on the cast, got into the canoe, set it just above the mouth of the brook, anchored and began fishing.

I lighted my pipe, sat down in front of the tent and watched him. If patience be a virtue, Bill certainly would qualify for any reward it chooses to confer. For fully fifteen minutes he continued to cast without getting a rise, then he hooked a nice trout—a half-pounder—and soon had it in the canoe. After that, while I was watching him, he took six more. Then, instead of taking a nap or going up the portage road to hunt for raspberries, I got my notebook and wrote down the story of the ghost of Dead Man's Camp.

* * *

Chapter XXI

Late in the afternoon we caught another salmon, a twelve-pounder. I said to Bill: "My wife prefers smoked salmon to boiled, fried or baked. Could you set up a frame of stakes, like your friend Angus, and smoke it over them?"

He smiled. "I'll do that," he said; "an' better that contraption made by old Angus, bless his soul. But first I'll do a little surgery." So when we got to shore, the good-natured fellow scraped off all the scales, removed the head and tail, split the fish down the back to one side of centre, and cut out the spinal column with its attached bones as deftly as any surgeon can perform an operation. Then he washed off all the blood, rubbed salt into the orange-coloured flesh, folded the parts together, enclosed the whole in birchbark and set the bundle in the tent so that no animal would molest it.

That night Bill asked me if I'd like to hear him sing "The Miramichi Fire",—the old ballad my mother had sung to me many times when I was a child; and Henry, our cook, had sung it one memorable night when Larry and I and Bill and Charlie had camped at Slate Island. I was quite ready to hear it again. So Bill began.

It was a vivid description of the most tragic happening in the history of New Brunswick. The fire started in the tinder-dry forest, and travelling with express speed extended one hundred and ten miles along the valley of the Miramichi, consuming an area of six thousand square miles. Five hundred human beings along the valley were either suffocated by smoke or perished in the flames, while countless numbers of domestic and wild animals and birds met a like fate. My grandfather was twelve years of age at the time. When past ninety, and I was a child of eight or ten, he told me that the whole sky was covered with a canopy of smoke turned blood-red by the sea of leaping flames. The flames caused a terrific wind. From the depths of the forest came prolonged rumblings and explosions as great pine and other trees crashed to earth. He told me that many of the settlers who escaped death did so by running to the river and wading in to their middles, holding their children in their arms; and that moose, bear and other wild creatures crowded in beside them. The heat was oppressive. Cinders and ashes rained down on the water, and the lye killed thousands of salmon and other fish. The next morning the shores were lined with them. He told me the people thought the end of the world had come.

Song of the Reel

When my grandfather had ended, my youthful mind was so convinced that the Miramichi fire had been sent by the Almighty as a warning of a greater catastrophe to happen in my lifetime, that I promised myself to be a good boy from that day forward.

* * *

The next morning, after breakfast, Bill washed the excess salt from the fish which he laid across two or three pieces of firewood so that it faced the sun, and asked me to sit beside it and keep off flies. Then he dug a little hole about two feet and a half in diameter in the sandy soil, and taking his axe went into the woods back of the camp. In a few minutes he returned with an armful of stakes cut from maple saplings. These, at a distance of ten or twelve inches one from the other, he drove into the ground in a circle about the fire-hole, so that they extended upwards about six feet.

As he worked he sang one of his favourite hymns, the refrain of which I well remember:

> *Brighten the corner where you are,*
> *Brighten the corner where you are,*
> *Some poor struggling sinner*
> *You may guide across the bar,*
> *Brighten the corner where you are*
> *Right in the corner where you are.*[87]

Again he went into the woods, and when next he came back he carried a couple of rolls of spruce bark, and with them completely surrounded the circle of stakes. Then from the lower edge of the bark he cut out a portion about twelve inches square. This, he explained, was the door of his wigwam. He cut some alder saplings the required length, carefully spaced them about three inches apart across the top of his wigwam and laid over them the slab of salmon with the flesh-side down. Now he made a little fire of dry wood and chips in the bottom of the fire-hole, when it was burning nicely

---

87 Early 20th-century evangelist and crusader against drink. GFC also quotes this hymn in *Six Salmon Rivers—and Another*.

Chapter XXI

laid over it some damp moss and covered the door with bark. The result was that the smoke was carried upwards against the slab of salmon. Then, with one of his winning smiles, he said: "I guess that'll do the job, Doctor."

* * *

You can always rely on a New Brunswick guide to turn his inventive genius to overcome all sorts of difficulties. Which reminds me that during the Great War of 1914-18 a certain general wanted a wide river bridged for the passage of troops, guns and equipment. He sent for the colonel of the Brighton engineers, a battalion composed wholly of hardened New Brunswick lumberjacks, river-drivers and guides recruited from the upper St John River Valley. The general gave the colonel three days to do the job. It should take that long at least.

The colonel returned to his battalion, had the men paraded before him and told them what was required. Then, in a ringing voice, added: "Now Canucks, we're going to have that river bridged by noon tomorrow, so let's get at it." So those New Brunswick lads—all descendants of Scots, Irish, Welsh and English—their colonel working with them in his shirt sleeves—began the job. They had a big circular saw; they made a crib to hold it, jacked up the rear end of a truck, removed one of the tires, fastened some belting from it to the axle of the crib holding the saw, and started the engine. With this hastily constructed apparatus they sawed out lumber the required length to form the floor of the bridge. In the meantime, empty oil drums were set in the water and over these were laid long lengths of deal securely fastened with heavy ropes.

Swiftly the work progressed. The men worked all night by electric flares, and by noon the following day the river was spanned.

The colonel (his name was Melville, from Florenceville, on the St John River) rang up the general and said: "The bridge is ready, sir. You can move over it at any time."

"What! What! Impossible!—You mean it's actually ready for transport? I gave you three days to construct it."

"Yes," said Colonel Melville, "but we took the liberty to do the job in less than that time." Then, with a bit of droll New Brunswick humour: "I hope you don't mind, sir."

"Oh—ahem! Not at all, Colonel Melville. But, dammit, the thing was impossible! Ahem—my sincere thanks and congratulations, Colonel Melville... You are quite sure the bridge will stand up to the guns and heavy transport?"

"It'll stand up to the combined weight of a herd of elephants," returned the colonel.

* * *

Every hour or so Bill inspected his fire, laid on more wood and chips and covered it with damp moss; and got up several times during the night to add more. By the following late afternoon the slab of salmon was smoked a beautiful seal-brown, and when I took a gobbet of it, and put it into my mouth, it was ambrosial, both in odour and taste, fit for the gods.

That night we sat up late, talking of this and that, while I repeated to him the yarn Harry Dale had told me years before about the strange untying of the horses in the hovel in the Kilmarnock woods, and of the equally puzzling actions of Smoky-Joe.

When I had ended, Bill drew a long breath and said: "Queer, wasn't it?—I mean about Smoky-Joe. I've heard of horses comin' untied in the woods. But that about Smoky-Joe is just about as fandanderous as the one I told you about the devil shakin' the man to pieces."

I suppose his "fandanderous" meant spooky or unexplainable. He—like the beloved Lewis Carroll—had an extraordinary facility for making up odd names.

* * *

We were up early the following morning, cooked and ate breakfast, broke camp, packed the dunnage in the canoe and then, after I was seated, Bill picked up his long-handled setting-pole and began the return journey upriver.

Scores of times in the succeeding years, I have relived in fancy that enchanting outing; as I have relived others. I have but to close my eyes to see the river; the innumerable rocks and pebbles which flooded its bottom; the stately trees that lined the hills and came down to the shore, their whole

Chapter XXI

form reflected in the water; the flowers along the banks; the birds and their songs; the little and big animals we saw. In fancy I can hear the dull thud of Bill's setting-pole on the rocky bottom; feel the motion of the canoe and hear the wash of the water against its bow and along its sides as he drove it forward with untiring strength. I remember the places at which we paused to get a drink of spring or cold brook-water—more thirst-quenching than anything else in this wonderful world. Then on again. At the Narrows—a place where the greater force of the river rushes between huge granite boulders, Bill had to do some clever manoeuvring—for the five-foot-wide passage is uphill all the way, while barely a canoe length above, sharp to the right, the current rushes with tremendous force, then with equal velocity makes an abrupt turn to the right, then another turn to the left between the two lower boulders. Surmounting the lower passage, Bill had to snub and hold the canoe until the bow swung at an abrupt angle towards the upper boulder between which and the shore—only three or four yards distant—the water tumbled in riotous fury. But he knew his business. As the avalanche of water hurled its might against the left side of the bow, he thrust down his setting-pole, straightened out the canoe, met the current head on, held it quivering for a few seconds then, with a few mighty pushes surmounted the crest of the cascade and in another few seconds was well above that dangerous place.

I had been apprehensive that the canoe might swing against the two lower boulders and be broken in two or upset. Now, in safety, I turned to Bill and said: "That was good work, Bill."

He grinned: "I always like bad water," he said; and taking a plug of tobacco from his breast pocket bit off a portion with his strong teeth.

Lewey Rapids was bad—too *bad* for Bill or any other canoeman, so we carried the canoe over the ledge of rock on the right to the basin above.

* * *

We paused at the camping-site below Lake Brook, made a little fire, "boiled the kettle", made tea, ate lunch. Then, filling our pipes we had a quiet smoke, and again embarked.

Coming opposite Lewey Mountain, I suggested to Bill that we climb it. He said: "OK—that will be fine."

We landed, passed the grave where the remains of old Lewey (or some other voyageur) rest within sight of the river, and entered the woods that led to the foot of the mountain. Reaching it we travelled wholly on great slabs of granite which, at some remote period in the world's upheaval, had been deposited from base to summit on its southern slopes.

Reaching the crest we had a panoramic view of flat country, high hills or mountains, and lakes. To the south were Miramichi and Napadogan lakes, set like blue sapphires in the primitive wilderness. Along the horizon squadrons of clouds drew their fleecy-white skirts in endless procession.

Below us, on the right, the long, low barren, covered with cat spruce, sheep laurel and other shrubs, stretched to the river which, two miles farther on, was crossed by the railroad bridge at Half-Moon Cove. On the left shore stood two or three small houses—the first we had seen since we had passed under the bridge a few days before. Suddenly Bill spoke: "See, Doctor, there's a moose!" I looked where he pointed, and presently—although it was half a mile distant—saw the big creature, its wide antlers spread back over its fore-shoulders, swinging with measured trot across the barren to the growth of timber below the western slope of the mountain whereon we stood.

Other than this the whole world about us seemed to sleep. We heard no sound of bird, nor saw any, until, just as we were about to descend the mountain, our attention was attracted to a solitary osprey circling high over the distant water. It swept in long curves, dipping, banking—the very epitome of poetic motion. I had often seen ospreys fishing in other waters, but this solitary bird in this slumbering wilderness seemed to intensify the profound and primitive solitude—as though the world had been pushed back to the dawn of time.

Suddenly it ceased its circling, remained poised in space a few moments, neither losing nor gaining height while its broad pinions beat the ether. Then, with legs and talons extended downwards, it dropped straight towards the water. We could distinctly hear the splash it made as it struck, and then it disappeared for a few moments, when it emerged with a large fish in its talons; and, holding it on a line with its body, flew on labouring wings to the opposite shore and was lost to view.

Slowly, stepping from one granite rock to another, we passed down the primitive causeway, and near the base of the mountain got a brief glimpse of a huge black bear before it vanished among the scrub bushes. "Lewey", said Bill, "is a great place for bears. They find spaces between the rocks an' den up all winter. I've trapped many of them an' shot a few."

* * *

Again in the canoe he poled steadily up-river. Above Half-Moon the going was easier until we came to Black Rapids, where Bill had to put his back into the work. Soon we came to Crooked Rapids where we saw a fisherman land a good salmon. Then on to the Forks I know so well, and the little camp that, far into the night, has so often echoed to laughter and song.

Twilight had settled over the river. We unloaded the canoe, which we took out of the water and turned bottom-up on the grassy landing, then carried the dunnage up the incline to the camp, opened the door, soon had a cheerful fire in the stove, then fried bacon and trout, made a pot of tea and ate a late supper.

Night closed in. There were three big rocking chairs, the seats of ash-splints. One of the broad arms contains the initials—N. P. G. July 12, 1921, which Doctor Grant had cut in the wood that far-off day. I sat down in it, Bill in one of the others. We lighted our pipes, smoked and talked. What about? Of course fishing, and running the river both when it was at freshet height and during its low, summer level, and in the autumn when the maples, which cover the slumbering mountain slopes, are a blaze of glory; a symphony of golds and reds and purples.

What a lovely, enchanting river. As Mr. Courtley, (then Commissioner of Canada's National Parks Sites) said thirty-five years ago: "I have seen most of the important rivers in Canada. The Miramichi is the most extraordinary of them all in its physiographic features."

"You know," said Bill, "it don't do to criticise a man's style of fishin' or his outfit. I mean if you're not guidin' him. If you are, then it's all right; 'cause if he don't know much about the game it's a guide's duty to tell him a few things. Oncet a feller I wasn't guidin' asked me what I thought of his rod, the way he was castin'. I told him square, and I don't think he liked it. Oh, he was a nice feller, but I had a feelin' he didn't want the truth. It made me think of my Aunt Libby, the great talker I told you about. Well, Aunt Libby was the best cook between Boiestown an' Newcastle. Her biscuits would melt in your mouth. She had a cousin, named Eliza, that used to come real often afternoons an' stay to supper. An' every time she put on some of her new-baked biscuits or rolls I guess they're called. An' each time Eliza ate one an' said how good they were. An' Aunt Libby always said: 'Oh, they're not as good as I baked a few days ago.' At last Eliza got fed up with Aunt Libby sayin' that, 'cause she knew darn well that her cousin was fishin' after more compliments. So next time she come of course there was the usual plate of biscuits or rolls on the table. She ate one an' didn't say how nice it was. (As a matter of fact Eliza told my mother that they wasn't up to par; an' she thought Aunt Libby had put in a little too much soda in them.) Then Aunt Libby said: 'Ain't they all right, Eliza?' 'Well,' says Eliza, 'they're not *too* bad. But I've had better.' At that Aunt Libby, who had a hot temper, blazed at her: 'Eliza, you know damn well they're the best you ever ate!'"

Bill paused a moment then said: "Well, Doctor, most people are like my Aunt Libby. When they ask you if you don't think their new baby is the sweetest an' prettiest thing in the world, they don't want you to say it ain't."

* * *

Bill and I had a good sleep that night. The following morning, about ten o'clock, he put his canoe into the water, picked up a couple of boulders about twenty or thirty pounds each and set them in the bow to balance the canoe, then shipped his pack, axe, smoke-blackened boiling kettle and sleeping bag. He would, he said, make Burnt Hill that evening, spend the night beneath his canoe, and complete the journey next day. He took my hand in his strong grip and said: "So long, Doctor. The whole trip has been wonderful. An' don't forget that if ever you want me again I'll be with you." Then, with a smile: "I hope I didn't tire you with my long yarns."

"I enjoyed every bit of them," I assured him.

He lighted his pipe, picked up his setting-pole, stepped into the canoe, pushed it off then, standing upright, poled downstream, *(24a)* leaving a long V-shape wake in the glassy water. *(24b)*

I was loath to have him depart. At the mouth of the Bogan he half turned and waved a hand in final farewell: I waved mine in return, then the canoe slid around the bend. A wave of loneliness swept over me... I can imagine that some of my readers (but surely not fishermen) may charge me

Chapter XXI

with being unduly sentimental. So be it. If loving my friends and feeling a deep regret that moves me almost to tears when they leave me be a sign of sentimentality only permissible in women, then I accept the charge. But genuine friendship is all too rare in this world, and worth more than gold or other possessions. It represents something that is of the spirit—infinitely precious; and life to me would not be worth living if I did not have it. As Emerson says: "I hate the prostitution of the name of friendship to signify modish and worldly alliances. I much prefer the company of ploughboys and tin-pedlars to the silken and perfumed amity which only celebrates its days of encounter by a frivolous display, by rides in a curricle and dinners at the best taverns. The end of friendship that can be joined… It is for aid and comfort through all the relations and passages of life and death. It is fit for serene days and graceful gifts and country rambles, but also for rough roads and hard fare, shipwreck, poverty and persecution."[88]

---

[88] From *Essays: First Series* (1841), "Essay VI : Friendship"

CHAPTER XXII

Perhaps no member of the human family can recall events of the past with greater clarity than the fisherman, especially he who has fished since early boyhood. He remembers the first brook he waded, armed with an alder pole and worm-baited hook, and landing his first trout. Having an observant nature, he remembers the fallen logs that spanned the little stream; the moss-covered boulders; the odours of wild mint, sweet birch and ferns—all the damp, enchanting smells that go with a brook. Perhaps it is possible that he knew little about the different species of birds (of course he knew the robin), but he remembers that often they added their melody to the lilt of the brook over its pebble-strewn bed.

We can find such memories recalled in haunting prose by such famous anglers as Henry van Dyke in his *Little Rivers* and *Fisherman's Luck*,[89] W.H. Blake's *Brown Waters*, his *In A Fishing Country*,[90] and in John Buchan's *Memory Hold the Door*, in which he tells of fishing some Highland burn or little river; experiences that were to him "not a pastime but a way of life."[91]

* * *

---

89 The former was published in 1895, the latter in 1899.

90 1915; 1922. Blake's *A Fisherman's Creed* (1923) was perhaps GFC's favourite angling book.

91 John Buchan, 1st Baron Tweedsmuir, a Scottish novelist, was Governor General of Canada from 1935 to 1940. His memoir, *Memory Hold-the-Door* (1940), describes his love of angling. His son, the second Lord Tweedsmuir, also an ardent angler, wrote the enthusiastic review of *Six Salmon Rivers* mentioned in an earlier note.

Song of the Reel

From the dormitory of the mind comes back a day when, fourteen years of age, I fished the lower reaches of Marven's Brook, and from beyond a sharp bend of the stream heard a voice singing some words I later learned were part of the deathless love song *A la Claire Fontaine:*

> *Unto a fountain clear*
> *I went one summer day,*
> *So cool I found the water*
> *I plunged into the spray.*
> *A long time have I loved you*
> *And I will love alway.*

Then I rounded the bend and saw a bare-legged, barefooted, hatless girl of perhaps seventeen years, standing on the tree-embowered bank fishing with alder pole and worm-baited hook. Her face was beautiful, tanned nutbrown; her golden hair plaited in a long braid; one unruly curl strayed over her brow. Even as I paused and gazed at her, entranced, she pulled a ten-inch trout from beneath a half-submerged log, deftly caught it in her left hand, removed the hook, and with her thumb in its mouth bent its head backward, thus killing it, and strung it on a forked branch that contained fully a dozen other fish. Then she turned and saw me. My unexpected appearance must have startled her, for her brown eyes widened. Then, with a bewitching smile, and in a low contralto voice no less musical than that of the brook, she said: "Hullo... What luck?"

I told her, and she said: "Good!" Then: "If you want to fish below me, will you please wade to shore so that you won't disturb my pool?"

So I slowly waded to the opposite bank, then paused to watch her thread another worm on her hook, again cast near the sunken log, again land a trout.

I passed between the boles of the trees and presently heard her lovely voice:

> *So cool I found the water*
> *I plunged into the spray;*
> *And underneath an oak tree*

Chapter XXII

In the cool freshness lay.
A long time have I loved you,
And I will love alway.

I fished Marven's Brook scores of times after that but never again saw her. Perhaps she was the reincarnation of Daphne, beloved of Apollo, who fled from his advances, was changed into a laurel tree, thenceforth the favourite tree of the Sun God. But in fancy I can still see that lithe form; the brown face and bare legs; the braided golden hair and the curl that fell over her brow.

* * *

Arthur Slipp was an ardent angler—almost as soon as he was able to walk his father had initiated him in the art—and an expert woodsman, for he had an uncanny sense of direction. We had fished Ayers, Fish and Trout Lakes, Nine Mile Brook, the Kilmarnock deadwater—all deep in the heart of the wilderness of north-central New Brunswick.

One evening, just as dusk was drawing her mantle over the forest, we had reached the end of the quick water on Nine Mile Brook where it merges into a long dead-water. To retrace our steps up the brook and reach the tote road that leads to Ayers Lake, where Arthur had a small camp of peeled logs, meant a six-mile hike. So pointing north-westwards Arthur said: "We can cut off three miles by going over the Munro Block. Will you follow me?"

"Anywhere," I said. So he left the brook, winding his way between the boles of the trees—a forest as primitive as it was before ever William the Norman landed on the coast of Kent. I followed close behind him and soon black night enveloped us. Once, during our climb up the side of the high ridge, Arthur stumbled and fell forward on his knees. A moment later he rose to his feet, turned and held out to me a deer antler shed by the animal the year before.

A half-hour later we reached a narrow trail which we followed around the lower end of the lake, and in fifteen minutes were safe in the little camp where we cooked some of our trout and with bread and tea had a hearty meal.

Song of the Reel

* * *

It was the latter part of June, more than half a century ago,[92] that Arthur and I boarded his canvas-covered canoe and began our trip down the St John River to the mouth of Big Pokiok, twenty-eight miles below our home town of Woodstock. We had a tent, blankets, frying pan, two boiling kettles and enough food to last a week.

After the ice breaks up in the spring on the numerous large tributaries and releases their spate of waters, the St John River often rises twenty feet in a few days, and a stupendous flood, that has often reached a volume of 200,000 cubic feet per second, rushes with resistless force to Fundy Bay, inundating islands and low-lying intervales on its way. Then the late-spawning salmon, that have been trapped by the ice during the previous early freeze-up, drop down to the salt water and re-clean themselves. It does not take long: only a few weeks, then, in the late fall or the next spring they speed back to their old spawning grounds once more to perform their allotted task.

But when the water has dropped to summer level the St. John—for its greater length—is a gently flowing river. The exceptions are few and far between; just enough to give it variety and excitement. It trips gaily, with a little song, over boulder-strewn or gravelly bars, to smoothen out into long, deep, still, mirror-like stretches that seem to be devoid of all movement; then, as though rejuvenated with its rest, ripples and chatters its way over yet another boulder-strewn or gravelly bar. Thus it was that far-off day that Arthur and I began our memorable trip.

How wonderful it is to be twenty-two years of age! All the world was before us and we were as happy as larks. I remember that we sang a good part of the way. Arthur paddled stern and I bow. Past island, intervale and upland; the islands ringed about with elm and butternut trees; the broad intervales and uplands under cultivation, but upon the distant ridges tall spruce, pine and fir trees stood in serried ranks, their branches silhouetted against the blue haze that stretched like a vast carpet along the far horizon.

---

92 Probably in 1906.

Chapter XXII

We disturbed several flocks of wild ducks—many of them mergansers which were fishing for salmon parr in the riffles. Occasionally a kingfisher plunged from a leaning tree after a small fish. Once we saw an osprey circling and dipping high over the water, searching with far-seeing eyes for its evening meal in the pellucid depths far below.

* * *

Shortly before dark we landed in the cove at Meductic flat where, even before the coming of the white man to the river, the prehistoric Indians had their village and palisaded fort, and before going on the war-path daubed their faces with red ochre, ate the dog-feast and danced and chanted their songs that extolled feats of valour against their enemies.

We set up our tent on the sandy beach just below the ancient cemetery of the Maliseets whose descendants are now scattered. After the peace that marked the end of the American Revolutionary War, numerous members of the Loyalist Regiments migrated to the St John River where they received grants of land, cut down enough trees to build log houses, then gradually pushed back the primeval forest and sowed their crops. Meductic Flat was granted to a man of De Lancy's brigade but, the Indians having refused to vacate their ancient village-site, commissioners were sent by government to reason with them. The commissioners landed and were met by the chief of the Maliseets and his tribesmen arrayed in feathered bonnets and all the panoply of war. After some parleying the spokesman for the commissioners said: "By what right do you hold this land?" The chief, tall and straight as an arrowshaft, half turned, pointed with a majestic gesture to the cemetery, and said in ringing tones: "There lie the bones of our fathers. There lie the bones of our children. I have spoken."

To such an answer the commissioner could make no suitable reply, and he and his companions departed with more haste than dignity.

Half a century later the Indians were induced to remove from Meductic. Some went to the mouth of Tobique, a few to a small reservation two miles below Woodstock, the remainder to a reservation a few miles above the city of Fredericton.[93] And then white settlers farmed the land that for untold centuries had been the site of their most important stronghold on the St John River.

* * *

We made a fire, boiled the kettle and had supper while darkness was settling over the valley. Afterwards we sat and talked until almost midnight. Just before getting into our blankets we stepped outside to view the night. How beautiful the heavens! We could faintly see the Galaxy or Via Lactea—the Milky Way:

> *A broad and ample road, whose dust is gold*
> *And pavement stars, as stars to thee appear*
> *Seen in the Galaxy, that milky way*
> *Which nightly as a circling zone thou seest*
> *Powdered with stars.*[L]

The Indians call it the road or trail by which the dead travel to the happy-hunting grounds. In her chair was Cassiopeia—that wife of Cepheus, king of Ethiopia—who earned the wrath of the sea god by boasting that the beauty of her daughter, Andromeda, surpassed that of the sea-nymphs, and was transferred to the heavens and placed among the stars.

Then, still gazing into the north, we saw the Pole Star, known by the Micmac and Maliseet Indians as the star that does not move. The star that—long before the Northmen had set their course by it to Iceland and Greenland—had been the constant guide of nomads of the desert-wastes before ever the compass, the astrolabe or the cross-staff had been invented.

> *Her constellations come, and climb the heavens, and go…*
> *Star of the Pole! and thou dost see them set.*

---

93   A scant century later, white politicians flooded the Maliseet's sacred burial ground and the whole rich intervale with the waters of the Mactaquac headpond.

L   Milton: *Paradise Lost*, [Book 7, ll. 577-581].

Chapter XXII

Alone in thy cold skies,
Thou keep'st thy old unmoving station yet,
Nor join'st the dances of that glittering train...
On thy unaltering blaze
The half-wrecked mariner, his compass lost,
Fixes his steady gaze,
And steers, undoubting, to the friendly coast;
And they who stray in perilous wastes by night
Are glad when thou dost shine to guide their footsteps right.[M]

Infinite peace lay over the valley and in our hearts. The world hardly seemed to breathe. Regretfully we withdrew our eyes from the heavens and went into the tent...

I awakened about one o'clock to find the camp-fire a bed of glowing embers, and Arthur not beside me. I called his name; no answer. I rose and went outside the tent, threw some pieces of driftwood on the coals, and again called his name. There was no answering: "Hullo—here I am." Only the notes of a cow-bell from the opposite hillside half a mile distant, the quavering "baa" of a sheep, and the chuckling of the Betsy Rapids along the farther shore. All else was as silent as the ashes of the Maliseets in the little cemetery behind me. A low mist hung over the river and suddenly, with sinking heart, I noticed that the canoe was no longer drawn up on the beach. Had my friend gone out on the river, perhaps upset in the rapids? I imagined myself going home as soon as day dawned and breaking the news of his disappearance to his parents. Quite sure that the worst had happened I walked back and forth in an agony of mind. Then I heaped more wood on the fire and sat down to await the dawn...

Perhaps an hour passed then, to my joy, I heard the sound of a paddle against the gunwale of the canoe, and its shadowy form emerged from the mist. I ran over the cobbly beach in time to receive from Arthur's hand our ten-quart water kettle. "Careful," he said, "don't spill it!" Then he drew the canoe up on the beach and we returned to the tent.

M Bryant: "Hymn to the North Star," [1825].

He had crossed Betsy Rapids, climbed the high hillside pasture, driven one of the cows into an angle of the cedar-rail fence and milked her. He gave a low chuckle as he ended the story of his adventure, and added: "I fancy the farmer will think she's going dry."

I reproached him for going off without telling me, told him how worried I had been when I awoke and found the canoe gone. He said he was sorry but, since I was so sound asleep, he hadn't wanted to rouse me. He admitted that he had had some difficulty getting around a long sheer-boom of logs that set out diagonally into the rapids from the opposite shore. "But," he added, "we'll have milk and cream for breakfast.

* * *

We awakened just as dawn on "gray-sandalled feet"[94] was stealing into the valley, and going down to the river washed ourselves, returned to the tent, laid some wood on the few yet-glowing embers of our camp-fire, fried bacon and eggs and made tea.

As we ate, the sun pushed his crimson crown over the far horizon and presently, in royal splendour, stepped off into the blue: an age-old miracle that ever aroused in both of us a sense of awe and wonder. It drove the last wreaths of mist from the river. The Betsy Rapids seemed less vocal than during the night. From a farmstead chimney up the opposite shore greyish wood-smoke told us that other civilised beings had awakened and were beginning a new day.

* * *

After washing up our few tin cups and plates and scouring the frying pan with sand, we walked up the beach to the mouth of Hay's Brook, fished it for a distance of almost two miles, caught three dozen trout that averaged about eight inches in length, then left the stream and entered a hayfield in which were countless wild strawberries.

---

94 I cannot find the source of this quotation. It may be a recollection of the line, "The dawn with silver-sandalled feet" in Oscar Wilde's poem "The Harlot's House."

Chapter XXII

Evidently the field had not been ploughed for three or more years, for the grass was thin with many white daisies, buttercups with petals of burnished gold, and those beautiful little flowers known as the blue-eyed grass with their bright yellow centres. And there were bluets, variously known as *Indian Ladies, Blue Bonnets* and *Blue-eyed Babies.*

We knelt close to the earth, where slender stems held sometimes one, sometimes as many as half a dozen of the ruby-coloured luscious fruit whose faint fragrance slightly resembles that of its cousin the rose. We gathered them one by one, staining our fingers crimson, and dropped them into our hats. Occasionally a nectar-laden bumblebee droned past us to plunder yet another flowering weed. White-winged as well as varied-coloured butterflies made short journeys—as though they were not fully awake. Twice we disturbed to reluctant flight two song sparrows which, although they and their kind have charted the airy highways from continent to continent with as much accuracy as ever did the mariner with his compass, still persist in the precarious business of nesting on the ground. From another field (hidden by a line of distant trees) drifted the sound of a mowing machine where the farmer was reaping his crop of hay. The sun looked like an immense crimson coin pasted against the background of blue. We saw no sign of any human being. We might have been stranded on a planet that had no other life than that of the birds, the butterflies, the droning bees, and the owner of the now distant, now nearer, but wholly invisible mowing-machine.

* * *

Back at the tent again, with our hats half filled with strawberries, with the trout cleaned and fried to a crisp brown in bacon fat, we ate with that relish which only youth knows. Then we had a goodly portion of the strawberries with cream skimmed from the milk which Arthur had dared the Betsy Rapids to drain from the udder of some unknown farmer's cow. Trout, strawberries with cream and sugar: ambrosia fit for the gods.

I have used previously Dr. Boteler's eulogy of fishing and the wild strawberries as related by Piscator to Venator, but it will bear repeating here: "Indeed, my good scholar, we may say of angling as Dr. Boteler said of strawberries 'Doubtless God could have made a better berry, but doubtless

God never did."⁹⁵ And so, if I may be the judge, God never did make a more calm, quiet, innocent recreation than angling."ᴺ

John Buchan (now gone to his eternal rest), erstwhile Governor-General of Canada, wrote: "If fishing, as I maintain, be not only a craft but a way of life, then a fisherman must begin young."⁹⁶

I believe that I fulfil this requirement. My father and mother were born on the Miramichi—one of the world's finest salmon rivers. Both as girl and young woman my mother had fished the brook which flowed through her father's farm, and caught many sea trout from the river during the spring run. So love of the sport was in my blood, and I began fishing at the age of four.

Marc Lescarbot (a French lawyer and student of antique literature), who came to Acadia in 1606 with the Baron de Poutrincourt, lived at Port Royal until the autumn of 1607, and wrote his *Histoire de la Nouvelle France,* takes Plato to task for his opinion regarding fish and fishermen. Says Lescarbot, in his quaint phraseology: *And in this exercise (fishing) did Mark Anthony delight himself very much; notwithstanding Plato's reason, who forming his commonwealth hath forbidden his citizens the exercise of fishing, as ignoble, and illiberal, and fosterer of idleness, wherein he did grossly equivocate, specially when he chargeth fishermen with idleness, which is so evident I will not vouchsafe to refute him.*

The dear old scholar also looses a shaft at Pythagoras, that long-haired Samian philosopher who believed that he was the reincarnation of all the gods, and also decried the use of fish for food.

And I find, says Lescarbot, by *my reckoning that Pythagoras was very ignorant, forbidding in his fair golden sentences the use of fish without distinction. One may excuse him that fish, being dumb, hath conformity with his sect in whom dumbness (or silence) was much commended... And I would fain demand of such a man, if being in Canada he had rather die for hunger than to eat fish. So many men, to follow their own fancies, and to say there be we, have forbidden their*

---

95 Quoted in *The Compleat Angler.*
96 In *Memory Hold-The-Door.*

N In *Six Salmon Rivers and Another.*

followers the use of meats that God hath given to man, and sometimes lay'd yoakes upon men that they themselves would not bear. Now whatsoever the philosophy of Pythagoras is, I am none of his.

Bravo! Dear Marc Lescarbot.

* * *

Early after twelve o'clock we ran the river to Pokiok, carried the canoe and dunnage up the high bank to the home of a Mr. Gilman, hired him to take the tent and other supplies through the woods to an old set of camps on Big Pokiok and, while he was harnessing his horses, walked a few hundred yards up the highway to view the falls.

Indian place-names are either descriptive of some physiographic feature or commemorative of some tribal happening of bygone days. Thus Pokiok, in the dialect of the Maliseet or St John River Indians, signifies narrow or constricted at its outlet. For here, little more than one hundred feet above the highway bridge, the stream narrows to a bare eight feet, and plunges over a perpendicular face of solid rock into the basin below; then, in a series of cascades between rock-walled palisades some seventy feet high, pursues its turbulent course over more declivities to pour finally its foam-flecked waters into the St John.

Few places in New Brunswick present a more wild, awe-inspiring aspect; and few people, whether local inhabitants or tourists, pass the place without pausing to stand on the bridge and marvel in silence at the beauty and the drum-like reverberations that ascend from that mighty chasm.[97]

There is an Indian legend, handed down from prehistoric times, that an enemy tribe killed or captured all but Sock-a-lex-is—a member of a small band of Maliseets who were encamped a mile below the falls. Sock-a-lex-is was a famous warrior, as fleet of foot as a fox. He had fought bravely, but finally, realising that death awaited him if he persisted in the struggle, he ran to a tree where his infant son hung in his cradle-board, slung the carrying straps over his shoulders and fled, pursued by the yelling enemy. Arrows whizzed past him but none struck him. He doubled this way and

---

97 No longer. In 1967 the Mactaquac headpond destroyed the Pokiok falls.

that but couldn't shake them off. He must put the gorge between him and his pursuers or both he and his young son would meet a merciless death. So, quickening his pace, he ran on, saw the gorge ahead of him and finally, his moccasined feet on the very brink, gathered every sinew and muscle into the effort and leaped forward. His feet struck the solid earth on the opposite side. He half fell to his knees, but regaining his balance, disappeared among the trees, while his baffled enemies set up a howl of rage. None dared follow him across that dread chasm, and late that afternoon he reached the ancient stronghold of his people at Meductic. Descendants of the infant Sock-a-lex-is are living today both in New Brunswick and the State of Maine, and all the menfolk are famous runners.

* * *

When we arrived at the old lumber camps, unloaded our belongings, and asked Mr. Gilman to call for us the following Wednesday morning, we set up the tent near a little boiling spring almost opposite the corduroy bridge that spans Big Pokiok, from whence a tote-road leads through more wilderness to Little Pokiok, which we had decided to fish for the small trout for which it is famous. Big Pokiok would come later.

We made a little fire, boiled the kettle, made tea, fried bacon and the remainder of the trout we had caught at Hay's brook earlier in the day. And when we had finished eating them we had for dessert the wild strawberries (left from our mid-day meal) which we had put in a wide-mouthed glass jar and covered with cream. True, the cream had slightly soured, but what cared we?

Why, dear reader, should I make your mouth water by relating our fare?—except it be that I want to get you out of doors beside a murmuring brook or little river on a carefree holiday; or if only in fancy to recall some enchanting hours in your own lives when your world was young…

That night we had no need to petition Morpheus to drown our "senses in forgetfulness"[98] for it had been a long, strenuous day. We slept the sleep of tired youth nor awakened until the sun had been up fully two hours.

* * *

---

98   Shakespeare, *Henry IV, Part II*, Act III, Scene 1, line 8.

Chapter XXII

Light-hearted, with only our creels made of basket-ash over our shoulders, and each with a light greenheart trout rod that cost but a dollar and a half, and equally cheap reels, we walked along the tote-road flanked by trees of yellow and white birch, spruce and fir and maple that towered far above us, forming twin palisades of green of various shades. We tramped over swampy places where the sphagnum soil had its being unnumbered centuries before the white man came to the shores of America. Occasionally we heard the ethereally-sweet notes of the white-throated sparrows or the wood thrush. Once, on a little rise of ground, we saw a hen partridge and her brood of chicks. She uttered a thin cry of warning and the young scattered into the woods. But she, dragging one wing along the ground, as though wounded, fluttered ahead of us a few rods until we were well away from the spot where her young had hidden themselves, then rose into the air and flew between the boles of the trees. Who taught her to employ such subterfuge?

We reached the brook spanned by a narrow corduroy bridge, baited our hooks with the lowly angleworm and fished downstream. The trout were hungry, fat and small; but then small trout have a much better flavour than those weighing a pound or more—just as a little pig tastes better than a two-hundred-pounder.

Before long the sky clouded over and a gentle rain began to fall. But we cared not. We began to sing. It was about a young man and a maiden who had planned to take a day-off at a country fair; but when he called for her the sky lowered and rain began to fall. She was sad, and so he consoled her thus:

> *Wait till the sun shines, Nellie,*
> *And the clouds go drifting by:*
> *We will be happy, Nellie,*
> *Don't you sigh!*
> *Down lover's lane we'll wander,*
> *Sweetheart—you and I,*
> *Wait till the sun shines, Nellie—*
> *Bye and bye.*[99]

---

99 Written in 1905, the year before this trip. Music Harry von Tilzer, lyrics Andrew B. Sterling.

Occasionally we came to a log dam that had been built to make a head of water which, when the gates were raised, sluiced log lumber down the brook. Standing on one of these, Arthur slipped and plunged into the deep pool, disappeared, came up and, thrusting the second joint of his rod between his teeth, swam down to the shallows where I stood. Now that I saw that he was in no difficulty, I laughed at his dripping figure, then said: "Cervantes has said: 'There's no catching trout with dry britches.'"

He grinned, then we began singing again.

> *Wait till the sun shines, Nellie,*
> *And the clouds go drifting by—*

Oh dear, such a long time ago. I would give worlds, Arthur, to relive those days again. But you, my friend, have taken a longer trail than that we traversed more than half a century ago,[100] and all I have is memories of the many angling trips we took to other singing brooks.

Wet to the hides, the rain dripping from our hat brims, we retraced our steps to the little bridge and footed the tote road to Big Pokiok.

The clouds vanished. The sun shone in all its splendour; struck gleaming facets from the globes of rain on grass and fern and shrub. A hermit thrush loosed a few flawless notes of praise. The odours from the armies of trees blended in a bewitching incense...

We made a roaring fire in front of the tent, dried our garments, cleaned enough trout for supper, fried them and appeased our hunger. That night we slept, if not the sleep of the just, at least that of youths on whose shoulders dull care had not set its burden.

* * *

Sunday morning dawned fair. We had decided to give the fish a day-off; not because either of us were averse to fishing on the Sabbath, but rather because we had enough trout to last until the morrow. And so, after we had breakfasted, we half filled the frying pan with coals from the fire, put over them some damp moss, set it inside the tent and smoked out our unwelcome

---

100   Arthur Slipp was GFC's age; he died in 1935.

Chapter XXII

visitors, the mosquitoes. Then we entered it, closed the flaps, sat down and began talking. Presently Arthur suggested that we sing some hymns, then he would give me a discourse, the theme of which he had thought of before he had fallen asleep last night.

Neither of us was religious in the usual acceptance of the term. Each of us had certain doubts which I shall not attempt to relate, but we both believed that religion should be reserved not only for the Sabbath, that God is not wholly confined within four walls containing stained-glass windows with obituary notices on them, but that He is at every turn of the road, and on every hilltop, and beside every lake, and river, and little brook, and on every highway for us to sense His presence and give Him silent worship. Some of the best sermons I have ever heard have been when seated alone in some beautiful cathedral or chapel, with the sun casting shadows of green and gold and blue over the empty seats and along the aisles. And perhaps, as has happened more than once, from the unseen organ loft the notes of the pipe organ pulsating like a benediction from floor to rafters far above. Words were unnecessary.

* * *

I do not remember what hymns my friend and I sang, but they were old ones we had learned in church and Sunday-school; and we sang them reverently. And when we had ended Arthur said: "My discourse, Fred, will be on the deceitfulness of riches. And my text 'For what shall it profit a man if he gain the whole world and lose his own soul?'"

As nearly as I can recollect it went thus: "You must know, Fred, that there is more sound wisdom in those few last words than is contained in all the man-made creeds since religion, of whatever form, was first preached."

I interrupted him to remind him that Socrates had enunciated and stressed the same principle many times to his disciples four hundred years before the birth of Christ.

"Of course," he said. "So did other ancient philosophers who believed in pagan gods. Please be quiet. Our Indian friends preserve silence and never interrupt when another is speaking."

Thus chastened I listened, and he went on: "Yes, and Epictetus says: 'You will do the greatest good to the state if you shall raise, not the roofs of the houses, but the souls of the citizens; for it is better that great souls should dwell in small houses than for mean slaves to lurk in great houses.'

"By what standard then, shall we measure a man's worth? I maintain, not alone by the wealth he has accumulated. Not alone by his endowments to church or university. Shelley says: 'Money commands labour, it gives leisure, and to give leisure to those who will employ it in the forwarding of truth is the noblest present an individual can make to the whole.' And Emerson wrote: 'Nothing can bring you peace but yourself. Nothing can bring you peace but the triumph of principles.' This is an irrefutable fact. I do not believe that Christ meant that it was *impossible* for a rich man to enter the kingdom of heaven. For a man may be rich and yet keep his soul. I believe that He meant just this: that it is impossible for the rich man who neglects the spiritual for the material things of life to enter the Kingdom. It will not even bring him peace in this life. Life, then, is a game—a game in which, in the final analysis—wealth, without spiritual values, counts for nothing. If a man thinks otherwise he is imperceptive, and deceives himself."

Thus my friend went on. When he had finished I thanked him. We are always thankful if another, whom we respect, justifies our own philosophy.

Had Arthur wanted to, he could have been a successful preacher, for he had a rich vocabulary, a resonant voice, and a compelling manner. But, he would never have been a strict conformist. He read law at Dalhousie University and got his degree in 1908, but never practised. He told me the reason: he could not bring himself to plead the case of a client he knew was guilty of any infraction of the law. Besides, he confessed to me, the profession would tie him to an office. He wanted to be free—free to fish, to travel the woods, and fish again. He began dealing in furs. Trappers as far north as Labrador sent him their catch. He did well, never violated a promise, preserved his soul's integrity, took his children on fishing trips and left a family who adored him. What more could a man ask in the way of success?

At the present moment I said: "It was a good discourse." Then I reached behind me, took my copy of *The Compleat Angler* from my knapsack, turned the pages until I had found what I wanted, and read aloud to him: "Sir Henry Wotton…was a most dear lover, and a frequent practicer of the art of angling; of which he would say: 'Twas an employment for his idle

Chapter XXII

time, which was then not idly spent…a rest to his mind, a cheerer of his spirits, a diverter of sadness, a calmer of unquiet thoughts, a moderator of passions, a procurer of contentedness…that it begat habits of peace and patience in those that professed and practised it." I closed the book, then said: "Therefore it would be more profitable for us—even the rich man—to take more days off and go afishing even though, in our absence, the bottom drops out of the stock market."

"Right," said my friend. He paused a few moments, then: "This being agreed—although I have neither bonds nor other material riches—it will be perfectly in order for us to return here this day two weeks from now. In the meantime I'll convince you that big trout can be taken from Big Pokiok where Davidson Lake vents into the deadwater."

* * *

And so, on Monday morning, we put lunch in our knapsacks, and with our rods and half a dozen trout flies, took the old hauling road to the dam which backs up the Big Pokiok for a considerable distance.

We found a flat-bottomed boat tied to a stake by a rope which we knotted about a sizable boulder to serve as an anchor, dumped out the rainwater, and with two crude paddles, left by the owner of the boat, began our journey up the expanse of deadwater. This was flanked on either side by a wide barren covered with clumps of cat-spruce, stunted tamarack and beautiful white birch trees; the usual Labrador shrub and sheep laurel growing out of the sphagnum moss. These low-growing shrubs were in flower, and bees busy gathering the nectar. And there were clumps of tall cat-tails and a few blue flags with their purple banners. There were scores of birds; among them the red-winged blackbird, and that lovely creature we know as the thistle bird; and the swamp sparrow, and its cousin the song sparrow and the white-throat. In a little cove we saw a great blue heron or crane, standing like a statue along the shore grass. Skirting the left-hand shore we paused to examine a cluster of those oddly-shaped plants variously called the Pitcher Plant, Side Saddle, and Hunter's Cup. Each plant had a stalk with a purple flower, and on the stalk numerous hair-like projections, each one bent downwards, which nature had formed thus to trap the insects that, not knowing their fate, seek the sticky substance at the bottom. Some sort of nectar, I suppose. At any rate we saw several insects that had been trapped within that mazy prison house, and held as securely as was Prometheus, chained to the rock on Mount Caucasus by the vengeful Zeus.

We were surrounded by a vast wilderness as primitive as when the last ice-age had retreated and nature had once more reasserted her sovereignty over most of North America. And with the joy of youth we began singing to the accompaniment of our swinging paddles and the wash of the water against the bow of the boat.

Only a short time before I had read *The Compleat Angler* for the first time and now thought of dear old Izaak Walton, and how he had said to one of his friends: "Let me tell you, there be many that have forty times our estates, that would give the greatest part of it to be healthful and cheerful like us; who with the expense of a little money, have eat and drank and laught and angled, and sung, and slept securely; and rose the next day, and cast away care, and sung, and laught, and angled again." And as I write this I remember that Charles Lamb several times spoke of *The Compleat Angler* in his letters and in *Essays of Elia*, and of one precious suggestion he made in a letter to Miss Fryer: "This is a book you should read, such sweet religion in it...though the subject be baits, and hooks, and worms, and fishes."[101]

* * *

Coming within sight of the outlet of Davidson Lake we saw a boat, like our own, with a man seated in it, moored close to the shore. We were to have company and hoped he wouldn't object to our fishing a short distance from him.

As we came nearer we saw he was bait fishing with a line attached to a long alder pole; we kept well out so that we wouldn't disturb his casting, then opposite him, Arthur said: "Do you mind if we fish a little above you?"

"Nope," said the middle-aged man. "Not at all. It'll be company. I like company when it's not too many. Where'd you come from?"

Arthur told him, and he said: "I'm Ben Griffin; have a camp four or five miles upstream... So your name's Slipp. Know your father well. Yes, come

---

101   Charles Lamb, letter to Miss Fryer, 14 February 1834.

Chapter XXII

on and anchor where you want." He reached down a hand, then held up to our gaze a two-pound trout. "I've got another like this," he said.

So we drew in near the shore above him, dropped the stone anchor, set up our rods, attached a leader of fine gut, and tied on one of the few flies we had—a dark Montreal with two blue feathers.

Ben was watching us. Said he: "Ain't you got angleworms?"

Arthur said: "No, not with us." And Ben said: "Well, no one has ever taken trout on this water with flies. It's been tried before… I can let you have some worm bait if you want 'em."

Arthur thanked him, as did I, but said we would try the fly first. Just then the cork on Ben's line disappeared beneath the water. He felt the tug, and, with both hands grasping his alder pole, gave a yank. For a brief moment we saw the huge body of a trout breaking water, then the line parted. Ben gave a heavy sigh and said: "That was a mighty fish. The biggest I've ever hooked," and drew in his line.

We spoke some words meant to be consoling. But evidently they didn't sufficiently comfort him for he took a bottle of whisky from his pack, removed the cork, poured a generous amount in a tin cup, drank it, smacked his lips, then said: "Pardon me… I didn't think… Will you lads have some?"

We thanked him but said we'd signed the pledge. (It wasn't too many years before I broke it.)

Ben said: "That's right." Then he took hold of the end of his line, gave it a quick pull and broke off a foot or more. "As I thought," he said. "It's as rotten as hell or that big fish wouldn't have got away."

As I write this I am thinking of some words written by the late Frank Wise of Montreal, who passed from this world last year at the ripe age of ninety-seven. (He had been an enthusiastic angler from his early youth): "You'll never choke on the bones of that big fish that got away."

I'm quite sure that if Ben had played the fish, instead of attempting to pull it in by main force, he would finally have had it in his boat. Speaking of it later, Arthur said that Ben would have made a good executioner, for he had pulled hard enough to break a man's neck.

I had a hank of good strong line in my pocket which I offered Ben. He flashed me a happy smile and thanked me. We eased our boat close to his and I handed it to him. Then, back again at our anchorage, Arthur and

I began casting. For perhaps ten minutes we kept it up without getting a rise. In the meantime Ben had taken a fish that would go a pound and a half. He said: "Look here, boys, I told you no one has ever caught fish on a fly in this water. I don't want to catch 'em all, so let me give you some of my bait."

He was a good sport. Again we thanked him, but said we were not yet discouraged, and continued our casting. Another ten minutes went by and, for my part, I was now inclined to change my fly for worm bait. But just then a beautiful fish leaped clear of the water, took Arthur's fly and, the reel singing its glad notes, went tearing up and down the pool.

Said Ben: "Well, I'll be hog-swallowed if you haven't got one!"

It took Arthur fully five minutes to bring the trout close to the boat, and even then it was full of fight. We had no landing net, so I got to my knees, reached a hand into the water, quick as a flash seized it ahead of the tail and flung it into the boat. It was, we all thought, a two-pounder, richly coloured with carmine and gold spots along the sides.

Shortly afterwards I had one on, and after I had exhausted its efforts to break loose, led it close to Arthur's waiting hand. It was about half the size of his fish.

For the next two hours we had good sport, hooking and tailing six more fish. Then they stopped taking our flies as suddenly as they had begun, although Ben, with his bait, took two more to add to his catch. Said he: "I've fished this water for forty years and more and never saw nor heard of a trout taken on a fly. Now you boys have broke the spell. Well…" He reached down, picked up the bottle of whisky, drew the cork, poured some into his tin cup and added: "Here's to your good luck!" drank it, gave a satisfied grunt, and restored the bottle to his pack and the cup to the bottom of the boat.

* * *

Later, at his invitation, we moored our boat close to his and ate lunch together. He had a small tin kettle half filled with boiled eggs and told us to help ourselves to them. We did, and in turn gave him some of our ginger cookies. After we had finished lunch he lighted his pipe and started talking. But it soon went out, and he relighted it a dozen times before he had ended telling us what a great moose country this Pokiok country used to be; and deer—"No better place for them even now." Yes, he had shot plenty of moose. "One—the biggest head—had an antler spread of sixty-two inches. It came out of the woods to the edge of the deadwater just at sunset." But he liked fishing best; had fished ever since he was six years old, when his father had first brought him to Big Pokiok. "It was a long tramp through the woods from the settlement," he said, "and when my legs got tired father lifted me up and carried me pick-a-back for a while. From that time on I was a fisherman and loved the woods. I..." he hesitated a moment, then went on: "I think it's the quiet that gets you. I've come here and not got even a nibble, but I always have a good time, and went back home with a new outlook—if you get what I mean. So I built a little camp five miles above here near a nice boiling spring. I've had sports that came fishing, and I guided 'em. Always kept a couple of boats. But some of 'em only wanted to catch fish, and if they didn't was disgusted. One fellow I had didn't see anything but the water, and was in such a hurry every morning to start fishing he'd hardly take time to eat his breakfast... You know there's some nice sunsets here—sky like I think it must be in heaven. One evening it was the prettiest I'd ever seen before or since; the deadwater the colour of June roses. I pointed it out to him, but he only said: 'Yes—yes—mind the boat, Ben, and never mind the damn sunset. I've seen plenty of sunsets before this.' Yes, boys, no doubt he had, but not with something inside of him—if it was. I prayed to God he'd never come back, and he didn't... But I had another fellow—an artist, and he saw every thing there was to see. I mean some nice things I'd never thought of. He was a sickly chap. He'd fish until he caught three or four trout, then set a board with a sheet of paper on it, on his knees, and paint whatever took his fancy. One evening he began painting this bit of dead water, and the barren and the trees and the sky that was all crimson and reflected in the dead water. Gosh! it was a nice picture and I'd have given an eye to have it for my own. So I asked him if he'd sell it. He looked sad, shook his head and said: 'I'm sorry, Ben, but I want to keep it to remember this trip. But, Ben, I'll make you a copy this coming winter and send it to you.'"

Ben paused, reached for his whisky bottle, poured himself a drink, swallowed it, then said: "But the poor fellow died late that autumn. Consumption it was. I was awful sorry when I read about it in the paper—not because of the picture, but because he was so darn nice, and saw the woods and Big Pokiok with something inside him. But that was only one thing that made him different from the other fellow I told you about." He paused a moment then said: "Look here, boys, why not come up to my camp and stop the night with me?"

We thanked him but said we wanted to fish Little Pokiok on the morrow and were leaving for home the next day. But we hoped to return in a couple of weeks and then, if he was at his camp, we'd be happy to visit him for a night.

He said he'd be there.

From the opposite shore a bittern (also known as the stake driver) sent out its booming: "Klunk-er-glunk! Klunk-er-glunk!" that sounded as though someone were pumping water from an almost dry well. A blue heron—possibly the one we had seen earlier—winged its slow flight only a few rods above the surface of the water. Its long, rubber-like neck was not held straight out like that of the wild goose and the duck, but curved backwards and its head thrust forward like that of a serpent. Possibly it saw us, for it banked awkwardly on flapping wings, its long legs, doubled backwards, reminding me of narrow-bladed scull-oars. It seemed not of this era, but the denizen of a by-gone age as it disappeared over the barren in the direction of Davidson Lake.

Said Arthur: "He that hath eyes let him see. He that hath ears let him hear."[102]

"Yes," said Ben. "But lots of people come into the woods and see nothing and hear nothing."

* * *

A little later we shook hands with Ben, bade him farewell and proceeded down the dead water and he went up to his camp. And as we paddled along I thought much of what he had said about the artist chap and his love of the deadwater and the barren and the informing wilderness:

---

102   Ezekiel 12:2.

Chapter XXII

> *Where the high soul slakes*
> *The thirst for greater beauty, beauty gives*
> *The need for inner stillness that yet lives...*[103]

A few hundred yards below the outlet of Davidson Lake we saw three red deer that had come to feed on the weeds that grow along the edge of the deadwater: beautiful creatures that seemed not unduly alarmed at our approach. Possibly they knew that the hunting season was yet distant. A little later we saw two more, and before we had reached the dam had counted eighteen in all.

We walked in Indian file along the narrow foot-path in the centre of the tote road, on either side of which were deep ruts made by the wheels of heavy wagons and the hoofs of horses during a century or more. Arthur was ahead of me, walking with that slight intoeing that is so characteristic of the Indians and which so many white men who travel the woods have acquired. And as we went, twilight settled over the forest, and all we heard was the pad of our own footsteps and the chuckling of the quick water over its rocky bed on our left.

Within a few rods of the tent Arthur dug a hole in the deep moss in which we laid our catch of trout and covered them. They would keep fresh in that cold bed.

* * *

Tuesday we again fished Little Pokiok for some small trout to take home, for as I have already said, they are sweeter than their bigger brothers. Then, on Wednesday morning, Mr. Gilman came for us. We loaded the tent and other dunnage on his wagon, and Arthur and I followed him on foot.

Reaching his home we carried the canoe and the rest of our effects down the hill below The Falls, then poled up the lovely river between island, intervale, and upland. The only bad water was Shogomoc Rapids around which we carried the canoe, then went on again, the thud of the setting-poles on the rocky bottom, the rippling of the water against the bow of the canoe the only sounds.

---

103   From "To Autumn", unpublished poem by GFC, MS in editor's collection.

Song of the Reel

It was almost dark when we reached Woodstock, and, leaving the canoe well up on the beach for the night, shouldered our packs, said *au revoir* to each other, and went our separate ways.

On the 12th of July we made another expedition to Big and Little Pokiok and spent one evening and night at Ben Griffin's little camp. I never saw him again. He passed away, in his late eighties, a few years ago, and met, I have no doubt, the artist friend who had promised to make him a copy of the sunset on Big Pokiok he had painted with such loving care.

CHAPTER XXIII

"You're wanted on the telephone—long distance calling," said my wife. So I dropped the book I had been reading and took the receiver from her hand. "Hullo—hullo," I said. Then over the wire came the slow drawling voice I knew so well: "Hullo, Doc—this is Myles speaking. The fish have come up the Upsalquitch. Yesterday I caught an eighteen-pounder. Come up as soon as you can—plenty of room for you. Can you make it tomorrow?"

I thought a moment. I had an appointment on the morrow, which was Tuesday. "I can't make it until Wednesday," I said. "But, Myles, my car is not working well, so I'll take the express train Wednesday morning, get off at St. Leonard, board the bus, get off at Robinsonville and hire someone there to drive me up to the Lodge."

"You'll not hire anyone to drive you up to the Lodge," he said. "Get off at Robinsonville and Ralph and I will meet you there with my car." (Ralph was his manager at Two Brooks Lodge, and the distance thirty miles). "Thank you, Myles," I said. "I'll be there—sure."

"That's the boy," he said. "There's a good run on, bigger fish than we've had for years. Goodbye for now."

* * *

Wednesday morning my wife drove me to the station to catch the 10.20 train. When it arrived, one of the trainmen, noting me struggling with my big pack basket, rod case and fly-box, said: "Where is it this time, Doctor?"

I had seen him many times, but didn't remember his name. I told him the Upsalquitch. "Well," he said, "let me put your things in the baggage car."

I hesitated a moment then said: "I haven't checked them."

"That's all right," he said. "I'll take good care of them, and put them off at St. Leonard."

"Thanks a lot," I said.

The train started off, winding its way up the lovely valley, always in sight of the river, along whose intervales and terraces I had during the last twenty-five years, dug out so many prehistoric Indian campsites, and for much longer than that had fished the pools for salmon. I saw several fishermen at the Hartland *(11a)* or Guimec Pool, others strung out at intervals for the next fifteen miles; and at the mouth of the Munquat—a wonderful run of water—three fishermen in waders. Here, all along the river, was salmon fishing. Why was I not among them instead of travelling two hundred miles to the Upsalquitch? The answer—I wanted not only fishing but the wilderness—its peace-giving solitude.

Not more than a dozen passengers were in the car. (People now travel mostly by motor.) But there were many express packages and bags of mail to be unloaded at all the stations, big and small.

It was not long before the trainman came in, sat down beside me and began talking. "Where do you fish on the Upsalquitch?" he asked.

I told him on Myles Brown's nine miles of water, and he said: "Oh yes, I know him. I've fished the government reserved water above Popologan Brook, a few miles below the Forks."

So he was a fisherman. That doubtless explained his kindness in relieving me of my pack and other gear, and saying that he would take good care of them. Fishermen are like that.

We talked of fishing. He had done a good bit—on the St John River, the Miramichi and the Tobique. And he liked to wade a brook and catch a "mess" of trout . He generally carried a frying pan with him, made a little fire beside the brook and fried some of them. "They taste better just out of the water," he said.

I agreed with him. And he said: "Lots of people consider a man's silly to go fishing, and get bit and pestered by mosquitoes, black-flies and midges."

"Yes," I said. "But every one to his likes. The dedicated golfer prefers *his* form of sport; the fisherman *his*. In turn other men prefer to watch a game of football, baseball, or go to a race track, rather than to play golf or go

Chapter XXIII

afishing. Some men prefer a crowd, others solitude. Some listen to the radio or keep their eyes glued to a television set all evening. Others like to read. Some people sit in a motor car and, with all the windows closed tight—as if they were mortally afraid of a little fresh air—drive about the country at a terrific speed for hours at a time. Personally, unless I can go slow enough to take in the various aspects of the landscape, and the brooks and rivers, I prefer to walk." I ceased, and he said: "That's right, Doctor Clarke." Then, for the train was approaching a little station, he got up, went into the baggage car, and, when the train came to a stop, helped unload the express consignments billed for that place.

He was soon back beside me and we again talked about fishing. I wasn't bored. What fisherman would be? Indeed the times I have been bored have been few and far between. I have too many interests. I like people but not crowds. You can't talk to crowds. Only politicians and ministers of the gospel can talk to crowds. Although—let me hasten to add—I sometimes enjoy being with crowds, and studying the different faces. But, like Sir Walter Scott, who said he was quite sure that, if incarcerated in the Bastille he would find something to interest him, so would I were I confined in our county jail. There would be so many stories to get from the other prisoners. I think it was Montaigne who said that, in his opinion, there was no man who has not deserved hanging five or six times. That's going it a bit strong. But most of us (who have never seen the inside of a prison) have at one time or another deserved it as much or more than some of those unfortunates who occupy the cells. Of course in my own case I wouldn't be able to go fishing—save in fancy. But perhaps by good conduct my sentence might be remitted and I could then resume my favourite sport.

* * *

When the train arrived at St. Leonard I got out, went to the baggage car and found my piscatorial acquaintance was unloading my pack basket, rod and fly box. This done, he hailed one of the waiting taxi drivers and put my things in the car. I thanked him for his kindness and shook his hand in farewell. He said: "Good luck, Doctor. A tight line. So long."

May the Lord bless him and keep him. And may he live long to enjoy many more fishing trips.

An hour later I boarded the bus and it started on its long journey over the Stewart Highway over which for many years I had motored with the Doctor, Charlie and Bill, to the Restigouche waters, or with other fishermen on to the enchanting Upsalquitch.

A buxom French woman with her infant on her lap occupied the seat opposite me. Presently the child began to cry. For a few moments the mother tried to compose it by crooning some lullaby. But, that proving ineffective, she unbuttoned her shirt-waist, exposed her ample breast and suckled her tiny progeny. To me it seemed the most natural thing in the world. We do not think it unseemly when we see a mother cow suckling its calf, or a cat its kittens!

A youth about twenty years of age, near the front of the bus, lifted a guitar from its case and strummed several melodies while he accompanied them in a low but distinct voice. I recognised one or two as French *chansons* that had been brought to Canada by settlers sent out to people his empire beyond the sea by that sun-monarch Louis XIV.

* * *

Descending the last long hill before we reached Robinsonville, I saw in the distance the high rounded mountain called Squawcap. I would like to climb it to its very top and feast my eyes on other high mountains from which so many of our rivers gather their cold purity and strength, and wind their course along valleys gouged out by the glaciers long ages since. "Here a cataract, there a rapid, now lingering in some corner of beauty, as if loath to go. Now shallow and wide, rippling and laughing in its glee, now deep, silent, and slow; now narrow and rapid and deep!"[104] Thus they traverse the valleys, winding among the mountains between vast ridges, and finally through intervale and on, on to the sea—and far out to sea. And the salmon, cruising along the coasts smell the waters of their nativity, and speed up the estuaries, past inland, intervale and upland, far—far up among the mountains where the cold brooks come down. And here, where they

---

104 John Brown, essay "Dr Chalmers" in *Rab and His Friends*, 1859.

Chapter XXIII

were born, they fulfil their destiny in due course. Thus it has been from time immemorial…

Myles and Ralph were waiting for me. We shook hands and, my dunnage loaded in the car trunk, I took my place beside Myles in the back seat.

CHAPTER XXIV

It was nearly six o'clock when we reached the landing from whence, on the farther shore two hundred yards upstream, I could see Two Brooks Lodge half hidden by the trees that lined the terrace on which it stood. On our left, only a few rods distant, a brook tumbled down a deep gorge to the river, and directly opposite another brook poured its cold tribute down an even deeper gorge. Thus the name *Two Brooks Lodge*. My dunnage was transferred to a long motor-driven canvas-covered canoe, and in less than two minutes we were climbing the long flight of steps that lead to the broad verandah.

Myles's wife, Millie, met me with smiling face and extended hand. She asked me if I preferred to occupy my old room, named the Dormitory, at the upper end of the Lodge. I said yes, so my things were taken to it. It is a big room about twenty feet by sixteen, with a capacious stone fireplace and a rug that almost covers the entire floor space. At the upper end is a door leading into the bathroom.

Three years previously, I had occupied the Dormitory with Darrell Longmore, of Toronto. I now wished he were with me. For he was an ardent fisherman, a gay companion and a good conversationalist.

After washing, I went to the cook house and shook hands with Jack—I forget his surname, but that doesn't matter, he was Jack and a wonderful cook—and the cookee and the guides, five in number, and Elizabeth, the kindly soul who waited on table, made beds and did other chores. Then I returned to the Lodge verandah. Millie and Myles were there, and an angler and his wife from Cleveland. I found in her, during the days that followed, one of the most persistent fisherwomen or fishermen I had ever met. Her husband was a splendid chap.

So we all had drinks and sat in the big cane-seated chairs and talked until Elizabeth rang the bell to announce supper was ready. Logs blazed in the stone fireplace. The table contained everything to captivate the most fastidious gourmet: cookies, little baked cakes, doughnuts the colour of antique mahogany, pickles of various kinds, pickled onions, olives, cheese and I forget what else.

Myles—huge, smiling, gracious—occupied the armchair at the head of the table; Millie was on his right. Did I say the meal was a supper? Rather was it a dinner—a feast—boiled salmon, vegetables. There was an enormous bowl of salad, for, although supplies had to be brought from Campbellton, forty miles distant, Ralph made at least two trips there every week, and the various vegetables he brought back were stored in the huge ice house and kept fresh.

Coffee or tea, whichever we preferred; ice cream or pie or pudding. Of course every morning for breakfast we were served fruit or tomato juice, hot or dry cereal, bacon, eggs and toast; and the main course for dinner varied from fish to beefsteak, roast lamb or chops or roast beef. The foregoing is an example of the abundance of food we enjoyed at Two Brooks Lodge. Why do I dwell on food? Simply because the majority of people like to eat!

We usually started out in the canoes about half-past eight in the mornings and fished until 12:30 or one o'clock, had lunch and whiled away the afternoons. Then, after the evening meal, fished until dark. After coming in, we usually sat on the broad verandah and talked over the day's luck or ill-luck, then perhaps an hour was spent in the great room in front of a woodfire in the fireplace, broad enough to roast an ox. Those of us who wanted to read had a choice of the latest magazines, and two or three shelves of books. But there was little reading done. We could do that at home. The main subject of conversation was fishing.

Two Brooks Lodge is one hundred feet in length. As I have already said it stands on a terrace that stretches back from the river bank about two hundred feet where the terrain ascends to a high hill covered with various species of trees; most of them black spruce. Indeed we are surrounded by hills, some of them almost mountains. Across the river, which at this

Chapter XXIV

point narrows to about a hundred feet, is a high knoll covered from base to summit with trees, the sombre tone of the evergreens relieved by slender white birches and poplars. It was an enchanting setting—a place where dull care never intrudes to enervate the mind. It is almost as primitive as it was at the dawn of time. How dear old Izaak, his friends Cotton, Joe Davers and Wotton would have enjoyed it! There isn't a permanent dwelling house from the headwaters, seventy miles up-river, until you reach Upsalquitch village more than twelve miles below Two Brooks Lodge.

On this trip I twice fished all the pools from the Promontory Pool to the Lower Rock Pool. I took thirteen salmon, the largest seventeen pounds, and never before had I caught so many large trout in this water. Indeed both salmon and trout were more plentiful than for many years past. I boxed and sent the biggest fish to my wife, and two others to friends in Fredericton by one of the fishermen who was leaving for home; and gave three to the Lodge.

Perhaps my most exciting fishing experience during my twelve days on the Upsalquitch occurred one evening I was fishing Big Indian Pool. I had taken a trout almost a pound in weight, and when I had got it into the canoe, darkness was settling over the river. Then I made a few more casts until I had about sixty feet of line out without any action. So I said to my young guide: "Let's pole back and fish the lower end of Caribou Pool where I raised that fish that didn't take." I began to reel in when I felt a tug that bent my rod in a bow. Quickly I took my fingers off the reel. The fish—a thirteen-pounder—sped like a thunderbolt downriver, leaped out of the water four or five feet, then swung towards the left-hand shore where there was a bad nest of submerged boulders. Burns had already pulled up the anchor and was paddling down the right-hand shore to get even with or below the fish. The boy knew his business. He knew that to keep the canoe stationary and play your fish is apt to end in disaster. For with the fish below you it has the advantage of its own strength plus the heavy current. Therefore it was his idea, as it was mine, to get below it. In this position the fisherman is more able to keep its head up-stream, not only with less chance of its breaking away, but of killing it more quickly.

This fish—fresh from Bay Chaleur and filled with energy—gave us a merry fight. Twice more we had to get below it. It ran upstream, down, back again, across the river, up opposite a small brook, jumped half a dozen times and used all the tricks it knew. But finally, after ten or fifteen minutes fight, I had it above me. Burns now stepped into the water, which came to his knees, and placing a small rock in the bottom of the net to make it sink more quickly, stood there in the semi-darkness, like a statue symbolising patience. Slowly I reeled in until I could see the fish, its head upstream, just above the stern of the canoe and about fifteen feet out. I exerted but a little pressure, for I didn't want it to rush out into midriver again or possibly take another run with the current, in which case we would have to follow and again get below it. Finally it was slightly below where I sat in the canoe, then it dropped back right over the mouth of Burns's net. With the quickness of an adder he lifted it out of the water, and, an exultant smile on his brown face, waded back to the canoe where he killed it with a couple of blows over the head. "Quick work, Doctor," he said, got into the canoe, pushed it out into deeper water with his setting-pole, started the motor, swung the craft around in a wide circle, and we sped up the lovely river.

The orange-coloured moon, well past its first quarter, hung over the tops of the pyramidal spruces and firs that lined the enclosing ridges. And, for the river makes wide turns, now it was on the right, again on the left. It cast its light over the tumbling waters, over the shallows.

Once from far up the hillside came the sharp bark of a fox, which was answered by an owl from the opposite shore. And instead of the metallic thud of the setting-pole on the rocky bottom (which had enchanted me so many times in former years) there came the continuous "pup! pup! pup!" of the motor and the swirling of the water beaten into foam by the revolving propeller.

For a few moments I thought of the fish lying back of me, and of how many of its kind I had taken when, thinking none were within reach of the fly, I had started to reel up my line, and then suddenly felt that terrific tug that told me one was on!

* * *

It was the season of the year when wildflowers are at their best. Along the river, wherever slate ledges sloped upwards, they had taken root and flowered in every cranny and cleft: the wild strawberry, the little star flowers,

Chapter XXIV

and what I thought was that other dainty inhabitant of the forest, the wood sorrel. And up the hillside were the massed umbels of the dogwood, white, so white.

Back of the Lodge, along the upward sloping ground, I discovered multitudes of those delicate little flowers locally known as twin-flowers or pink bells, but to botanists as *Linnaea borealis*. The flower that so much charmed the great Linnaeus that he bequeathed to it his imperishable name. The stalk is so slender, so threadlike, as are the two stems that radiate from its top, that they look too frail to sustain the insignificant weight of the one-third-inch-long inverted pink chalices. They clambered over and along the whole length of moss-covered, decayed logs, travelled beneath rotting limbs that had fallen from the trees above them, marched up the hillside into more open spaces. The air was filled with their faint fragrance, more enchanting than any flower in the exotic East.

There were the white blossoms of the bunchberry, the wintergreen and the partridge-berry. And here, too, I saw and marvelled at that beautiful orchid *Pyrola americana*, a dozen or more creamy-white flowers on each eight or ten inch stalk; and that other lovely orchid I took to be ladies'-tresses.

Then, down by the brook, I found a mass of the broad-leaf anemone; and, although the buds had not yet fully opened, several bushes of the dwarf wild rose. All more rewarding than if I had found a gold or a diamond mine...

A dozen times during my stay I visited my wildflowers. I say mine. For so far as I know I alone was their silent worshipper. And, more than once as I sat there, a song sparrow threaded the quiet with its rapturous melody.

"It is not all of fishing to fish."

* * *

During the last Saturday evening of my stay all of the guests, our hostess, and Elizabeth the waitress, gathered in the cook's big kitchen where the guides were putting on their annual performance. A bottle of Johnny Walker occupied the centre of the table. Ralph played his guitar, Jack (the cook) his mouth-organ, Dick Cleveland his violin. They played old and modern things that set our feet tapping an accompaniment on the floor. Oh, for fully two hours they kept it up; and finally the music proving irresistible, first

Song of the Reel

two, then four of the guests sprang to their feet and danced until exhausted. Then others took the floor, and, as well as was possible in the limited space, did a country dance until our heads went round.

About midnight the party broke up: good-nights were said and we trooped back to the Lodge.

For a long time I sat alone on the verandah. The pool below reflected a few winking stars. On the high knoll opposite me the tops of the spruces stood silent and black against the lighter horizon. There were no sounds save the chuckling of the waters which raced over the shallows a few rods upstream, and, below me, the faint music of the two brooks as they sang to each other across the intervening space that separates them. And I thought of those beautiful lines of Whitman:[105]

This is thy hour O soul, thy free flight into the wordless. Away from books, away from art, the day erased, the lesson done. Thee fully forth emerging, silent, gazing, pondering the themes thou lovest best.

Night, sleep, and the stars.

(25)

---

[105] Leaves of Grass, no. 283, "A Clear Midnight".

AFTERWORD

George Frederick Clarke and the Quest for a Good Life

Keith Helmuth

By the time George Frederick Clarke composed *Song of the Reel*, he had an unwavering and well-practiced philosophy of life, a store of memories to match, and twelve published books to his credit. He was in his ninth decade and *Song of the Reel* might well have been his last salute to the land and people he loved so well. The pinnacle of feeling to which this book rises, and the grace with which the writing visits and revisits its inexhaustible theme, provides everything one needs to understand the philosophy of life which George Frederick Clarke enthusiastically held and faithfully practiced.

But he had one more book to go; *Someone Before Us*[1] was published when he was eighty-five. While that last book is not as lyrical as *Song of the Reel*, or as his previous book on fishing the storied waterways of New Brunswick, it is fittingly important in another way; it tells the story of Dr. Clarke's pioneering archaeological work in the Saint John Valley of New Brunswick and his relationship with members of the Maliseet First Nation community.

Like his books on fishing, *Someone Before Us* draws on the memories of a life well lived, a life lived with curiosity and deep interest in everything he encountered—land, people, and history. The great French novelist Stendhal

---

1 *Someone Before Us*, now out of print, will be republished in a second expanded edition in the fall of 2016 by Chapel Street Editions, Woodstock, NB.

asks; "Is there anything stronger than love?" He answers, "Yes; *interest!*" George Frederick Clarke was a man endowed with a large measure of both love for the world and interest in all its doings, which is what makes his books good reading.

Song of the Reel is about much more than fishing, although without fishing there would be no story to bring that "much more" to light. With stories of fishing, human companionship, and wilderness solace, Dr. Clarke spins together the lines of description and feeling that puts the "much more" in the picture. He plays out his memories in a way that creates a philosophy of the good life and leaves no doubt he possessed the key to a satisfied mind.

The quest for the good life emerges with earliest literature and philosophy. The ancient Greek thinkers pondered this theme. Among the Romans, Cicero, in particular, contributes wisdom to this quest. Montaigne, great French essayist of the 16th century, is a treasure trove on the subject. Clarke knows and quotes this literature and is clearly determined to add his testimony to the tradition of this quest. You don't need higher education to know that a well lived life needs both shaping and tending, that we need to pay close attention to the relationships and activities that bring with them a sense of satisfaction and contentment. Clarke's fishing books make clear this wisdom is readily found on the river with wilderness guides and fellow anglers.

It is striking to think that George Frederick Clarke was born just a year after Ralph Waldo Emerson died. The influence of thinkers and writers like Emerson, Carlyle, Ruskin, Thoreau, and William Morris provided guidance for those in the generations that followed, and who knew in their bones that the great storm of "progress" was on track to destroy much of real value in both the human world and the natural environment. Following these 19th century thinkers, a cadre of poets, writers, artists, students of culture, and natural history scientists responded with a movement for the defense and conservation of wilderness regions and human communities. George Frederick Clarke grew up and developed as a thinker and writer within this conservation movement. He had a keen sense of how a good life is connected to a close association with both the natural world and with neighbours, friends, and family.

Although a dentist by profession, Dr. Clarke seemed to regard this work more like a useful trade; it was an important service in the community, he was good at it, and it provided an adequate income. But in his fishing books, you can tell from the number of times he writes, "A day off is day gained," that it is a perspective beyond work that provides him with the full sense of a good life. For Dr. Clarke, "a day off" fishing the Saint John, or perhaps a week on the Miramichi, was to align body, mind, and soul with the compass point of contentment. How well this comes across in *Song of the Reel*! In his other fishing book, *Six Salmon Rivers and Another*,[2] he is explicit. The other river is the river of contentment.

When Dr. Clarke graduated from dental college in Philadelphia, he was offered a partnership in the practice of one of his professors. Think about that! He could have stayed in the big city and built up a dental practice that would have made him moderately wealthy. Isn't that what an aspiring young professional should want? He turned down the offer. He came home to Woodstock and declared he did not want to live anywhere else. This is a remarkable level of self-knowledge for a person in his 20s. He loved the wilderness woodland of New Brunswick with its wildlife, lakes, rivers, remote deadwaters, high hills, wide valleys, long vistas, and its people. He must have already had a firm grasp on the kind of life he wanted, and had his sights well set on what was needed to achieve it.

His decision and sense of place, sets up an interesting contrast with other writers at the time like Bliss Carman and Charles G.D. Roberts who hailed from New Brunswick, but who migrated to places like Boston, New York, Toronto, and Europe to advance their literary careers. No such move appealed to George Frederick Clarke. The fact that his best writing grew out of his attachment to the people, history, and wilderness environments of his home region, is proof that strong roots nourish the creative soul.[3]

---

2 *Six Salmon Rivers and Another*, 4th edition, edited by Mary Bernard, 2015, Chapel Street Editions, Woodstock NB.

3 See *The Ghost of Nackawick Portage: The Collected Short Stories of George Frederick Clarke*, edited by Mary Bernard, 2015, Chapel Street Editions, Woodstock NB. According to Clarke archivist/editor, Mary Bernard, some of Clarke's best writing is found in his short stories about lumber camp life, log drives on the rivers, and wildlife.

Perhaps because Clarke's family heritage really was in the woodland, river and homestead farming life, the academic and literary culture of great cities did not tempt him.[4]

While Dr. Clarke was a dentist by profession, he was a writer by vocation, and the satisfaction he found in this craft was also central to his sense of what made for a good life. Fishing in rivers that ran and surged with the essence of life, and contemplating the wilderness by moonlight were restorative, but the writing was creative; and a sense of creative accomplishment is needed, in some form, for a fully rounded sense of a good life to emerge. Not everyone can be a writer, nor are most people artists in the usual sense, but most everyone can feel the satisfactions of creativity if they are attentive to the relationships and process that build up a sense of doing things right, of doing a good job at whatever you are doing.

Henry David Thoreau wrote, "I wish to live ever as to derive my satisfaction and inspirations from the commonest events, every-day phenomena..." This is pretty close to saying what it means to have a good life. When George Frederick Clarke returned from Philadelphia and determined that Woodstock, New Brunswick was to be his home, he set up a way of life in which fishing was a common activity. His schedule came to include regular excursions into the wilderness with fellow fishermen and with the guides who knew the wild rivers and were often fascinating storytellers. Fishing was a common activity for Dr. Clarke, but if the fish weren't taking the fly and none were landed, the deep satisfaction of just being in the woods and on the river with good friends was amply registered in his soul. If luck was good, if strikes came, and landings proved successful, the common activity was tinged with excitement and with the sense of living fully in the moment.

This is what is so extraordinary about *Song of the Reel* and its companion, *Six Salmon Rivers*. In one way of reading these books, they are about fishing, about poling up and paddling down various salmon rivers, and about seeking out remote lakes and lively brooks for trout. But in another way of reading they are also about how the experience of the being in the deep woods and

---

4 For the full details see *The Last Romantic: The Life of George Frederick Clarke, Master Storyteller of New Brunswick.* by Mary Bernard, 2015, Chapel Street Editions, Woodstock NB.

Afterword

on the river can rise to a sense of grace in the presence of the wilderness and its great commonwealth of life. Clarke's attention to sunsets, to spring wildflowers, to the night sky above the silhouette of spruce trees, to the tumble and murmur of a brook as it drops over a small ledge are transformed into memories that provide both the author and reader with a sense of the extraordinary within the common round. This sense of heightened and contemplative living is a central feature of the good life.

For some folks this kind of thing is perfectly natural, for others it may seem almost mystical. For George Frederick Clarke it seems to have been a little of both, perhaps best expressed by Ben Griffin in *Song of the Reel* when he talks about the sunset on the Pokiok deadwater "being the colour of June roses," and that those who see such things do so "with something inside them." That "something" is the kind of vision Dr. Clarke made his stock in trade as a writer. He never tired of quoting Izaak Walton's famous saying; "It is not all of fishing to fish." With *Song of the Reel* and *Six Salmon Rivers* Clarke has given us two of the finest renditions of how this fisherman's wisdom works out in the quest for a good life.

Keith Helmuth,
Woodstock, New Brunswick,
April 2016

INDEX

♦ A ♦

Arnold, Matthew, lines from "Balder Dead" . . 4
Ayers Lake. 237

♦ B ♦

Bear
—catches salmon 134
—mauls Angus Bruce 194–196
—steals salmon 149
Beechwood Dam 71
Betsy Rapids. 241–242
Big Indian Pool 267
Big Pokiok Stream. . . .245–248, 251–256, 258
Biggar Brook. 119–120, 127–129, 188
Black Dose (salmon fly) 11, 39
Black Rapids. 167, 231
Black Watch Regiment 37, 42, 179
Bonner, Ada 23–24, 26–27
Boyce's Rocks 210
Boyer, Russell 36, 61–64, 66–67
—his island and camp. 61, 64–65, 67
—recites "The Mary Gloster" 65
Bristol, NB. 135
Brown Fairy (salmon fly) 31, 39
Brown, Millie 265–266
Brown, Myles 259–260, 263, 265–266
Browne, Sir Thomas, *Christian Morals*. 3
Bruce, Angus. 179–181, 192–197, 215
—drunken cow 202–205
—mauled by bear 194–196
—parrot, crow and wife 180–186
Buchan, John. 39, 235, 244
Burns (guide) 267–268

♦ C ♦

Campbell, William Wilfred, lines from "The World-Mother (Scotland)" 2

Caribou Pool. 267
Clark, Charles (Charlie) 17, 21–22, 142, 177, 262
—Four Musketeers of Fish 20
Clarke, George Frederick
—childhood and youth. 23–24, 27–30, 38, 97–98, 107, 244
  —meets girl fishing. 236–237
  —Trip to Indian Lake 23–30
  —trip up the Pokiok . . . 237–243, 245–258
  —trout fishing 235–243, 245–258
—conservation. 110, 212
—dams 212
—finds Indian artefacts 134
—Four Musketeers of Fish 20
—song
  —"O there was a wee boy" 17–19
—unpublished poem "To Autumn" 257
Clarke, Maria
—sings "The Miramichi Fire" 225–226
—stories
  —about devil 107
  —devil shakes man to pieces 146–147
  —haunted horse-hovel 101–107
  —pedlar cures warts 148–149
—youth
  —fishes for trout 244
Clearwater stream 133–135, 193, 197
Cole, Earl, photographed 71
Cow Dung (salmon fly) 47
Crooked Rapids 119, 167, 188, 231

♦ D ♦

Dale, Harry 73, 92–97, 101–108
Dugout canoe 168–169, 173
—"Drunkard's Doom". 169–171
Dungarvon Whooper (train) 126, 201

277

♦ F ♦

First Nations Peoples 5, 14, 93, 214
—artefacts . 41, 114, 134, 173, 189–190, 208, 260
—crafts and customs 15, 43, 112, 114, 134, 147, 249, 257
—history and prehistory. 8, 15, 41, 135, 173, 207, 239, 260
—language. . . . 38, 43, 69–70, 109, 119–120, 168, 175, 196, 211, 214, 240, 245
—legends 26
  —Sock-a-lex-is. 245–246
—Maliseet 26, 31, 93, 168, 245
  —"The bones of our fathers" 239
—Micmac 26, 69, 172, 175, 214, 240
—white injustice. 111, 239–240
Fly Fishers' Club, England 2
Forks of Miramichi 20, 121, 134, 142, 168–169, 171, 231
—fishing camp. . . . 2, 17, 142, 169, 177, 231
—Forks Pool. 10, 118, 142
Four Musketeers of Fish. 20
Franquelin, Baptiste Louis. 173, 211

♦ G ♦

Gilbert, Helen, catches first salmon . . . 53–56
Gillalpen, Bill (guide) 117–135, 137, 139–141, 143–147, 149–150, 167–168, 173–176, 179–197, 200–202, 204–205, 207–210, 215–220, 223–232
—digs for artefacts. 190–191
—stories
  —devil shakes man to pieces 146–147
  —guiding Mrs J 120–132
  —haunted horse-hovel 101–107
  —Jim J.'s ghost 223–224
  —loup-garou 145–146
  —pedlar cures warts 148–149
  —talkative aunt Libby 120–121
Grant, Dr Nelson P. 1, 17, 19–20, 46, 142, 169, 177, 231, 262
—catches poachers. 169–171
—character. 20–21
—Four Musketeers of Fish 20
—recites poetry 20–21
Grant, Levi. 134–135
—story: tame bees 135–137
Gray, Thomas, lines from "Elegy in a Country Churchyard". 20
Griffin, Ben 252–253, 255–256, 258

♦ H ♦

Half-Moon Cove . . . 150, 167, 172–173, 210, 230–231
Harris, Moses, witnesses Miramichi Fire 225–226
Hazlitt, William
—*Lectures on the English Comic Writers*
  —"Merry England," 8
—*Sketches and Essays*
  —"On A Sun-dial". 3
Highlander (salmon fly) 39
Hutton, John E. *Trout and Salmon Fishing* . . 8

♦ I ♦

Indian Lake 23–26, 196

♦ J ♦

James, Henry, letter to Frederick Sturges Jr 3–4
Jock Scott (salmon fly). . . 10, 32, 39, 125, 192

♦ K ♦

Kedgwick River 3, 69, 141
Kennedy, Bill. 16–17, 22
—Four Musketeers of Fish 20
Kipling, Rudyard "The Mary Gloster". . 65, 98

♦ L ♦

Lamb, Charles, letter to Miss Fryer 252
Larry (author's friend) 117, 225
Lescarbot, Marc 244–245
Lewey Mountain 172, 207, 209, 211, 229–231
Lewey Rapids 210, 229–230

Little Pokiok Stream. 246–248, 256–258
Loler, Peter. 108
Long Stump Bar (pool) 175
Lower Rock Pool 267

◆ M ◆

MacGregor, Robin. 31–51
MacKenzie, Murdoch (guide and outfitter). .12, 20, 121, 168–169
Maplewood, NB. 23–24
Mar Lodge (salmon fly) 39, 47
Marven's Brook 97, 236–237
McKiel Brook 211
Meductic flat. 239
Miramichi Fire of 1825 225–226
Miramichi River. 2, 6, 10, 17, 20, 69, 107, 118, 121, 125, 129, 134, 142–143, 146, 149, 168–169, 171–172, 177, 180, 189, 209–212, 215, 225–226, 231, 244
—Forks 2, 10, 17, 20, 118, 121, 134, 142, 168–169, 171, 177, 231
—Main Southwest 53, 66, 93, 117, 142, 169, 175
Moriarity family 96–97
Murray, Allie (guide) 5

◆ N ◆

Narrows, The (Miramichi). 210, 229
Nixon, Joe (fish warden). 169–172
No. 1 Pool 11, 141
No. 3 Pool 10, 12

◆ O ◆

Ogilvy, John (Jock) (guide and outfitter) . . .10, 141, 193
Old Hen and Chickens, The, rocks 210

◆ P ◆

Palmer, Bessie 24–30
—recites *Ulysses* 28–29
—sings "Oh wert thou in the cauld blast". . . 29
Palmer, Pearl. 24, 27–29

Parmachenee Belle (salmon fly) 10, 224
Patterson's Run 71
Piscator (character in *The Compleat Angler*) . 243
Pokiok Stream, Big and Little 245–248, 251–257
Polchies, Noël 93, 109–111, 113
—child's snowshoes 112–113
—death 113–115
—spearing salmon 93, 109–110
—story, "Too good neighbours, Fred". 111–112
Polchies, Peter (Doc) 93
—spearing salmon 93, 109–110
Polchies, Susan. 113–114
Promontory Pool 267

◆ R ◆

Restigouche River 3–4, 11, 15, 22, 47, 74, 141, 145, 199, 262
—government reserved water 10–11
—the Lodge 4–5, 15
Run, The (pool) 11

◆ S ◆

St John River. 31, 38, 70–71, 73–74, 110, 115, 173, 238–240, 245
—Grand Bar. 31, 36, 41–42
Salmon
— black 143–144
—fishing technique 12, 34, 141, 192–193, 199, 218–219, 267
    —greased line. 33, 122, 132, 140, 192
    —mending line. 8–9, 140–141
    —tickling 133, 140, 180
—flies 8–9, 32, 34, 39–40, 47, 122, 125, 139–141, 199, 254
    —Black Dose. 11, 39
    —Brown Fairy 31, 39
    —Cow Dung. 47
    —Highlander. 39
    —Jock Scott 10, 32, 39, 125, 192
    —Mar Lodge. 39, 47

—Parmachenee Belle. 10, 224
—Silver Doctor. 39–40, 130, 201
—Wilkinson 40, 201
—life cycle and habits 64, 73–74, 93–94, 110, 141–142, 199, 204
—rods 40
—smoked/smoking 225–228
—spearing 93, 109, 115
Salmon Hole (pool) 120, 125–126, 171
Saunders, Michael (photographer) . . . 71–72
Shakespeare, lines from
—*Hamlet*. 21
—*Romeo and Juliet*. 21
Silver Doctor (salmon fly) . . . 39–40, 130, 201
Slate Island. 225
Slipp, Arthur. 237, 249–250, 257
—trip up the Pokiok. . . . 237–243, 245–258
Songs
—by Burns. 2, 29
—by GFC
—"The Wee Boy". 17–18
—hymn
—"Brighten the corner where you are". 226
—popular
—"Maybe you will say 'Maybe'" 27
—"Mother Machree". 2
—"Wait till the sun shines, Nellie" 247–248
—by Stephen Foster. 2
—traditional
—"A la Claire Fontaine" 236–237
—"The Miramichi Fire" 225
Squires, Fred C., poem about Charlie Clark
. . . . 21– 22
Stories
—Angus Bruce
—birds and wife 180–186
—drunken cow 202–205
—Bill guides Mrs J 120–132
—Bill's talkative aunt Libby. 120–121
—devil shakes man to pieces 146–147
—haunted horse-hovel 101–108

—Jim J.'s ghost. 223–224
—loup-garou. 145–146
—Noël Polchies, "Too good neighbours, Fred"
. 111–112
—pedlar cures warts 148–149
—St Kentigern and the salmon 95–96
—tame bees 135–137
Strange, James (graphologist) . . 57–64, 66–67
Sturges, Frederick, Jr., letter from Henry James
. . . . 3–4

♦ T ♦

Tobique River 70
Trout. 23, 111, 119, 193, 196–197, 224, 236, 242–244, 246–248, 251, 253–254, 260, 267
—fishing technique 26, 40, 140
—worms vs. flies 253–254
Two Brooks Lodge . . 259, 265–267, 269–270

♦ U ♦

Upsalquitch River . . . 69, 135, 142, 259–260, 262, 267

♦ W ♦

Walton, Izaak 45, 53, 221, 252, 267
—*The Compleat Angler*. .7–8, 39, 189, 251–252
—memorial window, Winchester Cathedral .7
Whitman, Walt, "A Clear Midnight" . . . 270
Wilkinson (salmon fly) 40, 201
Williamson, Henry *Salar The Salmon* 10
Wood, A. H. E., greased-line technique. . . 33
Woodstock, NB 33, 72
Wyers, Harvey (guide). 11–15